Paranormal

A New Testament Scholar Looks at the Afterlife

Paranormal: A New Testament Scholar Looks at the Afterlife

Valerie A. Abrahamsen

Shires Press
Manchester Center, Vermont

Also by Valerie A. Abrahamsen

*Goddess and God: A Holy Tension
in the First Christian Centuries*

*Women and Worship at Philippi:
Diana/Artemis and Other Cults in the Early Christian Era*

SHIRES ✺ PRESS
4869 Main Street
P.O. Box 2200
Manchester Center, VT 05255
www.northshire.com

©2015 by Valerie A. Abrahamsen

ISBN: 978-1-60571-258-1

Building Community, One Book at a Time
A family-owned, independent bookstore in
Manchester Ctr., VT, since 1976 and Saratoga Springs, NY since 2013.
We are committed to excellence in bookselling.
The Northshire Bookstore's mission is to serve as a resource for
information, ideas, and entertainment while honoring the needs
of customers, staff, and community.

Printed in the United States of America

To the Sisters of St. Margaret,

Catherine Joanne,

and Martha,

and in loving memory of

Alan O. Dann

Contents

Acknowledgments viii

Chapter 1: Introduction 1

Chapter 2: The Paranormal Scene Today and the Four Types of Evidence 13

Chapter 3: A Short History of Paranormal Research 41

Chapter 4: The Science of the Afterlife: Instruments and Investigations 73

Chapter 5: Western Religion and the Afterlife 103

Chapter 6: Themes and Findings 140

Chapter 7: Ethics and Comfort 182

Appendix I: Short Biographies of Nineteenth-Century Paranormal Researchers and Renowned Supporters 203

Appendix II: The Apostles' Creed Analyzed from a Paranormal Perspective 218

Appendix III: Comparative Chart of Attested Themes 234

Resources: Alphabetically by Author 238

Resources: By Topic 252

About the Author 266

Index 268

Notes 276

Acknowledgments

Conducting research on the afterlife and paranormal phenomena in a materialistic, Post-Enlightenment culture is a challenge. We are buffeted on all sides not only by skepticism and denial of anything that cannot be witnessed by our own physical senses or "proven" by scientific investigation, but also, at times, by outright hostility. The early researchers from the nineteenth century encountered this, as do current investigators, but I have been fortunate in having been met, for the most part, by great interest and appreciation. I have truly felt called and compelled to write this book and have been energized and inspired by the many people – and spirits – who have provided insights and information.

I am grateful to the parishioners and guests at St. Michael's Episcopal Church in Brattleboro, Vermont; to the members of the Thursday Rotary Club of Brattleboro; and to countless other friends and colleagues with whom I presented my findings as the book progressed. I was moved and gratified when listeners shared their personal stories of near-death experiences, after-death communication, and wondrous unexplained encounters, some of them stating that they had rarely been able to recount these stories before for fear of being met with criticism or censure. I am grateful to the clergy of St. Michael's as well who have kept an open mind about this material and allowed me to share it in adult education settings.

Judy McGee kindly read an early draft of the manuscript and gave me helpful feedback.

I have been blessed to have a wise, grounded, curious and totally supportive spiritual director in the person of Catherine Joanne of St. Joseph's Dwelling Place in Ludlow, Vermont. Catherine has not only guided me deftly through years of personal and professional challenges but has also remained open and inquisitive about the material I have been unearthing. A Roman Catholic layperson, she is as close as anyone can come to being a priest without benefit of ordination, and I am forever grateful for her ministry to me.

My wonderful godmother and cousin, Martha Rosewell, has been part of me my whole life and my friend and confidante for over two decades. She is the epitome of hospitality, graciousness, faithfulness, love and service, even in the face of tragedy and serious illness. Precious memories of Christmas and July Fourth holidays, stimulating conversations, and beautiful drives around Cape Cod will be with me forever.

I have been associated with the Society of St. Margaret, now in Duxbury, Massachusetts, for over 25 years, and have told the sisters that, when I stay with them and participate in their beautiful offices and services, I feel that I have one foot in heaven. I am deeply grateful not only for the love and support they have given me over the years but also for their open-mindedness about the afterlife and the paranormal material that I have uncovered. I do not know at this point in my life what I would do without "my" sisters.

Finally, I offer this volume in loving memory of my dear friend, Alan Osborn Dann, who went to the other side on September 7, 2014. I met Alan through our mutual work with the Estey Organ Museum in Brattleboro, to which he was utterly devoted; the museum could not have survived without his financial support, hard work and dedicated leadership. I also had the pleasure of singing with Alan and his wife, Dr. Deirdre Donaldson, in the Brattleboro Concert Choir and the Pioneer Valley Symphony Orchestra and Chorus for many years, and Alan took a keen interest in my various research projects. I was privileged to sit with Alan shortly before he succumbed to cancer, and I know he watches over us now with the love that abides for eternity.

Chapter 1: Introduction

- *After considering the strength of the evidence, I am absolutely convinced that an afterlife exists. . . . The evidence of near-death experiences points to an afterlife and a universe guided by a vastly loving intelligence.* – Jeffrey Long, MD
- *This possibility of spirit entities recording their voice on tape is beyond the comprehension of most people. But . . . the so-called dead have used our advancing technology to communicate at increasingly sophisticated and evidential levels. . . . One thing that is certain is that the communication between worlds that has already taken place proves there is no death and there are no dead.* – Tom and Lisa Butler
- *There are no trimmings on a man when he has passed the Second Death; only pure spirit remains. . . One thing only was I conscious of – and that was the Allness, the infinitude, the wonder of God's love. In that supreme moment I knew no such thing as separateness of existence. Personality had died, but individuality was reborn.* – Arthur Conan Doyle postmortem

Most people wonder, at least sometimes, what happens to us when we die. Even people in the modern (or post-modern) West who are naturally skeptical about the afterlife want to know, at some level, what happens to their loved ones at death, whether they are "all right," and whether they will meet again. Many people have had paranormal experiences that are impossible to explain rationally, yet those experiences are real for them and at times life-changing. People from all walks of life sense the presence of deceased loved ones and see them in their dreams. Many of us believe that the deceased, angels or other divine beings help us through difficult situations, while others experience negative, disturbing phenomena that they attribute to demons, evil spirits or the devil.

Despite the enormous growth in our culture of people who claim no religious affiliation per se (the "nones"), most adults in the United States still consider themselves spiritual, believe in some kind of God, pray, and seek answers to life's mysteries. The questions of a Divine Being, the ultimate purpose of our lives, and what transpires after death are intricately bound together.

In the scientific, secular and Post-Enlightenment world in which we find ourselves, there are opposing trends around these issues. Skeptics – or perhaps, more accurately, "deniers" – in the scientific and wider community often posit that anything that cannot be rigorously tested in controlled situations or experienced with the five physical senses – taste, touch, smell, sound and sight – do not exist. Critics on the skeptical or denier spectrum often disparage – sometimes in heated, hateful, and dismissive tones – any notion of survival after death, eternity and ultimate reality. On the religious side of the issue, scholars in a number of disciplines, such as New Testament, Hebrew Bible, church history, ethics, and theology, focus primarily on texts and tradition and warn us away from concern about the afterlife; the argument – not entirely illegitimate – is that our focus should be on this life and this world. Into this category of religion professionals also fall many mainline priests and ministers, who preach very infrequently on the afterlife for similar reasons. At the Christian fundamentalist end of the religious spectrum, the afterlife may well be an important focus, but the emphasis tends to be on fear of everlasting damnation or on the belief that tragedies occur because they are "God's will."

In this book, the question of life after death will be addressed with the goal of meshing current scientific and other research with religious and ethical precepts; the questions of eternity and the Divine will inevitably also come into play. The starting point is our culture's pervasive (and largely legitimate) trust in science, technology and progress. We will draw primarily on four types of evidence: paranormal investigators and scientists who work with paranormal phenomena; reputable psychics and mediums; people who have had near-death experiences (NDEs); and those who have experienced out-of-body experiences (OOBEs).[1]

Paranormal investigators have become widely known by the general public through one of today's primary influences: mass media. Thanks in part to cable and satellite television, the World Wide Web and other formats unavailable just 20 years ago, there are now dozens of ways to learn about the paranormal (some legitimate and some mainly for entertainment). Among the television series that feature ghost hunting, hauntings, paranormal investigations, and related topics are *Ghost Hunters*, *Paranormal State*, *A Haunting*, *Celebrity Ghost Stories*, *Ghost Adventures* and *Haunted Collector*. Many of these programs have emerged from the work of non-profit organizations whose missions and purpose had been well established for years prior to the arrival of the television cameras. Information about these groups can be accessed through their websites and books; the work of these groups is, on the whole, highly ethical, humane and compassionate. The results of their investigatory efforts often bring healing and comfort to those who appeal to them for help, and the organizations often work pro bono. Thus, while television and the media can sometimes be used to promote rampant consumerism, anti-social behavior, fraud, and over-indulgence, many of these programs, supported by the practitioners' work away from the cameras, are actually offering significant social benefits.

Investigators on several of the ghost-hunting programs are shown utilizing highly sophisticated electronic instruments of various kinds.

The instruments are not gimmicks: they have been designed and created by authentic scientists, inventors and engineers. Many of these instruments can be purchased by amateur "ghost hunters" through the Internet.

Apart from but related to the electronic instruments and the evidence that has been gleaned from them are the hundreds, if not thousands, of scientific experiments that have been conducted worldwide over the past century in university and other laboratories on extra-sensory perception (ESP), telekinesis, electronic voice phenomena (EVPs), telepathy, levitation, and other paranormal phenomena. Paranormal experiments and their results have been described in peer-reviewed journals such as *The Journal of Scientific Exploration, The Journal of the History of the Behavioral Sciences, The Journal of Parapsychology, Proceedings of the Society for Psychical Research, The Journal of Religion and Psychical Research,* and *The Journal of the American Society for Psychical Research*. It is significant that one of the most respected encyclopedias in the world, *Britannica*, presented as early as the 1960s a positive outlook on parapsychology and Spiritualism, based primarily on scientific experimentation. We will examine the early history of paranormal research, the paranormal scene today, and scientific instruments and techniques in some depth below.

Reputable psychics and mediums provide a second type of evidence for survival after death; some of these individuals also appear in television programs, have websites and have written books. Names that may be familiar include Theresa Caputo, Chip Coffey, Michelle Belanger, Maureen Hancock, James Van Praagh, John Edward, Noreen Renier, Phil Jordan, and Nancy Orlen Weber. Among the television shows featuring these men and women are *Long Island Medium, Psychic Detectives, Psychic Kids,* and *Ghost Whisperer*. These psychics and mediums use their well-honed skills to speak to the dead and probe the truths of what transpires "on the other side." These gifted practitioners are deeply spiritual, caring, wise, dedicated and self-sacrificing and use their gifts to help those who are grieving, ill, in despair, or seeking information about missing persons or murder victims. Some psychics routinely assist police departments in homicide and other investigations. Skeptics are often "converted" by the uncanny accuracy of what psychics and mediums sense and channel about situations and deceased persons. We will examine some of these individuals, discuss the problem of fraud and present the evidence for the reader to consider.

The third group of individuals who have had experience with the "other side" is that of average, normal people around the world who have had near-death experiences (NDEs). Since the 1970s, when medicine has made it more and more possible to resuscitate injured and ill people who have technically died, scientific studies have been conducted to study this phenomenon. Jeffrey Long, MD, published a major study on his Internet-based survey research in 2010,[2] and a neurosurgeon, Eben Alexander, has recently published his own experience with "near death."[3] We will examine their and others' tales below.

Finally, there is evidence especially from Eastern cultures for purposeful, non-unique out-of-body experiences. Some people have been known to travel outside of their physical bodies, witnessed events and conversations that can be separately verified, and have come back into their bodies with no ill effects.[4] In the West, the primary source for purposeful, documented OOBEs over time is Robert Monroe.[5] His books astoundingly parallel findings from the other sources under discussion, and the institute he founded in 1974 carries on his work on consciousness studies.[6]

In order to provide context for the current state of the research, we will briefly trace the history of paranormal investigation in the

West. In both the US and Europe in the nineteenth century, documented reports of paranormal experiences abounded, although they may be largely forgotten today. Some accounts involved luminaries like Queen Victoria, Thomas Edison, Abraham and Mary Todd Lincoln, Winston Churchill and Albert Einstein. The birth of the Spiritualism movement in the mid-1800s was a major catalyst for heightened interest in communication with the dead, which inaugurated experiments with séances, Ouija boards, automatic writing, electronics, and photography. While there was also widespread fraud and raw commercialism, the vast majority of the accounts remain verifiable.

Perhaps surprisingly, there is also early twenty-first-century evidence for reincarnation and extraterrestrial beings. While we will not explore UFOs in any depth, the evidence for reincarnation (from human being to human being, not generally from human being to animal) is attested in one way or another by all four of the types of evidence that we will explore.

As we will see, the current and past experiments, research, investigations, verifiable stories and experiences will attest not only to the fact of our actual survival after death as individuals but also to universal themes, values, and guidelines that resonate with us as human beings: forgiveness, unity, ethical behavior, eternal life, the Divine, service, peace, joy and love. These are the points at which science and the paranormal join religion for the betterment of humankind.

Since the dawn of consciousness, the issue of life after death has been addressed by most religions and philosophies around the world. We will examine the ways in which our ancestors in the West have communicated with the deceased and closely analyze the Apostles' Creed – a major statement of Christian doctrine – from the vantage point of paranormal research. In mainstream Christianity, the dominant religion of the West, the resurrection of Christ purports to hold one of the keys as to what Christians can expect – eternal rest and unification with God in Heaven. Christian funerals speak of the soul of the deceased going to a beautiful place where there is no grief or tears. Christianity grew out of Judaism and Graeco-Roman religion, both of which had notions of the afterlife. We also know from prehistory – Paleolithic and Neolithic times – that our ancestors developed ideas about the non-earthly realms. Human beings have long used their imaginations, as well as dreams and visions, to posit whether our souls – however defined – live on apart from our bodies and in what manner. Art and rituals were developed to send the dead on their way, to assuage the gods, to communicate with those "on the other side," and to comfort the living. The afterlife has been envisioned in a vast number of ways throughout the ages, from Egyptian banquets to happy hunting grounds to eternal rest to heavenly places where the citizens play harps to nothingness. For people perceived to be evil or who transgressed social standards, some kind of hell or eternal punishment is envisioned – unbearably fiery and hot or eternally cold. We will thus investigate strands of this religious history and compare ancient and traditional precepts with what has been learned from the scientific literature and modern investigations.

It is by deliberately linking modern science with traditional Western religion that I hope to make an original contribution to the vast field of the study of the afterlife. There have been a number of books on heaven, hell, Purgatory, beliefs about the afterlife, NDEs, parapsychology, Spiritualism, psychics, the occult, reincarnation, and other aspects of the paranormal. However, most of the books written from a religious perspective analyze people's *beliefs*, while many of the scientific studies ignore or disparage religion. One of the exceptions is *Life Beyond Death: Quest for the Unknown* from the

Reader's Digest Association in 1992.[7] In my opinion, this volume is somewhat hard to follow due to its layout, but it does deal intelligently with many paranormal topics for a broad audience. It is, however, over 20 years old. Another small book that treats these issues is *After Life: What it's like in Heaven, Hell and Purgatory* by Michael H. Brown.[8] The author, an investigative journalist, examines tenets of the Roman Catholic Church and stories of people who have had NDEs. The perspective is decidedly Roman Catholic; my use of religious language is less overt, and I will include considerably more peer-reviewed scientific literature.

Afterlife: The Other Side of Dying by Episcopal priest Morton T. Kelsey[9] treats many of the topics I discuss, from both religious and historical perspectives: heaven, hell, and Purgatory, NDEs, contact with loved ones who have died, dreams, parapsychology, and reincarnation. Kelsey's presentation is beautifully written and inspirational. However, it is nearly 35 years old, so I will build on many of his precepts and add substantially to the scientific evidence.

Several recent books treat paranormal and afterlife phenomena in intelligent ways without explicitly bringing religious concepts to bear. In *There is No Death and There are No Dead*, Tom and Lisa Butler, Directors of the American Association of Electronic Voice Phenomena, have traced the history of modern communication with the dead.[10] The book draws on the couple's years of experience with electronic voice phenomena (EVPs), much of which they published for lay and science audiences. The Butlers deliberately avoid overt religious themes.

Three recent books – Lisa Miller's *Heaven*, *Spook* by Mary Roach and Deepak Chopra's *Life After Death* – do look at religious aspects of afterlife exploration, with Roach and Chopra both also examining scientific evidence.[11] Miller, a journalist, does an excellent job of tracing many historical perspectives of heaven but seems not to be too convinced by any of them. Roach's approach is very entertaining and humorous but also highly skeptical of both religious and scientific evidence for survival after death. Chopra is completely in the camp of pro-afterlife (and reincarnation) conviction from both religious and scientific perspectives, although he comes from an Eastern outlook that may be somewhat foreign to Western readers.

As mentioned above, two medical doctors – Jeffrey Long and Eben Alexander – have recently presented their own findings on NDEs. Long has documented his web-based exploration of thousands of NDEs from around the world and outlined powerfully and elegantly the nine reasons he has come to believe in the existence of the soul after death. Alexander has written *Heaven Is Real: A Doctor's Experience of the Afterlife* outlining his NDE and retracting his previous dismissals of claims of heavenly out-of-body experiences. Another recent volume, and also a movie, is the account of four-year-old Colton Burpo's NDE, written by his father.[12] Other books appear on the market on a regular basis.

Very few New Testament scholars, my closest intellectual colleagues, have written specifically on individual survival after death and the science associated with it. The Right Reverend John Spong, retired Episcopal Bishop of Newark and a highly-regarded progressive (some might say radical) church leader, has probably come closest, tackling the issue of the afterlife in his 2009 book, *Eternal Life: A New Vision*.[13] A very compelling treatment, his conclusions differ somewhat from mine, and he includes virtually no scientific literature.

A remarkable and unique book that answers many questions about "the other side" is Ivan Cooke's *Arthur Conan Doyle's Book of the Beyond*.[14] Sir Arthur Conan Doyle, known best for the Sherlock Holmes detective character, died in 1930 but appeared in a number of carefully monitored and documented séances a few years later; the book is based on the wisdom that emerged via automatic writing that was communicated by the medium. Doyle was a long-time Spiritualist and wrote a definitive two-volume *History of Spiritualism*. We will draw heavily on both of these works, since the findings coincide remarkably with what has been learned from scientific and paranormal investigations, the work of twenty-first-century psychics and mediums, NDEs and OOBEs.

In dialogue with these previous treatments, what follows will focus on Western notions of the afterlife, introduce the reader to a vast array of scientific and anecdotal evidence and draw on my expertise as a New Testament scholar. Mine is a humble attempt to bring current scientific exploration of this enormous question to the attention of people in the West, especially people in religious circles, unchurched seekers, and skeptics who are willing to keep an open mind. I will attempt to present the science and other types of verifiable documentation alongside traditional religious views of life after death, the soul, God and eternity. I will of necessity deal with the evidence from a lay perspective, not being a scientist myself, and with the religious questions primarily from a Christian stance, not because Christianity is a superior religious framework (I do not hold to that notion) but because it the one with which I am most familiar and in which I have been raised and trained.[15] While much of the field of religion concerns theology and beliefs, my perspective will deal more with actual physical and anecdotal evidence from ancient people's lives as documented through archaeology and texts.

The scholarly treatment of religion does not mean that issues normally deemed in our culture as "personal," "private," philosophical or universal will not be considered. Rather, many of the larger and deeper concepts are revealed naturally, "on their own," as it were, because of the nature of the topic. When confronting the basic question of survival after physical death, one is automatically thrust into ultimate questions of life that our human ancestors have confronted for millennia – and which are usually confronted from a perspective we moderns consider "religious," "spiritual" or, more pejoratively, "superstitious." It should become evident that many ideas about the afterlife that are implied or alluded to by Western religions – heaven, angels, and the supremacy of love, to name just three – are in fact bolstered by the research. Therefore, to think about life after death is to "marry" science and religion/spirituality, without hesitation or apology. We will thus explore many themes that are encountered through the paranormal materials and that parallel or challenge religious, especially Christian, tenets.

To conclude this introduction and for clarification, I offer a few autobiographical points. First, I personally have not had any significant paranormal experiences. Therefore, I do not have a particular personal viewpoint to argue or defend, so I can remain relatively objective in presenting the evidence. Second, while I am not a medium or psychic, many of my beliefs as a progressive and feminist Christian, specifically from the perspective of the Episcopal Church, are supported by the scientific, experimental and anecdotal evidence. I hold strongly to the stance of many mainstream Christian traditions that Judaism and Christianity are, at base, forces for social justice and a "preferential option for the poor" and oppressed. My feminist convictions that all people should "have a place at the table," and of equality between the sexes, are supported by the afterlife evidence, as I hope will become clear.

Third, I have never been a skeptic or afterlife denier, having always believed in a soul and life after death, but I am now entirely convinced, after conducting this research, that there is survival of the individual after this earthly existence (not just an automatic "ascent" to heavenly bliss), that reincarnation is true, and that these are supported by science and observation. While none of us will truly know our fate in the afterlife until we get there, I believe I have a much clearer idea of what most of us can expect when we "cross over," and this book is an offering of that understanding.

Perhaps most importantly, I believe more than ever that what we do on earth matters; that "the other side," for most people, is one of beauty, growth and expanded consciousness; that those on "this side" can help those on the other side – and vice versa; that our animal friends and companions also survive and grow on the other side; that we are not alone, as earth dwellers, in the universe; that many souls reside on earth many times in some kind of reincarnation process, for the purpose of spiritual growth; and that there is a benevolent Divine Intelligence that can, must and will ultimately be accessed by all human beings – perhaps even by all Creation. Thus the scientific and anecdotal proofs of the afterlife can inform religious values in profound ways and vice versa, bringing healing, comfort and high ethical standards to our modern world.

Chapter 2: The Paranormal Scene Today and the Four Types of Evidence

- *"The only kind of evidence we accept is the kind that can be examined by others, whether it's a still photograph, a video recording, or an audio recording. If other people can't go over it and come to the same conclusions we did, it's not proof as far as we're concerned. Therefore, we go to great lengths to ensure the integrity of our documentation."* – Jason Hawes and Grant Wilson
- *"Theresa is a typical Long Island mom who has a very special gift. She talks to the dead."* – Theresa Caputo website
- *"[O]ur eternal spiritual self is more real than anything we perceive in this physical realm, and has a divine connection to the infinite love of the Creator."* – Eben Alexander, MD
- *"Think about how such knowledge – not belief or faith – would affect your own life pattern; the knowledge that you are indeed more than your physical body, that you do indeed survive physical death. . . [W]hat a difference that would make!"* – Robert A. Monroe

The proliferation of paranormal and afterlife investigations, organizations and television programs available to the Western public in the past decade and a half is astonishing. In the early 2000s, paranormal research societies, television shows, series and specials, books, and Internet sites exploded. Even National Public Radio offered a series on the afterlife in October 2013, interviewing a rabbi, a nun and a philosopher and inviting comments from listeners.[16] The interest in the afterlife and paranormal phenomena is rampant.

To some observers, this trend is alarming and dangerous. As long ago as the 1970s, Episcopal priest Morton Kelsey, a believer in life after death, addressed these concerns. He pointed out that prominent thinkers like Marx, Freud, and B.F. Skinner concluded that "religion [and belief in a future life] represent[ed] a return to the womb... [These men] were convinced that belief in a future life . . . keeps individuals from working to achieve" the goal of people sharing equally in material well-being. Further, "[w]ith the development of materialistic thought any existence not connected with the physical body became unthinkable."[17]

Kelsey explained further the fear that "men and women whose eyes are always turned toward heaven tend to forget this life" and deny it, rather than supporting and enhancing it.[18] Arthur Conan Doyle, two generations earlier, traced this fear among scientists, intellectuals and religion professionals to Western materialism: "There is only one school of thought to which [Spiritualism] is absolutely irreconcilable. That is the school of materialism, which holds the world in its grip at present and is the root cause of all our misfortunes."[19]

Even though material, physical existence is basic to true Christianity – which maintains that God (a spiritual Being) created both heaven and earth and that Jesus was incarnated into a flesh-and-blood human being – there is still in the West a fear among some that it is dangerous or at least misguided to dwell too much on what happens when we die.

Skeptics, critics and outright afterlife deniers often go even farther. They fear that generally sane people are falling into vast, unsupported delusions that make them misfits in a scientific, rational age; for deniers, nearly every example of paranormal testimony is rampant fraud, trickery and deception, usually for monetary gain. This negative attitude can be found throughout sources such as Wikipedia and even among religion professionals, as we shall see in future chapters.

If one believes that many of today's paranormal television programs and the groups and individuals behind them (along with the shows' producers and sponsors) are perpetrating fraud and pulling a great deal of wool over the public's eyes, it follows that the alarm and concern are justified. Heaven forbid (pun intended) that the entire population of the US be duped into believing in an afterlife due to what they might see on TV or the Internet! As we know only so well from the lowest points of human history – the mass hysteria of a Hitler or a Jim Jones, the vast "brainwashing" of people drawn to fanatical cults, the religious arguments of racial inferiority and slavery, the Crusades and the Inquisition – the argument goes that our rational age must at all costs avoid any kind of irrational belief, including religion and life after death.

While these arguments have some validity, and fraud, deception, many "fundamentalisms" and the complete surrender to irrational emotionalism must always be challenged, the criticisms of afterlife deniers are nearly as extreme as the views they criticize. Deniers and skeptics often throw the baby out with the bath water, emphasizing infrequent discrepancies and rare examples of fraud to the exclusion of decades of valid research and thousands of validated examples and experiments.

Unless all of these television programs have recruited actors to depict people who have experienced hauntings and have created lavish settings, which seems highly improbable, the evidence is compelling that what one sees on the TV screen or the web is real and not fraudulent. It would seem to be a herculean task, not to mention very expensive, for so many different cable and network television organizations to "stage" these programs, and one would have to wonder why. Widespread fraud is not beyond the realm of possibility in this world of unreal "reality" shows, camera tricks, and highly sophisticated cinematography, but one would truly need to question the motivation.

Further, it seems equally improbable that the myriad of documented university experiments, the books and in-person readings of psychics and mediums, the thousands of confirmed NDEs, and the work of the Edgar Cayce Foundation and the Monroe Institute are built on sand.

As we shall see, there are legitimate human and pastoral reasons for keeping an open mind in all directions. Despite objections to the television programs and to groups and individuals who investigate the paranormal, the fact is that millions of people – most of whom are by any measure rational, sensible and mentally sound – are not only fascinated by the paranormal but may indeed have experienced phenomena themselves. This in fact is often the reason that people have contacted an investigative group or medium in the first place. Sadly, many such inquirers have often been shunned and dismissed by their families, physicians, counselors and pastors due in large part to the prevalent views of skeptics, cynics and deniers.

It is impossible to document in this book all of the paranormal evidence currently available via modern media and technology. Rather, I will describe a selection of television programs, organizations, individuals and websites that meet several criteria: 1) they are generally available to the US public so that the reader can access them him/herself; 2) corroborating evidence can be attained from books, articles, public appearances, websites and other means; 3) there is little convincing evidence of fraud; and 4) for the most part they offer positive, beneficial perspectives rather than hateful or destructive ones. Through this examination, we will be introduced to the four types of evidence that support the reality of the afterlife and the survival of the individual soul after physical death: scientific techniques and methods; reputable psychics and mediums; NDEs; and OOBEs. As we shall see in Chapter 3, A Short History of Paranormal Research, the debates we are witnessing in the early twenty-first century are remarkably similar to those that took place in the nineteenth, at the dawn of our modern era. The reader is invited to weigh the evidence with an open mind – and an open heart.

Ghost-Hunting and the Use of Scientific Techniques

While some of the television shows and organizations that focus on the paranormal are geared toward entertainment, we will focus on those that purport to offer real assistance in dealing with hauntings, possession, and generally bothersome unexplained phenomena.[20] Specifically, we will consider *Paranormal State*, which presents cases of the Paranormal Research Society, originally associated with Pennsylvania State University and now based in Raleigh, North Carolina; *Ghost Hunters*, which focuses on cases of The Atlantic Paranormal Society (TAPS), based in Warwick, Rhode Island; and *Ghost Adventures* on the Travel Channel, featuring a team that uses a wide range of scientific instruments in its work.

The Paranormal Research Society (PRS) was founded in September 2001 by Penn State student Ryan Buell.[21] At the time, Buell, 19, established the group primarily as an outlet for his own investigative interests; he was joined over the next few years by fellow students who are familiar to those who watch *Paranormal State*, now in reruns: Eilfie Music, Sergey Poberezhny, Katrina Weidman, Heather Taddy, and Josh Light. PRS also benefits from the talents of psychics Chip Coffey, Michelle Belanger, Lorraine Warren (all of whom we will meet below), and Father Bob Bailey.

In 2002, PRS launched a paranormal conference, the "University Conference for Paranormal Research" (UNIV-CON). The conference did not draw many participants then or in 2003, but the 2003 conference introduced Buell and PRS to Jason Hawes and Grant Wilson from TAPS (see below). Many of the daily workshops at UNIV-CON were conducted by members of TAPS, and Hawes and Wilson became regular guests at UNIV-CON until 2007. By that year, attendance at the conference had grown to over 2,000, clearly demonstrating the interest in paranormal activity and investigations. However, the conferences appear to have ended in 2008, apparently because organizers no longer had the time to organize them.

The Arts and Entertainment network (A&E) learned about PRS and its work and contacted Buell about a documentary, which soon catapulted into a wildly popular television series. In April 2006, as Buell was graduating from Penn State, he and PRS shot a pilot for A&E and received news that the network had ordered a full season. As Buell returned to school for another degree, he and his team simultaneously conducted and filmed 13 investigations between November 2006 and Spring 2007. In October 2007 the pilot was shown during UNIV-CON 2007 to a sold-out crowd, and on December 10, 2007, *Paranormal State* debuted on television, with 2.5 million people watching the first episode.

In their investigations, the PRS team uses an array of techniques to diagnosis and handle the disturbance or situation. The investigators, who have had extensive training, obtain information from the victims or clients, as well as from neighbors and relatives; they visit local historical societies and libraries to understand the historical context of any events that may have influenced a haunting; and they carefully canvas the house, building and/or site, often with mediums, to know where the "hot spots" are. During "Dead Time," usually around 3:00 am when the crew turns off all their equipment so that the site is as dark and quiet as possible, the team members do the bulk of their on-site investigative work.[22]

Several examples demonstrate results related to the scientific techniques they employ. In one session, an old-fashioned telephone ringing sound was heard; at first Buell was annoyed, thinking a crew member had left his or her cell phone turned on, but despite a close examination, no explanation could be found. The sound, which occurred about five times, was captured on audio.[23] In another case, video surveillance during Dead Time captured a chair moving on its own; there was no physical explanation.[24] Similarly, motion detectors have "gone off [during Dead Time] when nothing visible (as documented by our cameras) was present."[25]

In late 2013, PRS celebrated its 12th anniversary, following its move to new headquarters in Raleigh, North Carolina. Buell had been diagnosed with pancreatic cancer in 2012 but battled it courageously and returned to work for the anniversary celebration after 18 months on leave.[26] We will encounter Buell, PRS and their research in future chapters.

The history and adventures of TAPS, the Atlantic Paranormal Society, are documented in a number of books written primarily by founders (and Roto-Rooter plumbers) Jason Hawes and Grant Wilson.[27] While Wilson has left the television series except for guest appearances, *Ghost Hunters* celebrated its tenth season on the air in 2014.[28]

For anyone who has seen a number of episodes of *Ghost Hunters*, especially over the past seven years, it becomes quickly apparent that the investigators are highly trained and professional. They treat their clients and each other respectfully (even as they joke around and tease one another occasionally), and they care not only about the living but also about the deceased with whom they come in contact. They always begin an investigation from a skeptical, open-minded stance; they listen carefully to their clients' stories of hauntings and disturbances but are always on the look-out for non-paranormal reasons for strange happenings. ". . . [T]he point is to try to debunk [the phenomenon] first."[29] This objectivity marks them as legitimate and not overly eager to ascribe as unearthly something that can be explained in normal ways.

In *Ghost Hunting*, Hawes outlines the goals that underlie their investigations. These include the following:
- "Eliminate all possible natural explanations"
- "Learn what the phenomenon does under other conditions, such as after prayer or when it is clearly addressed with questions"
- "Predict what the phenomenon might do if it were moved away from the venue in question."[30]

Using highly sophisticated instruments and devices, the team sifts through all the evidence they collect during an investigation, analyzes it with each other, and then presents it to the client. They are "determined to come as close to scientific accuracy as we possibly can. That's the only way we're going to produce reliable evidence and advance the study of the paranormal."[31]

In the course of their investigations, like the Paranormal Research Society and other teams, TAPS has obtained evidence of spirits from the other side through digital infrared cameras, electronic voice phenomena (EVPs), orbs that inexplicably register on film or videotape, and thermal-imaging digital cameras.[32] In interesting experiments documented in the television segments, entities have answered questions clearly and immediately by manipulating flashlights. The flashlights are placed in the darkened room at a considerable distance from the investigators and crew, and the team demonstrates for the spirits and the television audience that the flashlight can be turned on by twisting the end. The investigators ask yes-and-no questions, and the flashlights signal the answers. It is difficult to see how these experiments could be fraudulent, since no one is close to the flashlights and the answers to the questions are usually not known in advance to anyone on the team.

Finally, the Travel Channel carries *Ghost Adventures*, featuring Zak Bagans, Nick Groff and Aaron Goodwin. While this is a more flamboyant series, the three investigators (who do most of their own videotaping) and a few technical assistants nevertheless work from many of the same operating principles used by PRS and TAPS. One major difference is that Bagans tends to deliberately provoke spirits to achieve a reaction; in one episode a guest investigator actually warns him against using that tactic. In general, however, the *Ghost Adventures* team treats the living and the dead very respectfully, use highly sophisticated instruments (some created expressly for them), and obtain stunning results. In all-night lockdowns, they have personally been afflicted with marks on their skin by unseen forces, have been physically and emotionally impacted by otherworldly presences, and have found remarkable evidence for spirits on various instruments.

Whether they realize it or not, these modern-day investigators and ghost-hunting groups are studying the paranormal in ways similar to those used by the illustrious researchers of 150 and more years ago – and obtaining many of the same results.

Evidence from Reputable Psychics and Mediums

As we will see in Chapter 3 when we examine the history of paranormal research, there is no doubt that fraud and trickery can be found among people claiming to have psychic or mediumistic abilities. While skeptics, cynics and afterlife deniers might claim that *all* psychics and mediums are fraudulent, we will present here an overview of recent examples that are almost certainly authentic. Chapter 3 will show that our nineteenth-century ancestors were already paving the way with elaborate scientific experimentation at the level available to them at the time – and those investigators often faced the same virulent criticism and defamation.

First we need to briefly examine the terminology. While some practitioners use "psychic" and "medium" interchangeably, and we will do so in the service of simplicity, others are adamant as to which gifts and skills they possess. Generally speaking, a psychic is a person who is sensitive to parapsychological forces or influences,[33] while a medium is an intermediary between those in the physical world and those on the other side.[34] Additional terms for paranormally-gifted people include "seer," "intuitive" and "sensitive." Clairvoyance (from the French for "clear seeing") denotes the ability to perceive things by senses other than our usual physical five.[35]

The twentieth and early twenty-first centuries are witness to myriad accounts of gifted women and men – usually self-defined as psychics and/or mediums – who purport to connect directly with the souls of the departed. The accessibility of television shows, the Internet, articles, books and other media, would make it appear that they would be hard to miss; surprisingly, however, many Americans remain unaware of them. Listed below alphabetically are some of the more well-known practitioners in the West today.

- *Michelle Belanger*. A medium, NDE survivor and occult researcher based in Ohio, Michelle Belanger has written a number of books on the paranormal and has appeared in such shows as *Paranormal State*.[36] She grew up having paranormal experiences, nurtured her gifts over time, and now explains, "I hear the voices of the dead as whispers, not with my physical ears but with some internal faculty."[37] She has had experience with objects moving on their own in her presence and is part of a group of friends, House Kheperu, who "have memories of shared past lives."[38] While Belanger does not resonate with investigative technology, she admits that the combination of technology with her type of gift will allow us to "be that much closer to understanding the strange and shifting world that seems to exist just beyond the Veil."[39]

- *Theresa Caputo*. The "Long Island Medium," Theresa Caputo and her hit television show of the same name have reached millions of viewers since 2011 on TLC; she appears around the country without the cameras as well.[40] In almost every episode of the show, chance encounters in her daily life bring comfort and understanding to average, ordinary people who have lost someone dear to them. Caputo will sense a spirit "pushing through" to her and leading her to the person who needs to receive a message. She will validate the spirit's presence by a mundane or obscure observation that cannot possibly be known to or discovered by Caputo in advance. In some cases, the spirit will let his or her loved one know why the tragedy happened; in other cases, the entity will reassure the survivor that there was nothing that s/he could have done to prevent the death. In many instances, proof is provided to the survivor that the deceased knew exactly what was going on during a coma or on a death bed, and the entity also knows about significant events – marriages, births, graduations – that occur after he or she has crossed over.[41]
- *Edgar Cayce*. The "sleeping prophet," raised a Fundamentalist Christian in the late nineteenth and early twentieth century, Edgar Cayce gave thousands of Life Readings, while in trance, until his death in 1943. His foundation, the Association for Research and Enlightenment, still exists in Virginia Beach, Virginia, and books about his work remain popular and inspiring. The Life Readings he gave to clients provide fascinating insight into the lost

civilization of Atlantis, the life of Jesus, reincarnation, healing and other paranormal phenomena.[42] Cayce's revelations include: "Free will . . . is always stronger than preordained destiny."[43] "Karma. . . [is] a universal law of cause and effect which provides the soul with opportunities for physical, mental and spiritual growth."[44] "As the soul of an individual travels through the realms of being, it shifts and changes its pattern as it uses or abuses the opportunities presented to it."[45] "The Law of Grace is a perpetually available alternative to the soul – the working off of accumulated debts, by unselfish dedication to the welfare of others even less fortunate than itself."[46]

- *Chip Coffey.* Based outside Atlanta, Chip Coffey has been working as a psychic and medium only since losing his job as a travel agent in the aftermath of the tragedy of September 11, 2001.[47] However, he was aware of his psychic gifts since childhood and now has helped a number of children and adolescents with his television show and website, *Psychic Kids*.[48] He has astonished thousands with his accurate readings, and his experience in the aftermath of the 9/11 attacks at New York's World Trade Center is both astonishing and comforting: "As I looked down on the site where the two majestic towers once soared into the sky, tears streamed down my face. I felt the sadness and the loss, but then a new emotion swept over me: peace. In my mind, I saw thousands of angels flocking to the World Trade Center on that awful September morning. God had sent them there to take away the souls of those who died . . . far, far away from the horror and devastation."[49]

- *Pam Coronado and Laurie Campbell.* Pam Coronado and Laurie Campbell, mediums who have assisted law enforcement agents in solving murders, appeared together in the television show *Sensing Murder*. Coronado has also appeared in *We See Dead People* on A&E, *Miracle Detectives* on OWN and recently, *the uneXplained* on Biography and is currently starting up a foundation to help locate missing persons. She says, "I have combined the talents of skilled and tested intuitives with search and rescue professionals and law enforcement investigators in missing person cases that have gone cold or resources have run dry."[50] She is also president of the International Remote Viewing Association. Laurie Campbell works with researchers and scientists at major universities on consciousness issues and in studies to help prove that the afterlife exists. She works "with police departments as a criminal profiler to help solve cases current, open investigations and cold cases, some of which are over thirty years old." She is firmly convinced that "Death is not the end but a new beginning. Spirits . . . are with us always."[51]

- *John Edward.*[52] John Edward is a renowned psychic medium who has appeared in person and on television shows around the world. He has channeled spirits of deceased space shuttle astronauts, victims of the September 11th attacks, and hundreds of others. He notes that it is atheists who "are usually the loudest energies who come through once they get to the Other Side because they have so much to say after they realize, *Yikes – I was wrong, there is an afterlife after all!*"[53] He asserts "that we all decide when to leave our physical body and 'go home' or 'join God.'" This is generally a subconscious realization by the soul that it is time to move to the next phase of the spiritual journey.[54] Edward does not know if we decide *how* we will die,[55] but other information suggests that tragic deaths, especially of people who seem innocent, may be related to karma. Like other mediums, he does not usually remember the readings he gives and can usually stay emotionally detached so that the entities can come through with their messages.[56] As we shall see in Chapter 3 when we examine the nineteenth- and early twentieth-century psychic researchers, Edward has learned that spirits often do not come through well in a hostile environment: "If these energies are not 'welcomed' or think we're taking their attempts to make contact as a joke, they won't bother to come back. Why should they? Would you visit a friend or relative who slammed a door in your face?"[57] Also echoing the experiences of other mediums, both past and present, Edward has learned from the entities that they grow spiritually on the other side and that relationships that may have been damaged on this side can actually improve once one of the parties crosses over.[58]

- *Maureen Hancock.* Maureen Hancock lives and works in Bridgewater, Massachusetts, and focuses most of her gifts and energies on healing, after having successfully healed herself of a serious illness while pregnant with her first child.[59] Like other psychics and mediums, Hancock attributes her extraordinary gifts to a power higher than herself. A devout Roman Catholic, she calls on healing guides and guardian spirits not only from Christianity but also from ancient religions, Judaism, Buddhism, American Indian belief systems, and even her own family.[60] Her experience has taught her that "we create our own realities," that spirits go through an orientation to "heaven" when they first cross over, and that animals' "messages are just the same as human messages."[61]

- *Phil Jordan.* With his duel occupations as an ordained pastor and licensed funeral director in New York State, Phil Jordan has had long experience with death and dying. Following discovery of his psychic abilities by successfully locating a missing boy alive in 1975, Jordan began to assist law enforcement. As a Deputy with the Tioga County Sheriff's department, he helps with their missing persons, homicide, and arson cases. "He graduated from New York State Municipal Police Training Academy in 1976, and continues to work with the police agencies in all levels of government across the country.... Many of his accomplishments and successes have been documented in television episodes on Court TV/Tru TV, Biography, A&E and other major networks, in the United States, Canada, Great Britain, Europe and Africa." [62]
- *Noreen Renier.* Based in Virginia, Noreen Renier is a prominent psychic investigator who, like Phil Jordan, Pam Coronado and Laurie Campbell, has helped law enforcement solve dozens of missing persons cases and homicides and other crimes.[63] Renowned FBI profiler Robert Ressler has enormous respect for her, as do detectives around the country. Renier specializes in psychometry, whereby she holds an object connected to the victim, goes into a trance and relives the crime; she is able not only to venture into the mind and emotions of the victim but can also channel the perspective of the perpetrator and even modes of transportation. She has successfully worked with animals as well. In 1985, John Merrell, a founder of Northwest Skeptics, a group dedicated to discrediting the paranormal, brought a lawsuit against Renier for fraud; after many years of litigation, she prevailed,

with the Court of Appeals of Oregon even upholding the decision.[64]

- *James Van Praagh.*[65] James Van Praagh is an internationally-known spiritual medium and best-selling author who has appeared on countless television shows for over 30 years. According to his website, "he has been recognized as one of the most accurate spiritual mediums working today. His messages have brought solace, peace and spiritual insights, changing millions view of both life and death. He has received many awards for dedicating himself to changing the consciousness of the planet." He has channeled "evidential details from many famous deceased personalities like Marilyn Monroe, Slim Pickins, Rock Hudson, Frank Sinatra, Roy Orbison, Lucille Ball, Andrew Carnegie, Liberace, Princess Diana, Michael Jackson, Johnny Carson, Gandhi, Edgar Cayce, Benjamin Franklin and even Abraham Lincoln." Among the many wise messages he has received from these and his spirit guides are information regarding reincarnation, group karma, and pre-birth decisions. Group death occurs when a number of people "leave as a soul group," that is, they die together in a natural disaster, bombing, or plane crash in order to fulfill a karmic debt. Group karma can also refer to the karma of a group of people or nation.[66] Reincarnation, or the return to the physical world as another human being with the same soul, is affirmed time and again by Van Praagh, as it is for many others. A soul spends the time between incarnations "familiarizing itself with knowledge about the material level of existence." An Etheric Council, a group of highly evolved beings, assists souls to re-enter a physical life, although it is the individual spirit that makes the final determination (an example of the fact of free will). Each incarnation has a number of tests and trials that are "opportunities to develop and expand by living through adversity."[67] While not overtly political, Van Praagh, by working so closely with spirits on the other side, has reached many conclusions that might be termed progressive or liberal.[68]

- *Lorraine Warren.*[69] Lorraine Warren is a trance medium and psychic who can read people's auras; she and her late husband Ed, a religious demonologist trained as a visual artist, are best known for their work on the Amityville hauntings in upstate New York but have many other accomplishments to their credit. Their stance is decidedly religious: they believe that their work is in God's service and that often they are combatting forces that oppose God. They founded the New England Society for Psychic Research in 1952 for the purpose of investigating paranormal phenomena and assisting "stuck" spirits; the Society does not charge for its services and only asks that expenses be covered. The Warrens' and Society's website, http://www.warrens.net/Warrens-Bio.html, outlines their investigative approach in Ed's words: "Many times we use three or four clairvoyants in the same place. We take them into a house one-at-a-time, they don't know where they're going, what the case is about, etc. And if they all tell me the same thing, that they see a woman spirit in a certain room or a man or a child, then I know that we're on the right track. I do think scientifically, we do have scientists working with us, and I think theologically and scientifically. There are organizations of atheists, so-called skeptical investigators that say, 'There is no proof scientifically that God exists, that spirits exist, that miracles occur.' That's ridiculous, there's all kinds of proof."

- *Nancy Orlen Weber.* Nancy Orlen Weber is a psychic, healer and holistic educator based in New Jersey. Originally trained as a nurse, she began to realize her psychic gifts while serving as Head Nurse in the Acute Psychiatric Unit of the former Lincoln Hospital in the south Bronx. Working individually and in groups resulted in offers from psychiatrists to apply her abilities to research. In 1975, Weber opened her own practice and, in 1977, began working once a week with a psychiatrist's clients. She responsibly refers clients to appropriate practitioners, realizing that she is not always the person to continue the work. For her law enforcement work, she earned a police badge in 1982 and was awarded a Chief of Detectives badge from a Commissioner in New Jersey in 2006. In 2004, Court TV (now TruTV) aired *Psychic Detective*, in which Weber appears in four episodes. (The series remains one of the network's most popular shows.) She has also been featured on the two-hour special *Mediums*, the *Nancy Grace Show*, the *Ricki Lake Show*, and *The Other Side* on APTN, the Aboriginal Peoples Network. Her Lightwing Center of the LifeSpirit Seminary offers courses related to holistic practices.[70]

As we can see from these examples, psychics and mediums provide some of the best validation for the survival of the individual soul after death. Time and again, when a reputable, gifted medium channels a spirit, it is almost impossible for the information provided to the "seeker," the person receiving the reading, to be gained by normal means. Try as they might, skeptics and deniers have repeatedly been unable to find proof of fraud when a medium provides a seeker with information that could not possibly have been discovered by a private investigator, neighbor, friend, relative, Google search, or even ESP. The evidence is oftentimes so mundane and obscure, often known only to the seeker and the deceased, that the only viable explanation is that the entity on the other side actually is present in the seeker's life, can see what he or she is doing, and possesses expanded knowledge of life in the physical world.[71]

Readings of psychics and mediums, including those who use automatic writing while in a trance state, also provide highly reputable and often certifiable information about reincarnation and past lives. Van Praagh has channeled a number of souls that have been verified by the sitters themselves, and he has been regressed himself to grow spiritually.[72] Caputo too has undergone past life regressions to enhance her abilities and grow spiritually.[73] Recently some psychiatrists and therapists have begun to regress patients, with great success, in order for their past lives to inform their current lives and to ease symptoms ranging from fear and anxiety to loneliness and despair.[74] Psychics, mediums and patients who have been regressed gain enormous clarity from discovering their previous lives on earth; they are able to uncover the origins of certain phobias, attractions (to people, places, professions, and so on), and even understand marks on the body that correspond to points of injury in a past life. We will deal more with reincarnation in later chapters.

The imparting of knowledge and wisdom from the other side through psychics and mediums begins to address the "why" question and human tragedy, as we have touched on above. In countless examples, the spirit or entity provides a comforting explanation for what seems to us in the physical world to be a random, senseless tragedy. In many cases, as seen in *Long Island Medium*, for instance, a young child dies in order that another child can be born to that couple, or the husband who died while his wife was pregnant is reborn as the infant. Evidence about pre-birth decisions shows that, in our in-between state on the other side, we know who we will be and what will become of us in our next incarnation; as shocking as it may seem, *we* decide – for karmic reasons oftentimes – that we will die young, suddenly or tragically.

In two final examples, we see how psychics and mediums help mitigate tragic loss. Three young men die in a horrible car crash and fire, seemingly for no reason, but it is revealed through the medium that the three men had been US soldiers in Vietnam and had callously set fire to the car in which a young couple was hiding. It was the men's karma that caused their seemingly senseless death, and they testified through the medium (Van Praagh, in this case) to the fact that their debts were now paid and they were free.[75] Hancock describes a reading for the mother a four-year-old, Lulu, who died in July 2001 when a bike rack fell over and pierced her heart. Hancock explained to Lulu's mother that "Lulu is a highly evolved being who served her purpose here on earth and now is able to help so many more" on the other side.[76]

Evidence from Near-Death Experiences

Near-death experiences (NDEs) have been recorded since ancient times. However, due to great advances in Western medicine since the 1970s, they have become much more common. The pioneering work of Raymond Moody, with his 1975 book *Life After Life,* launched the examination of NDEs in the medical profession and brought NDEs to the public's attention. Years later, Dr. Jeffrey Long started the Near Death Experience Research Foundation and its website, NDERF.org, to "to collect as many NDEs as I could and to collect them through a questionnaire that would make it easy to separate and study their elements." In the first 10 years of the survey's existence, 1998-2008, more than 1,300 accounts of NDEs from around the world were collected and analyzed.[77] Other studies and reports of NDEs in the twentieth and early twenty-first centuries have included those of

Doctors Bruce Greyson, Michael Sabom, Kenneth Ring, Margot Grey, Michael Rawlings[78] and Eben Alexander[79] and the young boy Colton Burpo.[80]

As we will note in Chapter 4, The Science of the Afterlife: Instruments and Investigations, the objections cited by skeptics and deniers to explain away NDEs by various scientific means are systematically refuted by Long, Alexander and others. They have firmly come to the following conclusions about death, the afterlife and related paranormal phenomena after studying and/or having an NDE:

1. "[C]onsciousness leaves the body at death." That is, "having a vivid and conscious experience at the time of clinical death is among the best evidence available to suggest a conscious existence after bodily death."[81] One cannot have a highly organized experience while unconscious or clinically dead.[82] In Alexander's terms, "consciousness is the basis of all that exists. I was so totally connected to it that there was often no real differentiation between 'me' and the world I was moving through."[83]

2. The common report in an NDE of an out-of-body experience (OOBE), whereby the person near death can relate later, often in minute detail, events occurring around him or her and/or things happening to his or her body, is further affirmation of an afterlife, a conscious existence apart from our physical one. "Approximately half of all NDEs have an [OOBE] that involves seeing or hearing earthly events."[84] In a study of 617 near-death accounts, 46.5% described OOBEs "that contained observations of earthly events that would allow others to objectively assess the reality of their observations. Of this group of 287 OBErs, 280 (97.6 percent) were found to have had out-of-body experiences that were *entirely* realistic and lacked *any* content that was unrealistic."[85]

3. Studies of NDEs show that people born blind have entirely visual NDEs. While the dreams of people born blind do not include vision, and "[i]t is medically inexplicable for someone born blind to have a detailed and organized visual experience," those born blind who have an NDE "may immediately have full and clear vision."[86] Thus the NDE is a real experience of another dimension of reality, not a dream, hallucination or fabrication.
4. NDEs are not the result of too much or too little anesthesia.[87] "By conventional medical thinking, neither a person under anesthesia nor a person experiencing cardiac arrest should have a conscious experience like that of an NDE. Yet the NDERF study found many that do."[88] These survivors can recount in detail the attempts of the surgeons to resuscitate them and also report seeing a bright light, meeting deceased loved ones, and having thoughts and memories that are unusually clear.[89]
5. The Life Review is reported in many NDE accounts and is often transformative for the person for the rest of his or her life. In many of the accounts of the Life Review, the person sees fragments of his or her earthly life, often from a third-person perspective. They see how their actions affected others, both positively and negatively, they judge themselves (i.e., there is no higher God judging them), and in some cases they are aided by a spiritual guide. Of 617 NDEs studied, 14 percent included the Life Review. "*None* of the life reviews contained content that was considered unrealistic, either to the NDErs or to me."[90]
6. Many people who have an NDE report joyous reunions with deceased relatives and other loved ones. Sometimes the entities encountered are not immediately recognizable to the

NDE survivor but are revealed after return to physical life. Entities who were elderly at death often appear in the NDE as in their prime of life, while children often appear older.[91] In some cases, the spirits who appear to the person having the NDE are Jesus or the Virgin Mary.[92] These appearances could not be the result of wishful thinking, dreaming, hallucination, or fabrication.[93]

7. Young children who experience NDEs report content very similar to that of adult NDE survivors, so the content of NDEs is not the result of preexisting beliefs.[94] Furthermore, children who experience an NDE almost always report that they had less anxiety about death than people in the general population, "increased psychic abilities, a higher zest for life, and increased intelligence."[95]

8. There is remarkable consistency about the content of NDEs from around the world; they are not just Western occurrences.[96] Furthermore, *"Preexisting cultural beliefs do not significantly influence the content of NDEs."*[97] While the language of some of the surveys, English, may be somewhat misunderstood by a segment of respondents whose first languages are not English, Long and others have found that people's basic NDE is consistent not only in content and the order of occurrence but also in principles and values. Many respondents report conclusions such as "I was everything and everything was me" and "[c]onsciously living by love is the essence of life itself"[98]

9. Various scientific explanations for NDEs are ultimately untenable. Alexander discusses several: the evolutionary argument, that the experience is a "primitive brainstem program to ease terminal pain and suffering;" the distorted recall of memories from deeper parts of the limbic system; a

mimicking of the hallucinatory anesthetic ketamine; a "dump" of the chemical N,N-dimethyltryptamine (DMT); isolated preservation of cortical regions of the brain; the action of the subcortical regions of the brain; a "reboot phenomenon," whereby bizarre, disjointed memories are randomly dumped to create the visions that Alexander witnessed. Alexander handily disputes all of these theories, in consultation with other physicians, because his meningitis was so severe and because the theories do not "explain the robust, richly interactive nature of [my] recollections."[99]

Dr. Susan Blackmore of Plymouth University in England is one of the premiere scientist skeptics in the areas of NDEs, parapsychology, and psychic phenomena.[100] Early in her career, having had an OOBE herself, she set out "to show those closed-minded scientists that consciousness could reach beyond the body and that death was not the end." However, "Just a few years of careful experiments changed all that. I found no psychic phenomena – only wishful thinking, self-deception, experimental error and, occasionally, fraud. I became a sceptic."[101] Unlike Alexander, Long, Monroe, Assante and others, she concluded that OOBEs are hallucinatory, "merely products of disturbed functioning of the brain."[102] She no longer studies the paranormal, being "too tired" to try to devise experiments to disprove the next psychic's claim, so she has turned her attention in part to the issue of consciousness.[103] This field, as we have seen above, is also of great interest to Dr. Alexander, Deepak Chopra[104] and the medium Laurie Campbell, for instance, as it was to Monroe, but they take different approaches and come to different conclusions.

For Alexander, Long, Chopra, the researchers who study Campbell, and other scientists and physicians, and for the people around the world who have had NDEs, there is no better and more consistent, logical explanation for what has happened to them that the experience was real and a taste of what lies before all of us at "death." NDEs provide solace, hope and assurance not only of the survival of the individual after bodily death but also of another level (or levels) of existence where peace, joy and love abide for eternity.[105]

Evidence from Out-of-Body Experiences
In this section, we will rely almost exclusively on the work of Virginia businessman Robert A. Monroe. While OOBEs (as a phenomenon separate from NDEs) have been experienced fairly often in the East, Monroe is the primary Western investigator not only to document his extensive sessions but also to found an institute dedicated to training others to do the same.

Monroe began having OOBEs in 1958 when in his early 40s. After overcoming his fear that he might have been dying and after consulting with mental health professionals who confirmed for him that he was not going crazy, he learned over time not only to have OOBEs at will but also to record them for posterity and adventure further and further into unknown territory.[106]

Through his journeys and experimentation, Monroe discovered many of the same things that are witnessed through EVPs and other electronic media, psychics and mediums, and people who have had NDEs.

- Monroe was able to travel, in "spirit," to friends and relatives still in the physical world, witness what they were doing at given times, and have them confirm what he reported. In October 1962, to take one example, he had an OOBE in which he visited his friend R.W. in her apartment eight miles away. As she sat in a chair, he approached her. At first she did not notice him but then became frightened. He backed away and was pulled back into the physical. The next day he talked to her, and she told him that there "was something hanging and waving in the air. . . . It was like a filmy piece of gray chiffon." She had thought it might be Monroe, knowing about his experiments, so she apparently asked him to leave, and "it backed away and faded out quickly."[107]

- Monroe had several experiences in which he conversed during an OOBE with someone who died at approximately the same time.[108] He also connected with his departed father.[109]
- Monroe affirmed our survival of physical death, and the training his institute provides allows people to gain this knowledge for themselves.[110]
- He experienced oneness with the universe and other beings, along with immense love: "Most important, you are not alone. With you, beside you, interlocked in you are others. . . .[Y]ou are bonded to them with a great single knowledge. They are exactly like you, they are you, and like you, they are Home. You feel with them, like gentle waves of electricity passing between you, a completeness of love."[111] "One of the greatest enigmas of this whole affair is that someone – or more than one – has been helping me from time to time in such experimentation."[112]
- Monroe discovered the link between thought and action: "*Thought-action synchronicity.* Whereas in the physical state action follows thought, here they are one and the same. . . One gradually appreciates the existence of thought as a force in itself rather than as a trigger or catalyst. It is primarily an emotional thought force."[113]
- He connected with higher spiritual beings who helped him in various ways and imparted to him great wisdom.[114]

- He affirmed the truth of reincarnation and past lives on earth,[115] as well as the existence of beings who never existed in the physical world.[116]

Common Themes

As should be apparent, a number of themes emerge from some or all of these types of evidence. While these will be fleshed out more fully in Chapter 6, Themes and Findings, and a summary list is provided in Appendix I, we will briefly note some of them here.

- When we die, our basic personality survives. What survives is sometimes referred to as the soul. The "souls" of animals also survive physical death.
- It is possible for entities who have crossed over and those of us still in the physical world to communicate with each other.[117]
- There are other levels of existence apart from the physical, material one on earth, sometimes referred to as heaven.
- The evidence suggests that, for most people when we cross over at physical death, we experience the other levels of existence as "places" or conditions of joy, peace and love.
- Some entities encountered in the heavenly realm are beings that have never resided in physical, earthly form; these entities are sometimes referred to as angels and could account for tales of extraterrestrials and UFOs.
- Most people now residing on earth, and many entities on the other side, have had many prior earth lives and may have many more after this one. This phenomenon is usually referred to as reincarnation.
- Reincarnation is completely tied to the law of cause and effect, or karma. That is, the harm that we do to others in this

life, if not rectified in this life, must be overcome by good in another earthly existence (not necessarily sequentially in earth-time). The good we do in this life is never lost or wasted.
- The main reason-for-being of all souls is to unite in harmony with the universe, whose nature is perfect love and which has no beginning or end.

Because the evidence of paranormal phenomena that we have examined and the themes that emerge from them are both accessible to the Western public and still relatively unknown, not to mention roundly criticized by scientists, religion professionals and many others, we will examine in Chapter 3 the longer and quite illustrious history of paranormal research in the West. As we shall see, investigators ranging from William James and Arthur Conan Doyle to Ian Stevenson and J.B. Rhine have reached many of the same conclusions that we have examined here, and an array of important and life-affirming themes has emerged from their extensive, careful and well-documented research.

Chapter 3: A Short History of Paranormal Research

- *"The British Society for Psychical Research formally convened for the first time on February 20, 1882, representing a branch of science so new that the organizers felt compelled to invent a name for it. . . . The SPR . . . [was] founded because there were questions – of immortality and of humanity – that demanded investigation."* – Deborah Blum
- *"I am persuaded of the medium's [Leonora Piper's] honesty and the genuineness of her trance. I now believe her to be in the possession of a power as yet unexplained."* – William James
- *The powers of [Daniel Dunglas] Home have been attested by so many famous observers, and were shown under such frank conditions, that no reasonable man can possibly doubt them."* – Arthur Conan Doyle
- *"Between the deaths and apparitions of the dying person and the living a connexion exists which is not due to chance alone. This we hold as a proved fact."* – Nora Sidgwick

Research on paranormal phenomena, the afterlife, parapsychology, and near-death experiences has been conducted in the West for over a century and a half. While this may come as a surprise to many of us, a number of scientific journals have long published the findings of peer-reviewed scientific experiments in these areas – *Journal of Parapsychology, Proceedings of the Society for Psychical Research, Journal of Religion and Psychical Research, Journal of Scientific Exploration* and *Journal of the American Society for Psychical Research*, to name a few. The esteemed *Encyclopaedia Britannica*, in its 1963 edition, dealt favorably with the paranormal in its articles on "Parapsychology" (Vol. 17) and "Spiritualism" (Vol. 21), drawing in part on studies undertaken within various departments of American and other research universities.

In this chapter, we will provide an overview of research in the nineteenth, twentieth and early twenty-first centuries, the founding, mission and work of various psychical research societies, the findings of seer/clairvoyant Edgar Cayce and psychiatrist Ian Stevenson on reincarnation, and current experiments being conducted at universities in the US and abroad. We will also look into the claims of skeptics and briefly discuss the problem of fraud and deception.

Paranormal Research in the Nineteenth Century

A who's who of luminaries in the nineteenth century was drawn to the paranormal for many personal and professional reasons. Mostly men, they attempted to explain phenomena from their particular scientific points of view. They included naturalists, anthropologists, chemists, and physicists, and they were joined in their intellectual quests by philosophers, economists, poets, psychologists, Nobel Laureates and writers. Several of these greats were involved in the founding of the Society for Psychical Research (SPR) in England in 1882 and its US counterpart, the American Society for Psychical Research (ASPR). While generally respected in their scientific fields, thus proving their intelligence and their dedication to rational principles, some of these researchers were vilified by their colleagues for their stances on the paranormal; sadly, their experience is often shared by today's paranormal researchers. Short biographical sketches of the pioneer investigators of the nineteenth century can be found in Appendix I.

Concurrently with the work of these researchers were the people who prompted the formation of the societies – psychics, mediums and others who appeared to demonstrate phenomena that could not be explained by the science of the time, or explained away. In addition, a number of normal, everyday Europeans and Americans were reporting their own extraordinary experiences – appearances in dreams of loved ones whom the dreamer believed to be alive, only to learn that the person had died around the time of the dream; precognitive visions that were later deemed to be correct; hauntings; and objects moving by themselves. In an age of exploration, growing sophistication, the founding of universities, the rise of science, the aftermath of the Civil War, and the formation of alternative religious and spiritual groups, it is not surprising that intellectuals banded together to investigate unexplainable phenomena. In the words of British philosopher and economist Henry Sidgwick, the first president of the SPR, the Society was "founded because there were questions – of immortality and of humanity – that demanded investigation" and "because conventional science had tried to block even the most modest of inquiries along those lines."[118]

The SPR, which still exists in London, was founded to "understand events and abilities commonly described as psychic or paranormal" as well as "to examine allegedly paranormal phenomena in a scientific and unbiased way." The SPR does not ascribe to any particular set of beliefs and, in fact, many of its members are fairly skeptical.[119] The Society's headquarters includes a library and office, and it sponsors an annual conference, lectures, and two study days each year; the Cambridge University Library contains many of the Society's publications. Its peer-reviewed quarterly is the *Journal of the Society for Psychical Research*, and it also produces *Proceedings* and the magazine *Paranormal Review*.[120]

Among the early members of SPR was a wide swath of British and American intelligentsia and high society – Alfred, Lord Tennyson, the Rev. Charles L. Dodgson (aka Lewis Carroll), Samuel Clemens (aka Mark Twain), William Crookes, Alfred Russel Wallace, and William James. The Society's membership quickly grew to more than 200, attracting "painters, clergymen, politicians, spiritualists, and a cast of writers."[121] Sir Arthur Conan Doyle, famed creator of detective Sherlock Holmes, included a fair and comprehensive history of the SPR in his masterful two-volume *History of Spiritualism*, on which we will draw extensively in what follows.[122]

Although Henry Sidgwick was more skeptical than some of the other Society founders, he proved to be a strong leader and competently assigned the various tasks. Poet, classicist, philologist and psychologist Frederic Myers and psychologist Edmund Gurney were to investigate apparitions; William Barrett, physicist and parapsychologist, focused on thought transference; and Sidgwick's very capable wife, Nora (Balfour), was assigned to investigate ghosts.[123]

Eminent psychologist and Harvard professor William James invited William Barrett to Boston in 1884, where Barrett met with professionals in a number of fields, including theologians from Harvard Divinity School, to describe the work of the SPR. Barrett presciently warned them "to expect ridicule if they took up his challenge."[124] Within a year of Barrett's visit, the ASPR was founded, led by trained researchers using "purely scientific methods."[125] The ASPR remained open to non-scientists, so early members in addition to William James included James' publisher, Henry Holt; Gardiner Hubbard, founder of the National Geographic Society; Charles Everett, dean of Harvard Divinity School; philosophy professor George Fullerton from the University of Pennsylvania; and Minot Savage of Boston, a pastor and author.[126]

While the ASPR had a rocky start – its new President, astronomer Simon Newcomb, exchanged strident articles and letters in the journal *Science* with Edmund Gurney and William James over Barrett's experiments and other psychical work[127] – it still managed to survive and thrive, with headquarters now in New York,[128] and a great deal of work was accomplished by both the SPR and the ASPR as the nineteenth century waned.

As part of their task to investigate apparitions, Myers and Gurney placed ads in British newspapers soliciting accounts of their supernatural experiences from ordinary citizens.[129] What resulted, in 1886, was the massive two-volume *Phantasms of the Living*, co-authored with Frank Podmore. From over 5,700 responses to their questionnaires, Gurney reported the following results: 23 persons had had a "visual hallucination" within 12 hours of the person's death (quite a high number compared to the random chance of a trillion to one); more than half of 702 crisis apparitions appeared near the moment of death; and 25 of 702 occurred near the end of a fatal illness.[130] From their research, Myers and the SPR offered important conclusions and theories:

1. Telepathy (the transfer of thoughts and feelings from one mind to another) was a fact in Nature;
2. Phantasms (that is, impressions, voices, or figures of the dead and dying) were seen by loved ones with a frequency beyond chance; and
3. Telepathy might explain these phantasms: one mind acted on another's.[131]

The authors had no way of knowing that these conclusions would be substantiated time and again over the next 150 years and into our own day, as we will see further in this study.

There were other investigations and revelations as well. In 1892, Nora Sidgwick, by that time principal of Newnham College, which had been founded as an all-women's institution by her husband Henry, completed the Census of Hallucinations. The census, in which six countries participated (England, France, Germany, Russia, Brazil, and the US), documented survey results from thousands of people. Of the

17,000 death-day apparitions of loved ones reported in England, 2,272 respondents claimed to have seen an apparition near the time of death. The SPR reduced this number to 32, based on various criteria – which still resulted in odds that were well beyond chance. Nora calculated that the chance of any one person dying in England was 1 in 19,000, and the chance of a recognizable hallucination of a certain person was also 1 in 19,000. Thus for every 19,000 deaths, there should be only one such appearance. The rate of 32 out of 17,000 people surveyed was 442.6 times the chance rate of 0.723. A smaller number of persons in the US who had these experiences – 7,123 – was surveyed, with similar stunning results: the appearance of death-day apparitions was 487 times the rate predicted by chance.[132]

In addition to Nora's Census and reports from ordinary people recounted in *Phantasms of the Living*, members of the American and British Societies conducted various types of experiments on several psychics, mediums and clairvoyants of the day. Significantly, their work brought to light several examples of fraud and deceit. Madame Blavatsky – Helena Petrovna Blavatsky, founder of the Theosophical Society, who claimed to have powers of astral projection – was one of these. She was investigated in Bombay, India, by Australian researcher Richard Hodgson, who concluded in 1885 that Blavatsky was "one of the most accomplished, ingenious and interesting imposters in history."[133]

British author Frank Podmore examined the phenomena of telekinesis and poltergeists – 11 supposed cases in England – and published his findings in the *Proceedings of the Society for Psychical Research*. Even though he was one of the collaborators on *Phantasms of the Living*, he concluded "that the flying objects and crashing furniture could be attributed simply to girls seeking attention."[134] Unfortunately for reputable psychics and mediums, the 1890s evolved into a time of "creations of fiction writers – ghost, demons, creatures of the nights – stalking the pages of magazines and books."[135] It became difficult to discern fact and credible research from fiction.

James Hyslop, an American psychologist, philosopher and ASPR member, was outraged at scams being perpetrated on New Yorkers who visited the Occult Bookstore on West 42nd Street. The trickery involved questions that sitters would write on a piece of paper, which they would then crumple into a tiny ball or "pellet" and place in a bowl or tray. The medium would then supposedly answer a given question without virtue of looking at the pellet. Hyslop fooled the medium by putting a pellet on the table, ripping it to shreds in feigned embarrassment, then asking the spirit to provide an opinion on the question anyway; the medium could not oblige. Hyslop thus determined how the deceit was accomplished: when the medium could successfully distract the sitters, he or she could view the questions on the pellets without anyone noticing.[136]

This did not diminish Hyslop's absolute belief in communication with the dead, however, as he wrote in *Harper's*: he could find no fraud or deceit whatsoever in the medium Leonora Piper, whose gifts we will explore below. Hyslop also received messages from his deceased father that he could not debunk,[137] and he "honestly and fearlessly declared himself a convert to the Spiritualistic hypothesis" of the survival of the individual soul after death.[138] Following the publication of the *Harper's* article, Hyslop was roundly condemned by colleagues at Columbia University and effectively silenced.[139]

Many paranormal investigations undertaken by SPR and ASPR served to definitively affirm the authenticity and validity of several prominent mediums of the time – Leonora Piper, Daniel Dunglas Home, and Eusapia Palladino. The research was not without its challenges. Doyle's analysis of these mediums and investigations in his *History of Spiritualism* shows how difficult it was oftentimes to work with "human subjects," how conclusions could be twisted by critics and the press, and how advancing age, social pressures, religious values and other factors could adversely impact even the most credible and upstanding medium. As we shall see, however, the evidence for authenticity is overwhelming.

Daniel Dunglas Home (pronounced "hume") was born in Currie, Scotland, in March 1833. His psychic abilities began early in his life: he had visions of his 17-year-old brother's death at sea and a cousin's death; as a baby, when he lived with an aunt in Edinburgh, his cradle rocked by itself; he had a vision of his close friend Edwin who had died three days earlier, unbeknownst to Home, as well as a vision of his mother as she died. Home and the relatives raising him immigrated to Connecticut when he was 13, but the phenomena surrounding him over the next few years – rappings, knockings and a table lifting itself into the air – disturbed local religious leaders, and Home was forced to leave his house and strike out on his own.[140]

At 18, Home began conducting séances, healing sick people, and communicating with the dead in sessions in Connecticut and around New England.[141] He was unusual in demonstrating four different types of mediumship: direct voice, where spirits speak audibly; trance speaking – the spirits speak through the medium; clairvoyance, the ability to see things that are not visible; and physical mediumship, which included levitation.[142] Most other mediums tended to favor one or two types, not the full range that Home possessed.

Home did not charge for his services[143] but was able to support himself from gifts, donations and lodging from well-to-do admirers (including Harvard professor David Wells and William Cullen Bryant, editor of the *New York Evening Post*). While in the US, Home's fame grew as investigations into the possibility that he was a fraud came to nothing. He moved to New York and was dismissed as a "dire humbug" by *Vanity Fair* author William Makepeace Thackeray, but Home was not deterred. Despite being diagnosed with tuberculosis in

1854, Home then left the United States and sailed to England to continue his work.[144]

Home came to the attention of British chemist and physicist William Crookes, another early member of SPR and its president from 1896 to 1899. In addition to Crookes' very important work in his field – the discovery of the element thallium, the development of vacuum tubes, and his work with cathode rays and radioactivity – he studied Home's talents, primarily in his own laboratory in London, for more than 30 years. Despite harsh criticism of himself and Home from many quarters – including magician Harry Houdini[145] – Crookes courageously addressed the esteemed British Association for the Advancement of Science, as its president in 1898, with a forceful affirmation of Home's reliability. In that speech, Crookes maintained that Home, who died in 1886, had proved "that outside our scientific knowledge there exists a Force exercised by intelligence differing from the ordinary intelligence common to mortals."[146]

Crookes also investigated medium Kate Fox, although not under the auspices of SPR, and concluded that Fox too was authentic;[147] we shall hear more about Fox and her sisters when we trace the history of Spiritualism in Chapter 5. Crookes continued to believe in supernatural powers – telekinesis, telepathy, the possibility that the dead might return – and in the validity of his own and others' experiments until his death at age 86 in 1919.[148]

It was the long-lived American Leonora Piper (1857-1950) who was perhaps the most studied medium in the early days of psychical research. A New Hampshire native, neé Symonds, she married William Piper of Boston at the age of 22 and settled with him on Beacon Hill in Boston.[149] Piper proved herself time and again to investigators over a period of almost 25 years (1885 to ca. 1909), despite what deniers then and now assert. She had demonstrated psychic gifts as a child and young adult but wanted primarily to be a good wife and mother. She prayed about her gifts, as they became more and more obvious to herself and helpful to others, and began giving séances. Her connection with William James and other paranormal investigators began when the sitter she read correctly in 1885 turned out to be Eliza Gibbens, William James' mother-in-law.[150]

In 1887, Australian researcher Hodgson arrived in the US with a main goal (in addition to restoring order to the ASPR) of proving Piper to be a fraud. This was not to be. Channeling a spirit guide named Phinuit, ostensibly a spirit who had lived in early-nineteenth-century France, Piper correctly told a story of the death in 1871 of a cousin of Hodgson's. Phinuit further spoke correctly to Hodgson of a woman Hodgson knew who had died in Australia several years after Hodgson had moved to England; this communication correctly involved a book of poems. Following these two incidents, which greatly unnerved Hodgson, he had Piper and her husband followed, sure that somehow she was spying on him. The efforts came to nothing.[151]

Encouraged by William James, Hodgson then went full bore investigating Piper's gifts.[152] Hodgson "was building a detailed picture of work with a credible medium, leaving out nothing, documenting every disastrous sitting, every dubious encounter, and every moment of dumbfounding accuracy."[153] In 1889, SPR investigators succeeded in convincing Piper to travel to England to be further studied, after it was arranged that her young daughters would accompany her; her in-laws hosted her husband in a Boston suburb for the duration, further putting her mind at ease.[154]

Piper was hosted that year by researchers Frederic Myers, Oliver Lodge, and William Crookes.[155] The investigations were rigorous and trying for Piper – the scientists were anxious to prove her authenticity in every way possible, and Myers in particular continued to remain skeptical. After some exhaustive testing, Hodgson published preliminary results in the June issue of *Proceedings of the Society for Psychical Research*. While not knowing exactly what to make of the spirit guide Phinuit, he nevertheless concluded that Piper did enter into genuine trances when she channeled him. Hodgson reported that he had done a number of things physically to Piper while she was in trance, including pinching her until she bruised, but she had no reaction, only remarking in her waking state that she did not know how she had received the marks."[156]

After the appearance of the *Proceedings* article, Hodgson proceeded to conduct more experiments. It was in the winter of 1892 that Hodgson had a truly remarkable personal experience that he could not shake off. A friend of his, George Pellew, died when the horse on which he was riding in Central Park fell. Hodgson and Pellew had had many conversations about immortality, Pellew expressing the opinion that an afterlife was unlikely (even ludicrous). Pellew and Hodgson made a half-joking promise shortly before Pellew's death; Pellew said that, if he died first, "he would return and 'make things lively.' He would make himself so obvious . . . that his friends wouldn't be able to deny him."[157]

Five weeks after Pellew's death, a new spirit started coming through during one of Piper's trances and identified itself as George Pellew. It became the persistent spirit referred to as G.P., eventually replacing Phinuit. Hodgson was not convinced at first that this was not just "another peculiarity of Leonora Piper's subconscious," so he devised ways for many of Pellew's old friends and relatives to help validate what was being said through Piper. Hodgson also invited people that never knew Pellew in life to participate. The results were astonishing.[158] Hodgson concluded that he had made a mistake in thinking that G.P. was merely a trance personality; rather, after 130 sittings, "he'd been persuaded of the impossible – that the personality in the room was indeed a spirit, proof that his friend lived on."[159] In a paper published in December 1897, Hodgson concluded that the spirit personages "have survived the change we call death" and "have directly communicated with us, whom we call living, through Mrs. Piper's organism."[160]

SIDEBAR

Through the communications between Hodgson and Pellew, mediated through Piper, some knowledge of the other side emerged, not only the basic confirmation that souls survive what we call death. The afterlife, it was learned, is one "of gradual evolution which is a continuation of earth life and presents much the same features, though under a generally more agreeable form. It is not a life of mere pleasure or selfish idleness, but one where all our personal faculties are given a very wide field of action."[161] These observations from the nineteenth century are confirmed in our own day, as we shall see, through scientific evidence of various kinds, the work of reputable psychics and mediums, NDEs and OOBEs. In other words, there is a great deal of continuity between the findings of the early psychical investigators and what we can learn from many sources today.

SPR investigator Henry Sidgwick was not entirely convinced of the authenticity of Piper's gifts and communication with spirits, continuing to believe that telepathy between the sitters and Piper was somehow involved. One of the main stumbling blocks for Sidgwick was Pellew's supposed lack of knowledge about himself and his philosophical pursuits. Hodgson, foreshadowing some of the results gleaned from today's psychics, mediums, EVPs, ITC, NDEs and OOBEs, acknowledged Sidgwick's misgivings and countered them in several ways. For one thing, the medium had no knowledge of philosophy, so communicating such concepts from the spirit world to the living may have been particularly difficult. Hodgson also surmised, probably correctly, that "[e]motional connections – with their pure, personal power – might survive fairly intact through the translating mechanism of the medium. Intellect and sophisticated knowledge would be unlikely to fare so well." Further, just the challenges that take place between two *living* people as they converse should attest to how difficult it might be for a spirit on the other side to communicate with us in the physical world.[162]

Interestingly, Hodgson resurfaced after his death in 1905: he suddenly came through to Piper in the midst of one of her trances. His appearance was fleeting, and it seemed difficult for him to communicate. Piper's spirit guide at the time, Rector, intervened on his behalf, reporting, "Peace, friends, he is here, it was he but he could not remain, he was so choked. He is doing all in his power to return."[163] Another explanation as to why Hodgson was not emerging clearly was provided by deceased medium the Rev. Stainton Moses, as channeled through Piper:

> Dr. Hodgson says that I shall tell you that it was a great error that he kept himself so largely attuned to material life and material things. . . He did not view these psychic matters from the standpoint that I did . . . and did not seek to interpret anything wholly as spiritual. One that comes over as he came over, is transplanted from one sphere of life into another like a babe just born. He has been besieged since he is here with messages started from your side. . . This is all in vain: he cannot answer. He repeats that I shall tell you he realizes now that he saw only one side of this great question, and that the lesser important.[164]

Communication apparently became easier for Hodgson as time went on: he developed an ability to send messages to James Hyslop through Piper in "a series of evidential communications which convinced [Hyslop] that he was indeed in touch with his friend and fellow-worker."[165] Hodgson also communicated posthumously with Frederic Myers, who had crossed to the other side in 1901. In a series of odd communications between Piper, Margaret Verrall (a classics lecturer at Newnham College and an old friend of Myers'), and Verrall's daughter Helen, it finally became apparent to the people involved that hearing from the dead might indeed be a real possibility. The three women all began to receive messages via automatic writing that made little sense. In Boston, Piper was receiving messages from Myers in English. M. Verrall in England was experimenting with trying to reach Myers herself and was receiving messages "signed" by Myers in Greek and Latin. "Back and forth across the Atlantic, Nora Sidgwick, Oliver Lodge, and William James began comparing the messages. Taken separately, each woman's writing seemed a kind of stream-of-consciousness jumble of words and thoughts. Taken together, though, the messages seemed connected, as if ideas were relayed on some circuit impossible to detect." Nora Sidgwick "began to wonder for the first time if her Henry had been wrong, if there was a chance, after all, of proving conversations between the living and the dead."[166]

As we draw our survey of nineteenth-century mediums to a close, we will examine the interesting and controversial example of Italian medium Eusapia Palladino. Palladino was born in 1854 to a peasant family in Bari Province, Italy, orphaned early in life, and received almost no formal education. Until she died, in 1918, she demonstrated a wide range of psychic and paranormal abilities and was studied not only by SPR investigators but even earlier by Cesare Lombroso, a scientist from Turin. In séances held throughout Europe and Russia, Palladino levitated, materialized the dead, played musical instruments, and communicated with spirits through a spirit guide called John King.[167]

Palladino was a colorful person, to say the least, described as being "prone to scream like a fishwife," "never still . . . always twitching her fingers away," "sneaky," a "common cheat," "elusive,"[168] and possessing a nature that "was hysterical, impetuous and wayward,"[169] which did not engender trust. Whatever her basic character, however, she allowed investigators to conduct experiments on her for years that involved a great deal of physical and emotional discomfort.

In late 1893, French physiologist Charles Richet became involved in Lombroso's studies of Palladino. Despite early problems with the experiments and possible cheating on the part of the medium, other tests resulted in inexplicable results, including testimony from none other than eminent scientist Marie Curie: during the séance, Curie felt a hand even though she "kept an unbreakable clasp on Eusapia's fingers."[170] Pierre Curie also became involved in tests of Palladino's gifts, concluding that the work with Palladino presented "a whole domain of entirely new facts and physical states in space of which we have no conception."[171] Richet's experiments led him to coin the now well-known term "ectoplasm" from the Greek *ecto*, "exterior" and *plasm*, "substance."[172]

Richet, along with Lodge, Myers and psychologist Julian Ochorowicz, conducted a number of experiments at Richet's home in the Ile Roubaud in the Mediterranean, attempting every way possible to constrain Palladino and prevent her from manipulating any objects.[173] Various members of SPR – Lodge, Henry and Nora Sidgwick, and Hodgson – were completely convinced at this point that Palladino was a fraud. The SPR decided to have nothing further to do with her, causing a split in the organization, with criticisms flying back and forth in print over methods and possible explanations.[174] It seems beyond doubt that at least some of her demonstrations were due to fraud and trickery.

However, in 1908, the SPR began to re-examine Palladino's gifts and talents. The committee of three consisted of amateur conjurer Hereward Carrington, representing the ASPR; W.W. Baggally, another conjurer with a great deal of experience; and the Hon. Everard Feilding, a trained investigator. They conducted their experiments at the Hotel Victoria in Naples and used a number of methods to prevent Palladino from cheating. While they did catch her using some tricks, they nevertheless became convinced that she "produced genuine supernatural phenomena such as levitations of the table, movement of the curtains, movement of objects from behind the curtain and touches from hands." Other tests were conducted with mixed results, but Carrington remained certain that Palladino did possess some supernatural gifts and became her manager[175] as well as an internationally-known psychic detective. He long regretted that SPR had stopped investigating Palladino earlier.[176]

Doyle, in his usual fair and objective way, drew the following conclusion: "Her case is certainly a peculiar one, for it may be most truthfully said of her that no medium has ever more certainly been proved to have psychic powers, and no medium was ever more certainly a cheat upon occasions. Here, as always, it is the positive result which counts."[177]

The Early Twentieth Century

As the twentieth century dawned, the modern West was reaping the benefits (and encountering the drawbacks) of the Industrial Revolution and experiencing the wide expansion of electricity, the burgeoning of psychological theory, and the throes of a consumerist culture. The confluence of these developments gave rise to a wide range of experimentation with communication with the dead and scientific investigation of paranormal phenomena. These efforts in turn led in many cases to fraud, deception, and the ruination of the lives and careers of some legitimate researchers. Despite the setbacks and doubts, research persisted.

Tom and Lisa Butler of Nevada, Directors of the American Association of Electronic Voice Phenomena, have traced the history of modern communication with the dead in their 2008 book, *There is No Death and There are No Dead*.[178] From the earliest years of the twentieth century, people around the world, including scientists, have either accidentally or purposefully recorded voices from beyond – voices that could not come from a live person near the source of the recording or from other explainable sources such as radio interference. The findings have been documented in both books and scientific journals; as occurred in the nineteenth century, some of the evidence was also suppressed, as we shall see.

Thomas Edison was one well-known scientist who developed an avid interest in the potential for communication with deceased spirits via telephone, perhaps due to the fact that his parents believed in Spiritualism.[179] Although there is no evidence that he developed a machine that could be used to reach the dead, Edison nevertheless believed one was possible. He is quoted in the October 1920 edition of *Scientific American* as saying, "If our personality survives, then it is strictly logical or scientific to assume that it retains memory, intellect, other faculties and knowledge that we acquire on this earth. Therefore, if personality exists after what we call death, it is reasonable to conclude that those who leave the earth would like to communicate with those they have left here. I am inclined to believe that our personality hereafter will be able to affect matter. If this reasoning be correct, then, if we can evolve an instrument so delicate as to be affected by our personality as it survives in the next life, such an instrument, when made available, ought to record something."[180]

At around the same time, in the early 1900s, several articles and books further documented unexplained phenomena in different parts of the world – and results involving telephones! Two physicists in Holland, J.L. Matla and G.J. Zaalbert van Zelst, developed instruments that showed spirits being able to manipulate devices; they called theirs a "Manometer" and a "Dynamistograph."[181] David Wilson, an amateur wireless operator, had some success communicating with an entity on the other side via Morse Code, which he presented in the March 13, 1915, issue of *Light*; inventor and psychic investigator F.R. Melton reported results from a "psychic telephone" in *Light* and in a booklet, *A Psychic Telephone*, which included illustrations and instructions for the device's construction.[182]

Another example of the use of Morse Code to communicate with those on the other side concerns Grace Boylan and her son Bob. Grace and Bob used Morse Code to communicate with each other at their home prior to World War I, when Bob was sent to France to fight. As Grace read a letter from him, she noticed that the wireless was receiving a message. It was from Bob and read, "Mother... I am alive and loving you, but my body is with thousands of other mothers' boys near Lens. Get this fact to others if you can. It's awful when you grieve, and we can't get in touch with you to tell you we are all right. This is a clumsy way. I'll figure out something easier. I'm confused yet. Bob." Bob, along with others in his company, had died in the middle of a battle, where he could not have been able to communicate in Morse Code. Later, another message from him to his mother affirmed that there was no "horror in death." For many years he communicated with Grace through automatic writing. Grace's story is recalled in *Thy Son Liveth: Messages from a Soldier to His Mother*, published in 1918.[183]

SIDEBAR: WORLD BROADCASTING COMPANY

In 1933, the World Broadcasting Company conducted an experiment "to test the validity of the voices received during a direct voice séance." A medium and a number of parapsychology researchers attended, with skeptical engineers looking on. The results demonstrate a commonplace in the area of paranormal research: something remarkable truly happened, was witnessed by many, and was even recorded, but "the recording stayed at World Broadcasting, as they did not want to testify publicly that spirit voices had been recorded in their studio." The remarkable story continues:

[The engineers] devised test conditions that they felt would eliminate all possibility of fraud. Three microphones were set up for the séance. Microphone 1 was placed on the floor. Microphones 2 and 3 were installed on the opposite corners of the ceiling twenty feet in the air and twenty feet away from the sitters. The microphones on the ceiling were only sensitive to sounds that were within twelve inches and directly in front of them, assuring that they could not pick up voices that would be recorded on Microphone 1. Further, each microphone had a direct connection into the control room.

The medium and sitters were unaware of how the microphones had been set up by the engineers and proceeded with the séance. A spirit voice quickly showed interest in the experiment saying, *"We think they have worked out a very interesting testing procedure for us on their equipment."* The engineers in the control room asked who was speaking. The voice, speaking into microphone 1, told them that he was an engineer in the Spirit World who had colleagues with him. He then told them that they, the spirits in attendance, were all interested in cooperating with making a recording.

> The engineers in the control room requested that the person, calling himself a spirit and who was now speaking in Microphone 1, to speak directly into Microphones 2 and 3. Almost immediately, the voice answered within inches of both mics. The voice said that they wanted to provide a demonstration and proceeded to make a quick circuit of the three microphones while speaking a simple short sentence.
>
> Next, the voice introduced a colleague and told those present that he was an eminent research engineer in the science of sound. The spirit research engineer told the sitters and studio engineers that he and the other communicators were, *"Surviving personalities speaking to you from another dimension."* He then moved his voice from the normal level of the human male voice, 300 Hertz, to levels of 3,000 to 5,000 Hertz. While doing this, his voice trailed off to sound like, "An incredibly distant radio signal." The spirit engineer then descended through the frequencies so that eventually his voice sounded like, "a giant mumbling at the bottom of a well." And finally, "Like the lowest note on the longest pipe in a giant organ."
>
> The original spirit voice returned and thanked the sitters and engineers for helping in the experiment. He concluded with an offer of help and collaboration in future tests. The records of the experiment were sent to the American Society for Psychical Research.[184]

More work in the area continued in the United States, England and Italy in the late 1930s, the 1940s, and 1950s. A number of inventors created devices to channel spirit voices, some with remarkable success, and their results were reported in various books and journals.[185]

In the late 1950s and into the 1960s, extensive recordings were made by Friedrich Jürgenson of Sweden and Dr. Konstantin Raudive, a Latvian living in Sweden. We will hear more about them in Chapter 4, The Science of the Afterlife: Instruments and Investigations.

University Studies

While most research universities in the West have effectively ignored paranormal phenomena or disparaged their scientists who dared to venture into that area of investigation, there have been notable exceptions in the US and elsewhere, and many laboratories continue this work today. Here we shall briefly examine a few examples.

University of Virginia. At the University of Virginia (UVA) in Charlottesville, the College of Medicine houses the Division of Perceptual Studies (DOPS). Formerly the Division of Personality Studies, DOPS is a unit of the Department of Psychiatry and Neurobehavioral Sciences. It was founded as a research unit of the Department of Psychiatric Medicine at UVA by Dr. Ian Stevenson in 1967 (we will see more of Dr. Stevenson's research in Chapter 4). Utilizing scientific methods, the researchers in DOPS investigate apparent paranormal phenomena, especially children who claim to remember previous lives (reincarnation) and NDEs. The department's website indicates that the investigators are also interested in studying phenomena such as OOBEs, apparitions and after-death communication, and deathbed visions. Their research has been featured on National Public Radio and in a number of best-selling books.[186]

Jim Tucker, MD, is Bonner-Lowry Associate Professor of Psychiatry and Neurobehavioral Sciences at UVA and has written widely on reincarnation. In an interview with Dean Radin, PhD, on December 8, 2010, for the Institute of Noetic Sciences (IONS)

Teleseminars series, Tucker described some of his findings on young children, including unusual play, behavior patterns, specific phobias, and birthmarks or birth defects specifically related to the life and death of a previous personality. He also discussed the interpretation of the data and details about the methodology, as well as possible pitfalls of individual cases. Radin, Senior Scientist at IONS and an adjunct faculty member in the Department of Psychology at Sonoma State University, is himself well known for his best-selling books, *The Conscious Universe*[187] and *Entangled Minds*.[188]

The current Director of UVA's DOPS is Bruce Greyson, MD, Chester F. Carlson Professor of Psychiatry and Neurobehavioral Sciences. He has written and lectured extensively on NDEs, among other paranormal topics. At a conference entitled "Cosmology and Consciousness: A Dialog Between Buddhist Scholars and Scientists on Mind and Matter" in December 2011, Dr. Greyson presented the DOPS research on NDEs to His Holiness the Dalai Lama and to the monks of Dharamsal. In the same IONS Teleseminars series mentioned above, Dr. Greyson was also interviewed by Dean Radin where he discussed "how cumulative research into Near Death Experiences challenges both a classical physical view of reality and an exclusively neuroscience-based view of consciousness."[189]

The Handbook of Near-Death Experience: Thirty Years of Investigation by DOPS researchers Bruce Greyson, Carlos Alvarado, Nancy Zingrone, Edward F. Kelly, and Emily Williams presents information on NDE research. The authors "explore controversies in the field, offer specific accounts of NDE's from the research, and express their hopes for the future of investigation into this fascinating phenomenon."[190]

Duke University. From 1930 to 1965, Duke University in Durham, North Carolina, was home to the Parapsychology Laboratory. The lab was supported in its early years by Duke

President W.P. Few and directed by William McDougall, Chairman of the Psychology Department. The lab received private funding from benefactors such as Chester Carlson, the founder of Xerox, as well as grants from foundations and government agencies, including the Rockefeller Foundation (1950-54) and the Office of Naval Research (1953-59). At various times, collaborations were formed between the Duke researchers and those from other institutions, including Stanford and the University of Colorado.[191]

Joseph Banks Rhine and his wife, Louisa E. Rhine, were two of the most prominent investigators at the Parapsychology Laboratory. They both earned PhD's in Botany at the University of Chicago but became disenchanted with their work and increasingly interested in psychical research.[192] As we have seen above, the interest in the early twentieth century was mainly with mediums and proving the existence of an afterlife, but Rhine, realizing that the answer to that "depended first on investigating the ability of the living to gain psychic or psi information by other than sensory means (telepathy and clairvoyance)," he launched into work on the ability that he termed extrasensory perception (ESP).[193] In this way, he became "largely responsible for instituting an experimental paradigm in parapsychology." The first experiments in ESP were conducted in 1930, and Rhine's work caught the attention of a much wider public in 1937, with the help of the Zenith Radio Corporation. A broadcast of a series of ESP experiments with the simultaneous publication of a popular book, *New Frontiers of the Mind*, comprised the promotion tools. Zenith listeners and Book of the Month Club members were offered the first manufactured ESP cards, which were sold by Farrar and Rinehart, the book's publishers. Also in 1937, Duke University Press began issuing the *Journal of Parapsychology*, which was edited at the Laboratory.[194]

As might be expected, Rhine's work led to criticism and controversy. Rhine's scholarly book, *Extra-Sensory Perception after Sixty Years*, co-authored with several colleagues in 1940, was an attempt to counter the criticisms. However, after World War II, with the field of parapsychology taking fuller shape, Rhine's work began to be supported by that of Ian Stevenson at the University of Virginia, among many others who helped found, in 1957, the international Parapsychological Association. Rhine's papers show that he had a great deal of correspondence with notable psychologists and psychoanalysts such as Aldous Huxley, Julian Huxley, C.G. Jung, Timothy Leary, and Margaret Mead.[195]

Few and McDougall died in 1940 and 1938, respectively, which weakened Duke's support of the laboratory. Although the Rhines and others continued their work for more than two decades, "skeptics and conservatives dominated the academic environment around the Duke Lab," and Rhine realized that his research could only continue after his retirement under the auspices of an independent organization. In 1965, Rhine started the Foundation for Research on the Nature of Man (FRNM), receiving support from Chester Carlson, among others. FRNM moved off the UVA campus, and research continued on a national and international scale. FRNM was the parent organization for 30 years of the Institute for Parapsychology, its major research and education institute, and the *Parapsychology Press*, its publishing branch. Nineteen-ninety-five marked the centenary of J.B. Rhine's birth and 15 years following his death; in that year, the FRNM was renamed the Rhine Research Center in the Rhines' honor.[196]

University of Arizona. In June 2006, the SOPHIA Research Program was established at the University of Arizona in Tucson and "investigates claims of communication processes involving various spiritual levels, from deceased individuals, through guides and angels, to purported communication with a higher power or divinity. Its focus is on healing and life-enhancement."[197]

Dr. Gary Schwartz, director of the program, is professor of Psychology, Medicine, Neurology, Psychiatry, and Surgery at the University of Arizona; he also serves as director of its Laboratory for Advances in Consciousness and Health and its Center for Frontier Medicine in Biofield Science. Schwartz holds a doctorate from Harvard University and previously taught psychology and psychiatry at Yale, where he was also director of the Yale Psychophysiology Center and co-director of the Yale Behavioral Medicine Clinic. Schwartz is widely published in his fields, with 11 books and over 400 scholarly papers to his credit.[198]

The SOPHIA project, based in scientific theory and principles, has as its purpose "to investigate the experiences of people who claim to channel or communicate with Deceased People, Spirit Guides, Angels, Other-Worldly Entities / Extraterrestrials, and / or a Universal Intelligence / God. The ultimate objective is to investigate if these communications can be validated under controlled conditions." The program intends "to either validate the experiences or elucidate the psychological mechanisms behind these phenomena."[199]

The SOPHIA Research Program was preceded for many years by the VERITAS Research Program, which was housed in the Laboratory for Advances in Consciousness and Health (formerly the Human Energy Systems Laboratory) in the Department of Psychology at the University of Arizona. The VERITAS program focused on testing the hypothesis that the individual's consciousness or personality survives physical death. The Co-Director of the program, Julie Beischel, PhD, completed a post-doctoral fellowship in January 2008 and now directs and conducts research at the Windbridge Institute for Applied Research in Human Potential.

Her research focuses on survival and mediumship research as well as medium certification.[200]

University of Southampton, England, and SUNY Stony Brook. NDE and resuscitation research has been conducted for several years by Dr. Sam Parnia, first at the University of Southampton in England and currently at the State University of New York at Stony Brook. Parnia received his medical degree from the Guys and St. Thomas' Hospitals (UMDS) of the University of London in 1995 and his PhD in cell biology from the University of Southampton in 2006. His research in Southampton focused on cardiac arrest resuscitation, brain resuscitation and the cognitive sequelae of surviving cardiac arrest including NDEs and led to publication of his book, *What Happens When We Die*, in 2006.[201]

Among his findings and those of other researchers is that death is a process, not a specific moment. During this process, cardiac arrest occurs: the heart, lungs and brain all stop functioning. This condition, clinical death, is a time when approximately 10-20 percent of patients who are subsequently resuscitated have an NDE. As Parnia states, this critical time becomes "a unique window of understanding into what we are all likely to experience during the dying process."[202]

The AWAreness during REsuscitation (AWARE) study is a long-term, world-wide collaborative effort "to study the relationship between mind and brain during clinical death." Launched by the Human Consciousness Project, a consortium of scientists from around the world, the AWARE study is directed by Parnia and assisted by Dr. Peter Fenwick and Professors Stephen Holgate and Robert Peveler of the University of Southampton. Over 25 major medical centers throughout Europe, Canada, and the United States are involved in this research,[203] and they are publishing their results through peer-reviewed medical journals.

The AWARE study will utilize state-of-the-art technologies. Researchers will test the validity of OOBEs, which are often components of NDEs, as well as reports of patients seeing and hearing during cardiac arrest. Among the testing mechanisms is the use of randomly-generated hidden images that are not visible unless seen from above. Parnia states, "If we can objectively verify these claims [of lucid, verifiable thought processes and recall of events while the patient is clinically dead], the results would bear profound implications not only for the scientific community, but for the way in which we understand and relate to life and death as a society."[204]

As might be expected, this research is being met with criticism, primarily from the "skeptical community." While we will dialogue with skeptics and deniers in more detail below, the Wikipedia article on Dr. Parnia is an example of the skeptical genre. As Roach does in *Spook*, the Wikipedia author focuses almost exclusively on a few cases that might serve to disprove Parnia's (and others') theories, based on their scientific research, while ignoring the vast amount of supportive evidence.[205] Perhaps not surprisingly, one of the Wikipedia article's references of a supposedly significant point is one Keith Alexander writing in an online site called the Secular Web. Secular Web is owned by Internet Infidels, Inc., a non-profit organization "dedicated to defending and promoting a naturalistic worldview on the Internet. Naturalism is the 'hypothesis that the natural world is a closed system' in the sense that 'nothing that is not a part of the natural world affects it.' As such, 'naturalism implies that there are no supernatural entities,' such as gods, angels, demons, ghosts, or other spirits."[206] Alexander's article refuting many aspects of Parnia's research, which appears not to have been updated since 2008, does not cite Parnia's 2006 book, Jeffrey Long's 2010 study of NDEs, or the book or website of Eben Alexander. The article dialogues critically with Dr. Bruce Greyson, and its resource list contains many of prominent cynic Dr. Susan Blackmore's works.[207]

Despite criticism, and even outright hostility, these universities, institutions, foundations, researchers, scientists and physicians have the courage to honestly, carefully and systematically pursue paranormal and psychical research. Their search for truth can only serve to help humankind and well-meaning people everywhere.

Deniers, Skeptics and Frauds

As Doyle states throughout *The History of Spiritualism*, and as we have seen in our survey above, skepticism almost always followed those who investigated paranormal phenomena. Criticism, Doyle noted – harsh and unfounded – emanated from the world of science, the world of religion, and the American and British press. Even though Doyle was writing in the early twentieth century, his pointed comments could very well have been made today:

- "The crowning and most absurd instance of scientific intolerance . . . was shown by the American Scientific Association. This learned body howled down Professor [Robert] Hare [formerly of Pennsylvania University] when he attempted to address them, and put it on record that the subject [of Spiritualism] was unworthy of their attention."[208]
- "The opponents of psychic truth having upon their side the clergy of the various churches, organised science, and the huge inert bulk of material mankind, had the lay Press at their command, with the result that everything that was in its favour was suppressed or contorted, and everything which could tell against it was given the widest publicity."[209]

- "There is a certain type of scientific mind which is quite astute within its own subject and, outside it, is the most foolish and illogical thing upon earth."[210]
- "The clergy are so limited in their ideas and so bound by a system which should be an obsolete one. It is like serving up last week's dinner instead of having a new one."[211]

As we have stated, and as will be clear from upcoming chapters, it is important to identify and name fraud and deception when it occurs. Unless an audience knows in advance that the person whose performance they are attending is a trickster or magician, the work of psychics, mediums and others must be genuine and totally above board. It does the search for truth no good if a generally honest practitioner occasionally resorts to deception just to thrill an audience, give attendees their money's worth, preserve the medium's own reputation, or seek monetary gain. It is likely that this is what occurred in the cases of Palladino, the medium Henry Slade, and others who fell on hard times later in their lives and had no other means of support.[212]

It is equally untenable, however, for skeptics and vehement afterlife deniers themselves to play fast and loose with the facts and truth. As we have seen in Chapter 2, there is ample support now, from highly-respected scientists and physicians, that phenomena such as NDEs are real and often verifiable by today's scientific measures. Therefore, any commentator who focuses on one potential problem or discrepancy to the exclusion of all the innumerable positives and proofs is him- or herself a dishonest reporter and should be exposed as such.

Let us, then, ask some clarifying questions of the critics and deniers.

1. In the many cases of reported levitations, especially in the nineteenth century at the dawn of the Spiritualist movement,

how could so many stellar, highly intelligent witnesses be wrong about what they witnessed – including demonstrations in broad daylight – or be duped, or lie? Why would so many of these prominent men and women be converted to Spiritualism due to the phenomena they saw with their own eyes if there was rampant deception? One can perhaps see a handful of intelligent people "falling for" the supposed "tricks," but the evidence for widespread conviction is very difficult to attribute to deception. Furthermore, given what we now know about spirits and energy, which we shall explore more fully in Chapter 4, phenomena such as levitation, spirits passing through solid objects, detectable energy fields and the like can now be certified as real and verifiable, if not yet entirely explainable from a materialistic point of view.

2. In the many cases of mediums telling sitters mundane facts that the sitters themselves do not know – but which are usually confirmed – how can the argument be made that the medium is somehow reading the sitter's mind? Is it not more logical to believe that a spirit, an entity that has crossed over, who has an expanded consciousness and who is closely tied to the sitter, is the one who knows the facts and is channeling them through the medium for the benefit of the sitter, who is often bereaved and suffering? It has become apparent through the research that thought transference or telepathy is actually how spirits communicate between one another on the other side, and between spirits and those of us in the physical world.

3. Any number of prominent people testified in the nineteenth and twentieth centuries to having had visions of or clear, loving communications with loved ones who had died. Some of these trustworthy witnesses included Doyle, James, Hyslop, Hodgson, and Lodge. What purpose does it serve for

deniers and critics to attribute these incidents to wishful thinking or delusion – thereby not only denying the probability of life after death but also hurting and belittling the witnesses themselves – rather than to keep an open mind and give the witnesses the benefit of the doubt about the truth of what they reported? What purpose does harsh and damaging criticism serve the cause of truth and the betterment of humanity, especially as compared to the loving and comforting messages the witnesses say they received from their departed loved ones?

4. Why are clergy, scientists, the press and laypeople, then and now, so skeptical of the work of investigators such as Crookes, Hyslop, Lodge, Wallace, Rhine or Stevenson, even to the point of misquoting them or denying their belief in an afterlife? Should we not ask ourselves honestly why we cannot trust their wisdom and judgment, not to mention the results of their research?

5. One of the primary criticisms of paranormal research, both then and now, is that results are extremely difficult to replicate. Although many stringent tests have been made of mediums and other gifted practitioners throughout the history of modern research, any given experiment in one lab is not likely to yield exactly the same results in another lab. When one examines this problem from the standpoint of the reality of spirits and their existence on another plane, as explained by many modern psychics, for instance, one can logically attribute the problem to the motivations and goals of the spirits themselves or, as we saw in the case of Hodgson, to the deceased not being sufficiently attuned to things of a spiritual nature when they crossed over. The spirits often have different reasons for demonstrating their existence, or coming through

to someone, than the experimenter might have: goals and purposes on the other side are different from ours on earth.[213] Relatedly, spirits are sometimes inhibited from coming through by the negative attitudes of the investigators or attendees; if someone is merely skeptical and keeps an open mind, a spirit might be able to communicate, but outright hostility appears to diminish the energy needed by an entity for it to emerge.[214]

The history of paranormal research in the West is rich and fascinating. It has been, however, too long ignored in our Post-Enlightenment culture. The time is ripe, once again, to keep open minds and continue responsible research, at universities and elsewhere, about an area that is so vitally important to our lives as human (and spiritual) beings.

Chapter 4: The Science of the Afterlife: Instruments and Investigations

- *"[I]n the last hundred years, communication with the so-called dead has also been taking place through various mechanical and electrical devices. Today people record the voices of the unseen on electronic and digital devices and some experiments have even been carried out using lasers."* – Tom and Lisa Butler
- *"Scientific knowledge comes from systematic and objective observations, which help us make deductions we can trust. . . . In every investigation, we collect a wealth of data through different types of cameras, meters, and voice recorders, and from observations and reports of strange experiences. We sift through all of this as objectively as possible before we begin to draw conclusions."* – Jason Hawes
- *"We have reached a point in human history where many people now realize that science cannot provide us with answers to life's fundamental questions . . . and that materialism does not provide the route either to individual happiness or to a future for our planet."* – David Fontana

At the heart of our exploration of the afterlife is the modern, Western scientific evidence for the existence of paranormal phenomena, including the individual survival of human (and even animal) souls after "death." The various "ghost-hunting" investigation television programs that have been airing in the early twenty-first century have scientific techniques and instruments at their base, despite the skepticism of many in the scientific community itself; the techniques and instruments have been developed for decades with the help of established investigators, scientists and companies who have the courage to venture into risky areas of exploration.

In Chapter 3, we were introduced to some of the nineteenth- and early twentieth-century researchers and scientific investigations. Here we will look into the more recent devices and tools being used and examine the literature that documents scientific experimentation. We shall also look at basic biological, electrical, physical and other factors that underlie the paranormal phenomena that are captured on these instruments.

While many phenomena related to the afterlife are inexplicable by normal scientific principles, since they are based in a materialistic framework, we shall see that researchers are nevertheless able to postulate many logical and provable theories that match the evidence and, conversely, dismiss explanations that try to disprove the existence of paranormal phenomena. The literature, in legitimate scientific manner, lays out experiments that can be replicated by others. The findings are vast; readers are encouraged to consult the Resources to explore the evidence in more depth than can be presented here.

Our Physical World

The world around us is comprised of mass and energy. Human beings, animals and much of the rest of what we experience on a daily basis are comprised of molecules of some kind, as we are all aware. Even the air we breathe, though invisible to us, is real, made up of quantifiable gas molecules. Radio and television waves too are not visible to the naked eye but can be scientifically studied, and within human and other bodies electrical pulses are essential to life. We know now, which was not known to generations prior to the late nineteenth century, that bacteria and germs that can only be viewed with sophisticated instruments are the causes of disease and can be battled and conquered. In the far reaches of outer space, astronomers and physicists are able to map galaxies and conduct experiments with sophisticated devices that were the stuff of science fiction only a short time ago. Thus many phenomena in our daily lives which, in early ages of human existence, were viewed as miracles or acts of God, can now be seen, explained and dealt with rationally and logically. There is no longer widespread fear of the unknown in the West, and the vast majority of Westerners view the phenomena from the same vantage point.

We can expect, most of the time, that our lives are governed by this kind of logic – by predictable, natural rules and principles. If something of solid mass seems to move on its own, it is usually due to vibrations, a breeze, or the force of gravity. If a shadow is seen, we can usually attribute it to something moving across a light source. If a sound is heard, it can normally be traced to a logical source that just happens not to be visible at the time. When someone dreams of a loved one who has recently died, we often attribute it to our mind and emotions missing that person. In these ways, the laws of biology, physics and psychology are sufficient for explaining the "why" of a given phenomenon.

When, however, we experience or hear about occurrences that seem outside the normal natural laws, we are confused, in denial or sometimes frightened, as our human ancestors were millennia ago by phenomena that can now be explained. Contrary to prior generations around the world, however, modern Westerners are under pressure from the surrounding culture to dismiss any possibility that reality exists apart from our physical, material, scientific world. There is a strand of skepticism toward other realities that itself borders on quasi-religious fanaticism. From highly-educated intellectuals in the sciences, religion and many other fields to average citizens who stand firmly in the category of "I don't believe in ghosts," "I don't believe that we exist after we die," and "all that religious stuff is hogwash," the Enlightenment has done its job well in nearly erasing from the modern discourse any possibility that other – even better – "worlds" and realities might exist for all of us.[215]

In this chapter, we will ask that skeptics keep an open mind as we present the current evidence. It is the contention here that modern science can aid us in discovering extremely important "other worlds" that have been the bedrock of religious and philosophical belief systems for millennia.

Electronic Voice Phenomena (EVP)

In ancient times, before electricity, it was not possible for any type of sound to be "captured" and played back at a later time. Voices from the beyond were heard and experienced through dreams, hallucinations, trances and mediumistic sittings and séances, but many people who had such experiences were often mocked, dismissed or labeled as unbalanced or fraudulent. This is understandable, given what we know today about mental illness, the brain, and the prevalence of fraud.

In the early days of electronics, however, some voices that clearly did not belong to the people in close proximity to the instrument started to be captured, sometimes accidentally. One of the earliest experiences occurred around 1901. Waldemar Bogoras, in exile in Siberia, witnessed a shaman communicating with spirits in a dark room as the shaman beat a drum and entered into a trance. Bogoras set up recording equipment approximately 20 feet from the shaman and, after a few moments, spirit voices were heard. "They followed the shaman's request that they speak directly into the horn of Bogoras' portable Edison phonograph. . . . The recording showed a clear difference between the spirit voices, which seemed to come directly from the mouth of the phonography horn, and the voice of the shaman some distance away."[216]

More experiences followed. Francis Grierson in the US received communications from those on the other side through a telephonic device he invented; his book, *Psycho-phone Messages*, was published in 1921 and can still be found in a classic reprint edition. A few years later, around 1925, Brazilian Oscar D'argonell captured voices, as recorded in *Voices from Beyond by Telephone*. Author Edgar Wallace, who died in 1932, apparently came through subsequently on a 78 rpm record cutter. It was his stunned secretary who heard his voice and reported the incident, but unfortunately her report was not taken seriously.[217]

Experiments continued around the world, as we have seen from the historical overview in Chapter 3. It was in 1971 that the term "Electronic Voice Phenomena" was first coined in the context of the work of Latvian psychologist and philosopher Konstantin Raudive and Friedrich Jürgenson, a Swedish film producer. Jürgenson was recording bird songs near his villa in 1959 when he accidentally captured "a voice talking about 'nocturnal bird songs.'" He thought at first that he had picked up a stray radio broadcast but, after conducting more experiments, he realized that he was recording his deceased mother's voice – including one message telling him that he was being watched! Jürgenson's later publications on the voices he recorded included *Voice Transmissions with the Deceased*, *Voices from the Universe*, and *Radio-Link with the Beyond*.[218]

Raudive, who was living in Sweden at the same time that Jürgenson was publishing his findings, teamed up with Jürgenson, who taught him how to record the voices. It was Peter Bander, Raudive's editor for the English translation of his 1971 book with the title *Breakthrough: An Amazing Experiment in Electronic Communication with the Dead*, who initially used the term "Electronic

Voice Phenomena" in the introduction to his own book, *Carry on Talking*. *Breakthrough* was published by Colin Smythe, Ltd. In order to ensure the legitimacy of the voices described in the book he was about to publish, Smythe contacted Bander, senior lecturer in religious and moral education at the Cambridge Institute of Education and a psychologist, and asked him to listen to a tape he had made as a test. Bander heard a voice speaking in German, saying, "Why don't you open the door?" It was Bander's deceased mother, referring to a situation from the previous week in which Bander had insisted on keeping his office door closed and had been teased by his colleagues. Smythe did not know German, so Bander asked others to record what they had heard phonetically; they all heard the same thing, and Smythe was convinced.[219]

Both Raudive, who died in 1974, and Jürgenson, who crossed over in October 1987, have come through in spirit to various people a number of times in subsequent years.[220]

Over the intervening years, the term EVP has become widely used throughout the world, and controlled experiments have been conducted and published. Sarah Estep, a social worker and married mother of three, founded the American Association of Electronic Voice Phenomena (AA-EVP) in 1982[221] and was an early American investigator to use the classification system of recordings that is now routinely employed by paranormal investigators. A Class A sample is clear and recognizable; it "can be heard and understood over a speaker by most people." A Class B sample, "somewhat clear and definable," can be heard over a speaker, but not everyone may agree with the translation. A Class C sample is unclear and hard to understand, but listeners can acknowledge that an unexplainable sound was recorded.[222]

How do EVPs "work"? What mechanisms or principles might be involved in EVPs? What are the relationships between the electronics of the instruments used and the sounds and voices that are heard on the recordings, especially when the voices are not heard by the people in the instrument's vicinity until the tape is played back (and sometimes played back in reverse)?

In EVP, the voice that is heard in the recording may be "formed from available audio-frequency energy," which is basically just noise. Some noise seems to work better than others. "The most optimum noise appears to be broad-spectrum audio containing many voice-frequencies and providing numerous optional stable states."[223] In other words, since an entity on "the other side" no longer has physical vocal cords like those of us in the physical world, "available frequencies appear to be selected [by the entity] and given more power to emulate voice." The entity must consciously intend to communicate and is thus "able to reduce the amount of energy required to change the state of a system, thereby causing the system to assume a desired state." The working hypothesis of what an entity is doing to produce a voice recording on a physical instrument, then, is that a "trans-etheric[224] influence is initiated by an etheric personality as a subtle-energy expression of intention that acts on physical processes to select required energy states to form a desired effect."[225]

Related to the involvement of energy in entities producing voices or other sounds on recording equipment is the phenomenon experienced by many EVP investigators of a "click, pop, boom or crackling sound" heard right before an EVP message. These precursor sounds, which often precede a particularly clear Class A EVP, may be "caused by a dimensional breakthrough" when a spirit is entering the physical world (especially since the time dimension is different on the other side). It may also indicate "that the entities need and gather all available noise and energy to get their message through to us."[226]

In some communication sessions, entities have been asked "how they create the messages that are placed on recording equipment." The mechanism appears to be "thinking" the message they want to deliver then impressing it somehow on the recorder.[227] As we have seen and will explore in later chapters, this corresponds closely with the overall reality "on the other side" that communication between entities is through thought and thinking, not via language and speech as we experience them in the physical world.

As might be expected, people who adamantly deny the existence of an afterlife are not convinced of the existence of EVPs or afterlife explanations for them. The fact that voices do not always come through clearly, that experiments cannot be replicated exactly as in other scientific experiments, and that the devices sometimes work for certain investigators and not others, among other factors, cause scientists and laypeople alike to doubt the very existence of the voices or to suspect fraud. As we saw in Chapter 3, the nineteenth-century investigators faced the same criticism and disbelief.

The work of Paola Presi, C. Tajna and Dr. Renato Orso in Italy bears significantly on these challenges, and several angles of investigation were pursued along these lines in the 1980s. Professor Ferdinando Bersani, a skeptical physicist at the Centre for Parapsychological Studies in Bologna, attempted to disprove the otherworldly origin of voices. He "claimed that if any ordinary acoustic event is artificially fragmented and cadenced it could be interpreted in a linguistic manner if the perceiver is expected to receive a message." To defend the otherworldly origin supposition, Paolo Presi, one of the founding members of "Il Laboratorio" (Interdisciplinary Laboratory for the Biopsychocybernetic Research), conducted experiments and concluded that, under conditions of "selective attention," "even loud acoustic stimuli could go unperceived at consciousness level." He further concluded from his research that the "messages involve an explicit intention on the part of the sender to have them heard" and the "messages received are objective (not illusory)."²²⁸ Doyle discussed the same situation in *History of Spiritualism*: experiments worked better when persons involved in them were at least open-minded, rather than totally hostile to the afterlife hypothesis.²²⁹

To examine the willingness of the (otherworldly) sender, C. Trajna, an engineer, conducted research using mathematical linguistics. By examining one thousand economic advertisements from Italian newspapers, he plotted a graph with the number of words in the ad on the X axis and the incidence, in percentage, of the ads with a given number of words on the Y axis. The resulting graph demonstrated the advertiser's willingness to transmit information about his or her product. With this as the starting point, Trajna examined "a statistical sample of a thousand supposed paranormal messages" recorded by investigators such as Jürgenson, Raudive and others. The resulting diagram was the same as the one created using Italian advertisements, showing "that the messages retained a certain intention to communicate," whatever their origin.²³⁰

Similarly, the research conducted by Dr. Renato Orso of Turin and technicians from the Acoustic Department at the Electrotechnical Institute "Galileo Ferraris" proved "the acoustic objectivity of such messages." A sonograph even respected in judicial proceedings was used in several controlled experiments. Five clear voices from beyond were chosen for examination and, prior to the experiment, "processed with a parametric equalizer and a dynamic expansion processor." Several important conclusions were drawn:

- The voices of the non-physical entities "have an acoustical structure similar to human voices."
- The speech rhythm is similar to ours in the physical plane.
- "The transfer of information or 'message' is based exclusively on the sequence of the vowel formants and the integration,

made by the listener, of the missing consonants or the pauses of the same length of the Italian stop consonants."
- There was an almost complete absence of proof of physical vocal cords, as determined by frequency and vibration, meaning that there was no "productive speech apparatus" at work in creating the voices.[231]

The Italian researchers thus were able to conclude that the entity "is involved in the process" of forming the voices and can "overthrow known physical laws."[232]

As should be evident, a great deal of scientific experimentation and analysis has been done in the past several decades, in many controlled situations, to explore and explain EVPs. General characteristics of EVPs can thus be discerned. They are distinctive; they are complete words and phrases; they are appropriate to the circumstances, often being clear answers to questions posed by the investigator/s; and the voices are often recognizable as those of deceased loved ones.[233] In some cases, EVPs can be the thoughts of living people while asleep; these are usually achieved via pre-arranged experiments[234] and mesh well with the evidence collected by Monroe with his out-of-body experiences, which we explored briefly in Chapter 2 and will examine in more depth in Chapter 6.[235] Time and again, investigators worldwide have proven that the recorded messages are not radio broadcasts or other stray signals.[236]

The types of evidence captured over the past 100+ years are wide-ranging, fascinating and compelling. Readers and television viewers are invited to examine the recording samples that have been captured; beyond the examples presented here and elsewhere in this book, they are simply too numerous to cite. They include communications to people from their recently-deceased family members; to people from those they barely know who have died suddenly or tragically; to pet owners from their pets;[237] to scientists from fellow scientists who have crossed over; to psychic investigators from spirits who "haunt" certain locales; and to psychic detectives from murder victims. In addition, the Butlers present detailed instructions in *There is No Death and There are No Dead* for conducting one's own experiments; almost anyone can learn to capture EVPs. Skeptics are urged to keep an open mind about these stories, and religious leaders are urged to keep the stories and facts in mind as they counsel parishioners who have lost loved ones or raise questions about what happens when we die.

ITC: Instrumental Transcommunication

Instrumental transcommunication (ITC), which includes EVP, can be viewed "as a set of energy dependent phenomena."[238] It is linked to the Survival Hypothesis, which "holds that there are levels of reality differentiated by changes in characteristics of energy. . . Physical death is when a Self transitions out of a physical lifetime into a nonphysical lifetime. The personality of that human continues in a different aspect of reality. . . EVP and mediumship are thought to be evidence that nonphysical entities can occasionally penetrate [the] veil" between realities.[239]

Instruments and devices that comprise ITC and thus support the Survival Hypothesis include tape recorders, telephones and cell phones, cameras, video recorders, computers and even household appliances. Tom and Lisa Butler, in *There is No Death*, have extensively described their own and others' experiments using various devices, so it is not necessary to track the evidence here in great depth. An overview of some of the findings is important, however.

- Those on this side of the veil – the physical world – have reported receiving phone calls from deceased friends and relatives. Some of the calls are described as sounding hollow, as if in a tunnel.[240]

- Entities from the other side have come through clearly and intelligently via answering machines.[241]
- Faces and other features of famous or familiar deceased persons have been captured on cameras and video machines. One example shows a man with his dog; an owl is depicted in another example;[242] and yet another image depicts a woman in Egyptian headdress, closely resembling the photograph of Queen Nefertiti in the Egyptian Museum in Berlin.[243]
- In the 1980s, researchers started reporting images of the dead appearing on televisions. Klaus Schreiber and Martin Wenzel in Germany use opto-electronic feedback systems to obtain images, and there is corroborating evidence via audio-video contact with Schreiber's two deceased wives.[244]
- A number of scientists have designed sophisticated equipment and conducted experiments with the help of scientists on the other side.[245] Some of the living investigators include Hans-Otto König in Germany, who receives information in dreams;[246] Jules and Maggy Harsch-Fischbach of Luxembourg, who obtain high-quality TV picture sequences and incoming calls on an answering machine "from a scientist collaborator in the spirit world;"[247] Manfred Boden of Germany, who obtained unsolicited computer print-outs from spirits;[248] Fritz Malhoff in Germany, who "established contact with Spirit Group Cloverleaf on the other side" to collaborate on research on physical mediums;[249] and Larry Dean and Patricia Begley who work with a spirit guide named Choi to conduct video ITC experiments and capture photographic images.[250]

The Scole Group was founded in 1993 in Scole, England, by four friends, Robin and Sandra Foy and Alan and Diana Bennett. Diana went into a trance, and soon a voice named Manu spoke through her, explaining that "he was the gatekeeper between earth and the other side." Representing thousands of minds from the spirit world, he told the Scole Group that his group wanted to use creative energy to work together "to pioneer methods of communication between the two dimensions." He assured them that there would be no danger to the medium and that there would be a tremendous number of phenomena produced during their sessions. The Scole Group, joined by other scientists, witnessed, over time, the results of this collaboration, including the materialization of coins and jewelry. Photographic experimentation produced pictures, messages and writing on "factory-sealed, unopened photographic film that had been placed in a locked box." Video cameras recorded images on a blank videotape in a camcorder that was focused on a brown ceiling.[251] The group sat together for four years; *The Scole Experiment* by Grant and Jane Solomon, published in 1999, described their work.

After the experiments ended, Diana and Alan Bennett continued to develop their own spiritual gifts in different ways, including healing. In one experiment using crystals, they "linked together mentally and shared a journey," in full light, into wondrous and beautiful otherworldly dimensions. With help from spirit guides, the Bennetts have conducted a number of experiments that have produced images of people and animals. Their experiments continue.[252]

The International Network for Instrumental Transcommunication (INIT) was formed in 1995 with a major goal being "to ensure that ITC spread with an ethical/moral base as well as a technical one."[253] One of the co-founders of INIT, Mark Macy, then went on to found, with researcher Rolf-Dietmar Ehrhardt, World ITC, a vibrant organization with a comprehensive website at http://www.worlditc.org/. The mission of World ITC is "to promote decency in human relationships, to sustain resonance among ITC researchers and to forge a link with the light, ethereal realms of existence."[254] World ITC's site contains images of people who have come through from the other side, including scientists and investigators; articles presenting theories of how ITC works and how spirits make contact with the physical world; tips for investigators; an overview of a number of work groups that pursue different tasks around spiritual issues; excerpts from books on the paranormal written by some of the luminaries in the field; and professional, measured responses to angry and negative remarks by skeptics and afterlife deniers.

Another important finding that has been confirmed through ITC is that animal souls survive death just as our souls do and that animals' consciousness is often expanded in the afterlife, as the human consciousness is often expanded. Just as researchers have captured EVPs of animal sounds, as mentioned above, visual images of animals have been recorded from the beyond through ITC.[255]

EMF Recorder/Meter/Device

An Electromagnetic Field (EMF) is "a physical field produced by electrically charged objects."[256] A number of instruments capture and record these fields, the sources of which can include power lines, television sets, appliances and other items that surround us daily in the natural world. Some of the recording devices used by paranormal investigators include Gauss meters, the K-2 meter, and Mel meters (see below). When there is no obvious physical reason for an EMF to be detected in an area under investigation, it is postulated that entities in the spirit world emit electrical energy that affects the EMF and/or "absorb energy from available power sources in order to facilitate their crossing over" into our physical world.[257] Television viewers of such shows as *Paranormal State*, *Ghost Hunters* and *Ghost Adventures* see energy absorption in some episodes when the electronic equipment being used suddenly malfunctions for no known reason.

A REM pod is a type of EMF meter. One new model "uses a mini telescopic antenna to radiate its own independent magnetic field around the instrument. This EM field can be easily influenced by materials and objects that conduct electricity. Based on source proximity, strength and EM field distortion (4) colorful LED lights can be activated in any order or combination." This device was originally designed for the Ghost Adventures Team, which has had very interesting results, as featured several times on *Ghost Adventures*.[258]

Mel Meter

The Mel Meter is also a type of EMF device. Created by Gary Galka of DAS Distribution Inc., it is named after Galka's daughter Melissa. Melissa, who was born on Valentine's Day 1987, was killed in a car accident in 2004 when her car hit a tree. Gary and Cindy Galka sense Melissa's presence especially around Valentine's Day every year. With the help of the Mel Meter, they can hear her voice (as confirmed by comparing what is recorded on her cell phone greeting, which has never been erased) and experience her continuing love and existence. From beyond the grave, Melissa confirms that she is at peace.[259]

The *Ghost Adventures* team of Zak Bagans, Nick Groff and Aaron Goodwin filmed an episode of the show on what should have been Melissa's 25th birthday, Valentine's Day 2012,[260] so viewers can see for themselves how this encounter played out. The investigators not only captured Melissa's voice on tape several times but also felt a cold spot in her bedroom and smelled perfume. Gary Galka is featured in other episodes of the *Ghost Adventures* using some of the instruments he has developed.

Heat Sensors and Infrared Devices

A digital infrared camera is "used to capture images invisible to the human eye at the 'hot' end of the light spectrum. It is capable of feeding information to a computer, where its infrared images may be stored on a hard drive."[261] Investigators have picked up and recorded a number of these types of images that cannot be explained away; they are not human or animal, and they have also been shown not to be dust particles or caused by wind or breezes.

A thermal camera visually records temperature differences. *Paranormal State* has an episode in which "the thermal cam revealed a handprint on the wall, even though we'd documented through surveillance that no one had placed their hand on that spot."[262]

Spirit and Ghost Boxes

While spirit and ghost boxes may sometimes be terms used interchangeably, some investigators make distinctions. "A ghost box utilizes environmental queues through software to give the spirits a voice while a spirit box emits raw radio frequencies."[263] A spirit box uses both AM and FM radio frequency sweeps to generate white noise. Voices from the other side can tap into the energy produced by the white noise to come through the static and be understood.[264] Various companies market these devices to the paranormal community.

Ovilus

An Ovilus is an electronic device created by engineer Bill Chappell that contains an EMF detector and a database of words "that work in tandem to generate what some consider to be messages from disincarnate beings."[265] Chappell, who operates Digital Dowsing, LLC (www.Digitaldowsing), is an engineer in the robotics and semiconductor industries and has taught at the college level. He uses microprocessors and electronics to solve complex problems involving motion control and satellite telemetry.[266]

He was approached when in his late 40s to explore the possibility of building a device to communicate with the dead. Initially amused, he tested his device in April 2007 at Waverly Hills Sanatorium in Louisville, Kentucky, and came to firmly believe that there is more to the world and universe than we perceive with our five senses. He has since dedicated his skills to the pursuit of answers to these profound life questions and has created and marketed a series of Ovilus instruments in this quest, the most recent being the Ovilus X Rev B.[267]

The Ghost Box Ovilus X, as seen on *Ghost Adventures*, converts environmental readings into actual words in answer to investigators' questions. The results are based on underlying theories that suggest that beings on the other side alter the physical environment such as electromagnetic frequencies and temperature. The Ovilus X uses these frequencies to enable the entity "to choose a response from a preset database of 2,048 words."[268]

One can see the Ovilus instruments and spirit and ghost boxes at work in episodes of *Ghost Hunters*, *Ghost Adventures*, and *Paranormal State*. Investigators ask questions in a locale and are able to receive clear, intelligent answers via the Ovilus. The next generation of combination instruments can be viewed at http://www.ghoststop.com/Spirit-Box-RT-EVP-p/evp-rt-evp.htm?gclid=CMu74LSN67YCF cfd4Aodvw4Afg.

Alpha Device

Alexander MacRae of Scotland has developed several generations of biofeedback devices that detect changes in the Galvanic Skin Response (GSR) of mediums. This "Alpha" device, first used in the late 1970s, detects color changes as the GSR changes and also produces audible tones that mark frequency changes in GSR. A test in March 2003 at the Institute of Noetic Sciences in California produced several EVP messages. Because the lab itself was shielded from all radio waves, laser beams and infrasound and ultrasonic waves, MacRae is certain that "[t]here is no way known in our present science that the EVP could have been recorded in this laboratory by physical means."[269]

Frank's Box

Ryan Buell discusses an experimental device that was used in some investigations of the Paranormal Research Society. The box, designed by Frank Sumption, a paranormal enthusiast with an electronics background, "generates a random voltage and the base acts as an antenna allowing it to tune in to A.M. frequencies. The signal is filtered for the audio, which is amplified and fed through a speaker, which, in turn, is received by a microphone connected to . . . another speaker."[270] It was considered by some to be "a telephone to the dead," whereby spirits could somehow use the box to communicate with investigators.[271]

The PRS team brought in Chris Moon, a paranormal investigator, on one investigation to demonstrate the use of the box. In response to the question, "How many spirits do we have here with us?" as they visited Willard Drug Treatment Center in upstate New York, the box clearly responded with "There are seven here." Buell then asked, "What are the spirits' names?" The box responded, less clearly, with something resembling "Lucy." Historical research conducted by the PRS team disappointingly encountered dead ends due to privacy regulations around the site's previous incarnation as an asylum, resulting in an absence of confirmation of the physical-world existence of a Lucy. However, psychic Chip Coffey, who was brought in to do a reading, felt he was connecting with a female spirit. Chip

Moon concluded that Lucy may have been a nurse who died caring for the inmates.[272]

While the PRS team was not particularly impressed with Frank's Box, Chip Coffey confirmed some of the information that the box and Chris Moon were obtaining. Moon "claimed that while we try to communicate with the other side, technicians on the other side work to communicate with us. He was teamed with a specific spirit technician, or operator . . . Larry," who was "supposedly communicating through the box." While Buell is skeptical about this,[273] the claim parallels those documented by many investigators, as we have noted earlier in this chapter, that spirits on the other side collaborate with like-minded people in the physical world.[274]

The Visionaries of Medjugorje
Since 1981, in the village of Medjugorje in Bosnia-Herzegovina (former Communist Yugoslavia), the Virgin Mary, mother of Jesus, has been appearing and giving messages to the world.[275] In the 1980s, a number of medical and scientific studies were performed on six adolescents and young adults who regularly witnessed an appearance of "Our Lady." At regular times of the day, the young people, who regularly fasted on bread and water in advance, entered the chapel and, standing, started reciting prayers (Our Father [the Lord's Prayer], Hail Mary and Glory Be). Their eyes gazed on a crucifix above them. At some point, their gaze would become more intense, "[t]heir faces become almost imperceptibly brighter and turn towards the invisible speaker. They kneel down very naturally, all at the same moment." It is at this point that they would enter the first phase of the ecstasy, with their lips moving but no sound coming out. Suddenly, they simultaneously continued with the Lord's Prayer at "who art in heaven," since the Virgin has already started the prayer with "Our Father." After the Lord's Prayer, the visionaries recited the Glory Be

along with the Virgin (as reported by them later). In the third phase, their "voices disappear again for a second period of contemplation or conversation," followed by the simultaneous raising of the eyes and heads, bringing the experience to a close.[276] The visions as examined in the 1980s lasted between 62 and 102 seconds.[277] The visionaries reported that they were speaking to a real person, not a vision or image.[278]

While there is widespread skepticism and even hostility on the part of the Roman Catholic establishment, the site has become one of the most popular Catholic pilgrimage sites – the third most important apparition site in Europe; over a million people visit annually. Perhaps as many as 30 million pilgrims have come to Medjugorje since 1981.[279]

Despite vicious charges of fraud, lies and manipulation, the examination of the visionaries, conducted by a team of medical doctors and scientists, provide a wealth of information that is hard to ignore or dismiss. The team, comprised of graduates of the faculty of medicine at the University of Montpellier, France, included a cancer surgeon; a professional in ophthalmology; an ear, nose and throat physician; an assistant clinic head in cardiology; and a member of the Yugoslav Society of Neurophysiology. Also included was an electrical engineer, the technical expert.[280] The tests conducted on the visionaries included electro-encephalograms, electrocardiograms, and eye, touch, vocal and hearing tests. The tests were conducted prior to the appearance of the Virgin, during the appearance, and immediately afterwards. Some of the results of the tests included the following:

- Vicka, a 20-year-old visionary at the time of the 1984 experiments, did not flinch when she was poked with a needle during the ecstasy. Even though the poke drew some blood, "Not a muscle in her face moved [when touched]. She continued her conversation with Our Lady, unperturbed."[281]

- Ivan, 19, had no reaction when inflicted without warning with a noise of 90 decibels during the ecstasy (90 decibels being equivalent to a combustion engine at high revolution), even though he had previously jumped at a noise of 70 decibels before the ecstasy. Following the 90-decibel experiment, he reported hearing nothing.[282]
- When an object was placed in front of 18-year-old Ivanka's open eyes during the ecstasy, she showed no reaction.

All reports, including those of physicians and scientists who studied the youths on other occasions in the mid-1980s, demonstrate that the visionaries are normal and well-balanced people. "They appeared to be discreet, well-mannered, careful in their dress and in their speech and absolutely mindful of the surroundings in which they found themselves."[283] Their experiences leave them joyful, calm and at peace. Examiners routinely conclude that there are no clinical signs of individual or collective hallucination; no individual or collective hysteria; no neurosis; and no catalepsy. The experience is not a pathological ecstasy,[284] nor is there any element of deceit. Rather, "We would be quite willing to define [the phenomenon] as a state of active, intense prayer, partially disconnected from the outside world, a state of contemplation with a separate person whom they alone can see, hear and touch."[285]

While science cannot explain precisely what is happening to these young people (at least one of whom, Ivan Dragicevic, travels the world 30 years later spreading the loving messages he receives),[286] scientific experiments of all kinds – controlled and witnessed by many – verify that something extraordinary of a positive, beneficent nature does take place.

The Work of Ian Stevenson

Dr. Ian Stevenson was a rare example of a paranormal investigator who was supported by a mainline institution; he has greatly expanded the careful research on reincarnation and past lives. From 1957 until 2002, Stevenson was Carlson Professor of Psychiatry at the University of Virginia Medical Center in Charlottesville; he died in 2007.[287] Born in Montreal of Scottish and British parents, he was educated in Canada and England before beginning medical studies at McGill University in Montreal, where he earned his MD in 1943. Early in his career, when he held positions in New Orleans and New York, he published on a wide variety of medical subjects, establishing himself as prolific, meticulous, wide-ranging and a bit of a maverick.[288]

At the University of Virginia, when Stevenson became more interested in stories of past lives and expanded his research, Chester Carlson (1906–1968), the inventor of xerography,[289] provided Stevenson with the funding necessary to conduct past lives research in India, Sri Lanka and elsewhere. Despite opposition from most of his colleagues in the medical establishment, Stevenson won the support of the President of the University of Virginia, as we saw in Chapter 3. When Carlson died in 1968, he bequeathed one million dollars to the University to support Stevenson's paranormal research. Eventually the Carlson Professor of Psychiatry chair and the Division of Perceptual Studies were established as a result of the Carlson bequest.[290]

While Stevenson's primary area of paranormal research was reincarnation, disseminated in scores of books and peer-reviewed articles on the subject, he also conducted studies and published papers on ESP, NDEs, mediumship, apparitions, and xenoglossy, the ability to speak in a foreign language that the individual does not know in this life.[291] Reincarnation and its corollaries – karma and the law of cause and effect – cut across the paranormal evidence and has far-reaching ethical ramifications, as we shall see.

Methods and Literature
As has been indicated in the above discussion, investigators in the various paranormal fields use methods and instruments that can be duplicated by others. The methods and principles are described in peer-reviewed articles and books. Experiments have been undertaken in the US and abroad for decades, and procedures have been refined over time, as in all legitimate scientific endeavors. As we have seen in Chapter 3, scientific methods were used to investigate the paranormal as early as the nineteenth century.

Tom and Lisa Butler, in *There is No Death* and numerous articles, trace some of the early history of research as well as their own and others' more recent experiments, especially with EVPs. In Chapter 9 of their book, "Our Experience with Video ITC and Other Phenomena," they provide details of their trials and results, including how they use computers, angles at which to place equipment to get the best results, and help they have received from spirits on the other side. Their Chapter 10, "Recording EVP," offers specific techniques, such as recording in controlled conditions, the type of equipment to use, preparing oneself with meditation and prayer, keeping a log, and editing EVP samples. Chapter 13, "How to Record Video ITC," focuses on video recordings from the other side, and their Appendix B, "Techniques for Editing Sound Files," discusses in some technical detail noise reduction and noise filtering. Their techniques can also be found on the Association TransCommunication (formerly AA-EVP) website, http://atransc.org/.

Investigators from The Atlantic Paranormal Society (TAPS), the team featured on *Ghost Hunters*, outline their research methods in *Ghost Hunting*. They set up and record experiments so that other investigators can duplicate them. They seek first to debunk reported phenomena: what kind of natural process or event could have caused the phenomenon? Jason Hawes outlines how the subject of an investigation can be carefully observed in various settings and under different conditions. "In every investigation, we collect a wealth of data through different types of cameras, meters, and voice records, and from observations and reports of strange experiences. We sift through all of this as objectively as possible before we begin to draw conclusions."[292] These procedures can be seen clearly – although fleetingly, to fit in one-hour or 30-minute television segments.

Ryan Buell in *Paranormal State* explains that, over time, the equipment used by the Paranormal Research Society has become more sophisticated but basically consists of camcorders, audio recorders, a monitor system of strategically-placed "stationary video cameras wired to a central set of monitors," motion detectors, EMF detectors, and a thermal camera.[293] Viewers of the television program can see these instruments in action and can watch the investigators analyze the evidence they collect.

A final word can be said about the various journals in which much of the paranormal research has been published. The SPR, whose work we have examined above, "was the first society to conduct organised scholarly research into human experiences that challenge contemporary scientific models."[294] Its peer-reviewed quarterly journal, the *Journal of the Society for Psychical Research*, "has been published continuously since 1884, promoting the Society's aim of examining 'without prejudice or prepossession and in a scientific spirit those faculties of man, real or supposed, which appear to be inexplicable on any generally recognised hypothesis.'"[295] The ASPR publishes the quarterly *Journal of the American Society for Psychical Research*.[296]

The *Journal of Parapsychology* is a publication of the Parapsychological Association (PA). First established in 1957, the PA "is an international professional organization of scientists and scholars engaged in the study of *psi* (or 'psychic') experiences, such as telepathy, clairvoyance, psychokinesis, psychic healing, and precognition." The PA has been an affiliated organization of the prestigious American Association for the Advancement of Science (AAAS) since 1969.[297] The *Journal* is published out of the Rhine Research Center in Durham, North Carolina;[298] we were introduced to investigator J.B. Rhine in Chapter 2. The ethical and professional guidelines PA of can be viewed at http://www.parapsych.org/section/42/ethical_and_professional_standards.aspx.

The *Journal of Scientific Exploration* is the quarterly, peer-reviewed journal of the Society for Scientific Exploration. "Since 1987, the JSE has published original research on consciousness, quantum and biophysics, unexplained aerial phenomena, alternative medicine, new energy, sociology, psychology, and much more."[299]

Finally, The *Journal of Spirituality and Paranormal Studies*, formerly known as The *Journal of Religion and Psychical Research*, is a publication of the Academy of Spirituality and Paranormal Studies, Inc. Founded in 2005, the Academy is based in Bloomfield, Connecticut. Its mission "is to discern, develop and disseminate knowledge of how paranormal phenomena may relate to and enhance the development of the human spirit."[300] The Academy's Board of Directors and Advisory Council include PhD-trained researchers and scientists, university professors, and ministers in several denominations.[301]

It should be apparent that research in paranormal fields is a serious, scientific undertaking by many respected professionals who have high ethical standards of practice and publication. Readers are encouraged to consider articles from these groups in the same spirit that they consider findings from other professional societies and investigators.

Skeptics and Deniers

In order to try to explain away some of the evidence that has been collected using the devices and instruments we have examined, skeptics – or, more correctly, afterlife deniers – have postulated a number of possible explanations. Technically, by definition, skeptics have a healthy outlook on phenomena that cannot be readily explained; they are open-minded and curious: "Healthy skepticism invites the demonstration of an opposing point of view." Deniers on the other hand (or disbelievers, in psychic Chip Coffey's view) "already *know* that they are right and you are wrong... [T]hese people can be extremely hostile and aggressive in their response to anyone who believes in or has had experiences of the paranormal."[302]

Wikipedia, the online encyclopedia, is a handy source for articles of all kinds, but on paranormal subjects, it appears to be heavily slanted to the views of skeptics and afterlife deniers. A Wikipedia article on psychic detectives, for instance, offers a number of cases of psychics being incorrect in attempts to locate missing persons, identify killers, and aid law enforcement.[303] The author of this article baldly states, "As skeptics point out, however, not one of the alleged paranormal powers has been proved to exist."

In an article on parapsychology, the Wikipedia author says:
Former stage magician James Randi is a well-known investigator of paranormal claims. As an investigator with a background in illusion, Randi feels that the simplest explanation for those claiming paranormal abilities is often trickery, illustrated by demonstrating that the spoon bending abilities of psychic Uri Geller can easily be duplicated by trained stage magicians. He is

also the founder of the James Randi Educational Foundation and its million dollar challenge offering a prize of US $1,000,000 to anyone who can demonstrate evidence of any paranormal, supernatural or occult power or event, under test conditions agreed to by both parties. Despite many declarations of supernatural ability, this prize remains unclaimed.[304] Interestingly, while Randi refers to most of parapsychology as a pseudoscience due to the way in which it is approached, he nonetheless sees parapsychology as a legitimate endeavor that "must be pursued" and from which real scientific discoveries may develop. Also, exposing fraud, one of Randi's main goals, is thoroughly legitimate and an aid to the public.[305]

One of Randi's research fellows, Dr. Karen Stollznow, viciously pans medium Theresa Caputo and her show, *Long Island Medium*. She calls Caputo "yet another psychic medium who claims to be able to talk to the dead," and says the following about many of the ordinary people featured on Caputo's program: "As believers, these people are pushovers." Stollznow dismisses the conversion of skeptical men Caputo encounters in a motorcycle shop because "these are her husband's friends at his place of work and she could easily have inside information about them." Stollznow also doubts the legitimacy of a reading for the woman who grooms Caputo's dogs, since she has been a customer for years. With regard to "the too-specific private readings with clients at their homes," Stollznow insists that Caputo "has all of their personal information and comments provided at the time of booking."[306] In a number of episodes of the show, however, Caputo states explicitly that, for clients she sees in her own home, the only thing she knows in advance is their name and phone number. She has also insisted that she does no research on her clients, which is very believable, given her apparent (and admitted) weaknesses in technological areas. Caputo's practices, results and statements entirely parallel those of the other reputable psychics and mediums we have been discussing.

A website called Paranormal Skeptic Academy, which has as its focus the criticism of Ryan Buell and *Paranormal State*, boasts juvenile links called "Dumbass Review" and "The Dumbass Media Empire." One comment insults people who believe in the paranormal with this remark: "We are not professional skeptics but we accept mainstream scientific knowledge and rely on experts to help inform our opinions but what keeps us from sliding into [conspiracy theorist] Alex Jones territory? Is it anti-psychotics? Mind controlling vaccinations? It's something more sinister than that, something that we all should possess but very few actually have…critical thinking skills."[307]

Without direct reference to this Academy, Buell responds to skeptics who try to prove that *Paranormal State* is staged: "I can't speak for the other shows, but other than some honest mistakes, and time-crunched editing . . . it's not true so, in our case, no one's able to back up that accusation. In fact, an employee of James Randi, the world's best-known debunker, told me they tried to debunk our show but couldn't."[308]

From their standpoints as physicians, Stevenson, Alexander and Long have addressed much of the scientific skepticism about paranormal phenomena and attempts to disprove the existence of an afterlife; we outlined Alexander's and Long's arguments in Chapter 2 and have seen how Doyle dealt with similar criticisms in the early twentieth century. Ian Stevenson, in a 1981 "comment" in *American Psychologist*, addresses a review of Ronald K. Siegel's October 1980 article, "The psychology of life after death." Stevenson confronts Siegel's misreadings and errors point by point, using facts and statistics. Stevenson calls attention to Siegel's logical fallacies, "cursory reading" of Stevenson's many publications, and Siegel's "real inability . . . to distinguish between" "trash books" on the paranormal and scholarly ones. Stevenson further points out that Siegel "annoyingly attributes to all parapsychologists views that one of them may hold."[309]

In Appendix B of *Proof of Heaven*, Alexander lays out nine hypotheses that skeptics have offered to help explain what happened to him in his week-long coma. He disputes all nine, maintaining that they could not "explain the robust, richly interactive nature of the recollections," they "bore no resemblance whatsoever to my experience in coma," the theories did not mesh with the absence of his cortex, and they "failed to explain the auditory-visual interleaving."[310]

Jeffrey Long, as we saw in our discussion of *Evidence of the Afterlife* in Chapter 2, drew similar conclusions after examining thousands of NDEs. He refutes the theory of some scientists that people who have NDEs are not truly near death or that they suffer from hypoxia. To the explanation that the visions seen in an out-of-body experience associated with a person's NDE are only memory fragments, Long states, "A review of 287 OBE accounts reveals that they are fully realistic, without *any* apparent error, in 97.6 percent of the cases."[311] Skeptics might further argue that NDEs are the result of too little (or too much) anesthesia. To this, Long replies, "By conventional medical thinking, neither a person under anesthesia nor a person experiencing cardiac arrest should have a conscious experience like that of an NDE. Yet the NDERF [Near Death Experience Research Foundation] study found many that do."[312]

Long also tackles the skeptics' theories about the Life Review that many NDEers undergo. One possibility is that the Life Review is a psychological defense mechanism, and another is that it "results from the dying brain producing electrical discharges in the part of the brain responsible for memories." Long shows that some NDE memories are not pleasant, thereby casting doubt on the psychological defense theory, along with the fact that sudden unconsciousness does not give a defense mechanism a chance to develop. Long takes on the work of Dr. Susan Blackmore and Dr. Wilder Penfield, both NDE skeptics, pointing out that "[m]ost of the experiences Penfield reported in fact bore little resemblance to actual NDEs." Long concludes, "The skeptical argument that NDEs are somehow related to electrical brain stimulation or seizures needs to be relegated to the status of urban legend."[313]

The most straightforward explanation for legitimate paranormal phenomena, and the one that consistently fits the findings, is that we survive physical death, exist afterwards on a different plane of existence, and can sometimes "break through" to communicate with those on the physical plane through electronic and other means. This in effect is the Survival Hypothesis and the basis of Spiritualism. The quest for answers and scientific explanations continues, since many phenomena remain unexplained by what we consider to be natural laws. Given what has already been learned, however, it is highly likely that answers will continue to be found as this work progresses, as more people in both science and non-science fields begin to trust the evidence, and as cooperation between experimenters on "this side" and "the other side" of life/reality is further explored and strengthened.

Chapter 5: Western Religion and the Afterlife

- *"He descended to the dead. On the third day he rose again."* – Apostles' Creed
- *"Rest eternal grant to them, O Lord; And let light perpetual shine upon them."* – Requiem Mass
- *"Spiritualists believe that God or Infinite Intelligence is ALL That Is, expressing through all creation by love, light and law. . . . [T]he spiritual realm . . . is love, light, law, peace, cooperation, sharing, and growth."* – National Spiritualist Association of Churches

From the earliest ages of the human species, perhaps even prior to the emergence of *homo sapiens*, our prehistoric ancestors observed the death of their peers and elders, found ways to dispose of the remains, developed art and rituals around death, and built tombs and memorials. Many of these ancestors practiced methods of communicating with those "on the other side," often by creating classes of people such as priests, shamans, witch doctors, and seers who had particular gifts in this area. More recent peoples in the West, such as ancient Egyptians, Hebrews, Assyrians, Phoenicians, Greeks, Romans, Celts, Angles, and Saxons, also developed ideas about the afterlife and methods for communicating with the deceased.

It is difficult to know for sure what Paleolithic and Neolithic peoples actually knew or believed about death and the afterlife, but the fact that they did communicate with the dead – or at least performed tasks that indicate to us that they *thought* they were doing so – can be combined with what we know from later peoples to provide context for Western beliefs and practices around paranormal phenomena. It is important to study the practices of our earliest ancestors not only because it is interesting from historical and anthropological points of view but also because they have things to teach us about the afterlife and viewing the world in more spiritual ways. In our highly scientific, materialistic, Post-Enlightenment mentality, which envelops us in skepticism about things we cannot experience with our own five senses, or that science cannot prove experimentally, coming to a greater appreciation of how our ancestors dealt with vital questions of life and death can inform our own ways of thinking and behaving. It therefore behooves us to ask seriously whether, in the area of the survival of our souls after death, our ancestors may have actually known or perceived *more* than we do, not less.

Human beings seem to have always wondered about death and the afterlife. It is theorized that religions and religious belief systems emerged in large part because of this basic question of our existence (along with the observation of nature and of the life, death and rebirth cycles of both human and animal species). The near-universal idea of some kind of God, Goddess or divine figure can probably be traced to our ancestors' growing self-consciousness and awareness of mortality.[314] While we can rarely be sure what goes through the minds of animals, we can be fairly certain that it is mainly human beings who have developed full-blown systems of belief and morality due in large part to the knowledge that one day we will depart our current material (fleshly) form.

In this chapter, we will examine ways in which our prehistoric, pagan, Jewish and early Christian ancestors might be able to teach us about life after death, "heaven," reincarnation, and communicating with those who have crossed over.[315] Also, because religion professionals and leaders generally treat the afterlife, reincarnation and paranormal phenomena from the skeptical viewpoint, which differs from the approach of most of our ancestors, we will dialogue with some of these current leaders' writings from the perspective of the paranormal evidence. Finally, the Apostles' Creed is an ancient basic summary of the Christian faith, whose tenets have influenced much of Western culture; an analysis from a paranormal perspective is offered in Appendix II.

Prehistoric Culture and the Afterlife
Archaeologists and anthropologists have published widely in the area of prehistoric burial practices and afterlife beliefs in the European context. There is considerable evidence from the Neolithic era, which spanned roughly the years between 7000 and 3500 Before the Common Era (BCE) in Europe and the Middle East. Is it possible to discern whether our Neolithic ancestors "knew" and experienced death and the afterlife in ways that confirm what we can know, in our Post-Enlightenment age, from science, modern mediums, NDEs and OOBEs? In other words, if it appears that Neolithic peoples communed with deceased spirits and may have believed that some part of human beings went to another, perhaps better, "place" after bodily death, can we view their culture as something to be respected and emulated in this regard?

Archaeological evidence from dozens of sites in Old Europe[316] shows that the primary deity worshipped in the Neolithic era was a powerful female deity associated with nature. The most significant attribute of this goddess is that she was the earth – primordial Mother, Nature, Life. She was not only the creator of everything in the world – human beings, animals, plants, trees, rocks, mountains – she *was* the very earth from which all life emanated. To these early humans, the earth pulsated with her energy; she was completely in control of all growth, weather, birds, animals, birth, death, the sun, the moon, and the planets. This Earth Mother/Goddess provided all people's needs – and the needs of all living things – but, through storms, natural disasters, fierce beasts, and accidents, also caused destruction and ended life. She was self-generating and functioned as Giver of Life, Wielder of Death, and Regeneratrix.[317]

Evidence found at excavated sites such as Sitagroi in northern Greece, Çatal Hüyük in Turkey, and Crete shows that prehistoric cultures were socially complex and quite different on many levels from later civilizations. The symbols painted and incised on ritual and everyday objects found at these sites point almost exclusively to the high regard for the feminine and the female life force. Architectural and burial evidence from these sites shows that these were settled agricultural communities that experienced a large growth in population.[318] The Neolithic culture of the Mediterranean, Middle East and Old Europe – a true "civilization" – boasted towns with temples several stories high, a sacred script, four- or five-room houses, and professional ceramicists, weavers, and copper and gold workers. A network of trade routes facilitated the exchange of commodities such as obsidian, shells, marble, and salt.[319] Significantly, we should note that the society that the nature goddess' worship engendered was, for all intents and purposes, egalitarian. The society was matrilineal and matrifocal but not matriarchal; that is, descent was through the mother and a new husband lived with his wife's family, but women did not dominate.[320]

The symbols and signs on prehistoric artifacts such as ceramics, monuments, jewelry and coins can be "read" to some extent. The goddess in the guise of the snake, for instance, is a powerful illustration of the goddess' power and scope of influence. The non-poisonous snake was a major image signifying the vitality and continuity of life, the guarantor of life energy in the home, and the symbol of family and animal life. Its hibernation was viewed as analogous to death, while the shedding of old skin represented a kind of immortality, a continuum of life. The return of the snake in springtime signified the rebirth of the natural world. Thus the image was intimately connected with the cycles of death and rebirth in nature and, therefore, with the goddess.[321]

Birds depicted on artifacts also signified aspects of the goddess; prime examples included the dove, duck, swallow, owl, peacock and vulture. Doves, for instance, were raised in the goddess' temples, carved on her monuments and depicted on her jewels and coins. In the writings of the ancient Greek writer Homer, the goddesses Athena and Hera assume dove form; until the twentieth century, doves, along with the cuckoo, "were believed to be prophetic birds, omens of death, and spirits of the dead."[322] These are birds of spring, the time of regeneration; this cyclical nature of birds, like that of the snake, is linked with the goddess' overseeing "of the cycles of time, life and death, spring and winter, happiness and unhappiness."[323]

It follows, then, that this goddess was viewed as all-powerful and thus involved in almost every aspect of life, not only in the large-scale events – birth, marriage, childbearing, death – but also in more mundane daily activities. She was believed to oversee one's everyday work, one's play, the seasons, relationships within one's community, and the creation of clothing and homes. By extension, she dictated ethical behavior: cooperation, not competition or violence, was paramount for the survival of all species. In contrast to many strands of androcentric, historic, war-defined religion the world over, the goddess belief and praxis system emphasized joy, creativity, beauty and harmony, both between people themselves and between people and nature. The taking of human life would have been viewed, most likely, as anathema to the deity, and the taking of animal and plant life in the service of humankind would have been accompanied by devout prayers and rituals. The rituals concerned three major themes: thanksgiving for the abundance of the earth, supplications of forgiveness for the taking of animal and plant life, and petitions for the continued survival of those flora and fauna, on which humanity depended.[324]

Burial practices further aid us in speculating what may have been in the minds of our Neolithic ancestors. The deity they revered cared for and protected them not only in this world but in the next. The evidence from Çatal Hüyük and similar sites – where the deceased are buried under platforms in the structures of the living[325] – suggests that the people of Çatal Hüyük believed their "dead" to be very close to them, although in another "dimension." Furthermore, the development of a complex script to the goddess, as postulated by Gimbutas, also supports the notion that people revered a being that existed in a different form than the physical (a spiritual or otherworldly form, if you will) and that that being, usual female, was involved with both the physical and the non-physical (the "dead" or spiritual) form of humans.

From this brief overview we can see that the evidence strongly suggests that Neolithic peoples had a holistic view of life and death that intersected with and informed daily life and ethical behavior.[326] Can we also conclude that our prehistoric ancestors were in touch with a kind of reality that our age has largely lost sight of? The paranormal evidence we have been examining certainly suggests that a reverence for all of life – both this-worldly and otherworldly – along with communication with spiritual beings can lead to an ethical, highly-evolved society that holds promise, joy and hope for its members. Those of us in the twenty-first century can, then, learn real life lessons from our ancestors who lived nearly 10,000 years ago. What we moderns might dismiss as superstitious or mythological, or at best see as quaint, can and should be reexamined from a more nuanced perspective.

Judaism and the Afterlife

Judaism is both an ancient and a living religion and has influenced Western thought both through its own heritage, beliefs and practices but also as the "mother" of Christianity. While it is often viewed as a monolithic religion that has changed little since antiquity, it has actually evolved over thousands of years and in relationship with polytheistic belief systems. Just as there are at least three strands of Judaism in the US and the West today – Orthodox, Conservative and Reformed – there were many variations of Judaism as far back as its origins in the ancient Middle East, during the Graeco-Roman era, and through the Middle Ages. Therefore, the notions of the afterlife in Judaism are complex, and this overview will merely scratch the surface.[327]

What we know about Judaism and the Jewish people at their origins in very ancient times comes from two primary sources: Hebrew Scriptures (known to Christians and other Westerners as the Old Testament) and archaeological investigations in the Near East. Jewish history can be divided into several eras, each of which produced differing notions of death, the afterlife, and immortality. The Exodus from Egypt, when the patriarch Moses led the Jews out of slavery, is the central event of Jewish history. The event and the entire story around it are so influential that they have become a template of liberation not only in the rest of the Bible but also for African-American slaves in the US. In the words of scholar Michael Coogan, "The Exodus entails not only the actual events in Egypt but all those encompassed within the period from Moses to Joshua, from the actual escape from Egypt to the conquest of the land of Canaan, including the wilderness wanderings."[328] It is difficult to date the Exodus historically, but literary and archaeological evidence lends credence to a possible date in the mid-thirteenth century BCE.[329]

The Jews' forced exile to Babylonia around 600 BCE is another pivotal time in their history. The deportations, as described in 2 Kings 24, numbered in the thousands starting around 597, under the orders of Nebuchadrezzar.[330] These events followed on the heels of the destruction of Solomon's temple in Jerusalem approximately 10 years earlier. The Exodus and the exile, as well as many tragedies that followed, traumatized the Israelites and greatly influenced their ideas, philosophy and literature. The prophet Ezekiel is associated with the exile, and the prophets Jeremiah and Isaiah were instrumental in the restoration of the Jews in Jerusalem upon their return.[331]

Notions of the afterlife and the soul were significantly different in Judaism before the exile than after. Because pre-exilic notions were dismissed and repudiated by religious leaders during and after the exile, pre-exilic ideas in Jewish literature are vague and scanty. Notions can, however, be discerned from Biblical passages that reflect the time prior to the exile: the Israelites, along with other Near Eastern peoples, believed that human beings continued to exist in some fashion after death. In particular, the spirit of the deceased went to Sheol, a land below the earth. There was no concurrent idea of a judgment of the dead based on the person's behavior in life; rather, all souls were thought to go to Sheol, and the nature of Sheol and "life" there remained vague.[332]

The notions of what transpired in Sheol seem to have been more positive before the exile, since the later texts criticize the practice of necromancy, the consultation of the dead by a medium or through other means. Prior to the exile, Israelites believed "that the dead continued to play an active role in the world of the living, possessing the power to grant blessings to their relatives and to reveal the future." Necromancy was apparently quite popular among the non-ruling groups but later came to be vehemently derided and forbidden by religious authorities. This negative perspective, as reflected in the prophetic and legal literature of the Bible, is the legacy left to Jews and to Western monotheistic culture: opposition to necromancy was supported especially by the group that worshipped Yahweh (God) alone, the rationale being that "blessings and the telling of the future were prerogatives of Yahweh, not of the dead, and that consultation with the dead for such purposes was an abomination against Yahweh."[333]

This stance appears to have influenced Jewish beliefs about the afterlife and the dead in general. During and after the exile, the Jewish leadership, which adhered to the "Yahweh alone" (monotheistic) theology, took the debate one step further, arguing that not only was it inappropriate for people to consult the dead but that it was also impossible. "A new theology developed that argued there is no conscious existence in Sheol at all. At death all contact with the world, and even with God, comes to an end." It is likely that most Jews did not necessarily believe this, but it became official doctrine in the post-exilic period[334] and survives among many people down to the present.

In the years after the exile, especially in the Hellenistic period from 332 BCE when Alexander the Great conquered much of the known Western world, Jewish thinking about death and the afterlife came more explicitly under the influence of the Platonic idea of the soul's immortality.[335] Intersecting and competing ideas about heaven or the heavens, Sheol, the conflict between good and evil, resurrection, and the end times began to take shape during this time, not only in Judaism but throughout the Graeco-Roman world. In some Jewish literature of the period, these ideas started to emerge, although they flowered more fully in Christian thought. The Pharisees, a group of Jews that zealously revered Jewish laws and tradition, held to the notion of a blessed future after death, while the Sadducees, a group of

Jews focused on Temple rituals, "retained the conception of a universal Sheol."[336]

The notion of resurrection, found in the Hebrew Bible in Daniel 12:2, held "that at the end of time the soul would be rejoined with the body and each person would then receive reward or punishment." A related but competing idea was that the immortal soul, upon release from the physical body, went immediately to its punishment or reward; this idea is depicted most vividly in the extracanonical book, the Testament of Abraham, around 100 CE.[337]

What may be of particular interest to the modern Westerner is that the notion of evil as somehow apart from or opposite of God and "his" goodness does not originate in Hebrew Scripture. Rather, the Hebrew Bible generally attributes supposed evil, tragedy, and suffering to God himself. Creation – God's Creation – is seen overall as good, and God directed evil, along with the good, in order to accomplish his ends.[338] Anger at God for tragedy, then, as can be seen dramatically in the story of Job, is a natural, acceptable reaction.

A later tradition in Judaism, that of Kabbalah, which took root in Spain in the twelfth century, is a form of mysticism that retains its influence today. Kabbalah teaches reincarnation, which is not supported by rabbinic authorities, although most authorities do accept the Kabbalistic texts; the writings contain commentaries on the Hebrew Bible, the most important of which is called the Zohar. Mystics meditate on the text, which often results in an out-of-body experience. The Zohar teaches that souls must continue to return to earth until they attain perfect righteousness.[339]

If we compare some of the ideas about the afterlife of the Israelites and the Jews, both ancient and modern, with those we have found in the paranormal literature, we find many overlaps. While the notion of Sheol as a place disconnected from Yahweh or the Divine is generally not experienced by NDEers or encountered by mediums, we do find evidence that souls may go, for a time, to a place of relative nothingness, usually in order to rest. We also have evidence for disturbed souls – those who have been particularly materialistic or mean-spirited toward others in their earthly existence – going at death to a dark and dreary place at a level that is closer to physical existence than the more peaceful and joyful locale visited by other souls. As for reincarnation, the mystical tradition contains very similar notions, which we will explore below in the Christian context.

While the notion of resurrection at the end times is not explicitly found in much of the paranormal literature, there is considerable evidence for a perfect, blissful "final existence" for *all* souls – although not in the judgmental way that is usually envisioned. Further, the idea that God or some kind of Divine Being is responsible for both good and evil is also present: through reincarnation and the law of cause and effect, the supposed innocents among us experience evil or misfortune oftentimes to atone for wrongdoing in past lives. Free will is also attested in the paranormal literature, which indicates that we all choose, both in our physical lives and in pre-birth decisions, what we will do, become and accomplish. Contrary to some strands of Jewish belief, the paranormal evidence suggests that it is not a Divine Being or God per se who metes out judgment or punishment but rather the way the universe works as each of us progresses spiritually toward union with the Divine.

We can therefore learn important lessons about the afterlife from Judaism, just as we learned from the beliefs of our Neolithic ancestors. There seems to be at least a kernel of truth in ideas and theologies that may appear at first glance to be opposites. Let us turn now to a short overview of death, the afterlife, immortality and other themes in the ancient Western world – ancient Greece, Hellenism, the Roman Empire and early Christianity – and see where the discrepancies and overlaps are when compared with the paranormal evidence.

The Afterlife and the Soul in Greek Thought and Early Christianity

The examination of the afterlife in ancient Christianity hinges in part on the concept of the soul, which developed prior to the Christian era. If there is no soul – no entity of the human being that survives bodily death – there is no question about the afterlife, but as we have seen, the notion of the soul in some form is pervasive in the ancient Western mindset. While the question of the soul and the afterlife is vast and complex, based in Greek and Roman thought as well as Judaism, we will see that an ancient, highly respected philosophy of the soul was essentially turned aside by orthodox Christianity, and this stance has influenced us down to the present time. However, we will also see that the ancient ideas mesh in many ways more with the paranormal evidence than with mainstream Christianity and need to be reconsidered.

The Greek philosopher Plato (429-347 BCE) is a necessary starting point for this discussion. His enduring influence on philosophy, governance, theology and Western thought in general are astounding, nearly three millennia later. For our purposes, his ideas and writings about the nature of the soul, immortality and reincarnation are the most crucial.[340]

For Plato, the human being is made up of two distinct parts, body and soul, which are fused during a human lifetime but separated at death. The soul is immortal and exists both in the present and for eternity. The real self of a human being resides in the soul, and the home of the soul is in the heavens with the gods. Plato's beliefs are based in logic and tied to his ideal theory of forms: it is obvious to all that the body is temporal and does not survive death, but the soul is eternal: "an essential character of a soul [is] to be alive, to partake of the form life. It refuses to partake of the form death." A parallel thought, for illustration, are the forms of warmth and cold: "Heat is never cool, and cold is never warm." Pushing the rational argument further, since the soul does not partake of death like the physical body does, it lives many lives on earth: "the dead return to life, just as the living die. If this were not so, if the process of dying were not reversible, life would ultimately vanish from the universe." Thus, for Plato, the work of a true philosopher (and in today's context, the work of persons who desire to live good lives) is to attempt to free the soul from dependence on the body, since the appetites and passions of the body "interrupt our pursuit of wisdom and goodness."[341]

It then follows, in Platonic thought, that there are persons who do not live or do not choose to live good lives – there are good souls and bad souls. Plato asserted that persons always desire the good, but oftentimes the "real" good is obscured: a bad soul is pursuing something that is not real. It is therefore imperative that one pursues knowledge of the good and the real, so that death of the body becomes a true liberation and the soul attains "a supreme beatific vision" and wisdom.[342]

As Christianity developed over time, many of Plato's notions remained, but that of reincarnation and the transmigration of souls was gradually – and eventually officially and firmly – rejected and replaced by that of resurrection and a Final Judgment. The soul continued to exist in Christian thought, but it no longer inhabited a number of different physical bodies on earth, as Plato had taught. Rather, in Christian belief, persons were believed to live in only one earthly body or incarnation and given only one chance to "repent and be saved" so that their immortal soul would not be damned to an eternity in hell.[343] The death of Jesus and the ensuing tales of his resurrection became entangled with the forgiveness of sin: early Christian theologians portrayed Jesus as Christ and Savior who died and "rose again" for our sins, and each person must believe this and repent in order to attain the heavenly reward and abide forever with Jesus and God. Right belief – or "orthodoxy" – became essential for salvation; insiders who believed would earn everlasting life, but outsiders (non-believers) would suffer eternal damnation.[344] (We shall see much of this play out in Appendix II when we analyze the Apostles' Creed in light of the paranormal evidence.)

Resurrection in itself is a large and complex topic, and confusingly it becomes related to the soul, the body, the afterlife and reincarnation in ways that can make many spiritual concepts (at least in a Christian context) untenable for the modern mindset. The resurrection of Jesus specifically refers to his returning to a physical, bodily form of life after his crucifixion, and several resurrection stories are recounted in the Gospels. In theological terms, the resurrection of Jesus removes the sting of death, yet it is difficult to see how it does so, since our deceased loved one does not appear to us after his or her death in the way that Jesus appeared to his friends. The related Christian belief that we somehow reclaim our physical bodies in heaven, maybe only at the very end of time, seems just as preposterous to modern Westerners.[345]

In Christian polity, the resurrection of believers came to be something that one could not discuss rationally but rather had to take on faith. None of us can know how God will give us a body back, either at our death or at the end of time: we just have to believe that it can and will be done. No longer are Christians allowed to believe that their souls have lived in earlier bodies on earth and may live in other physical bodies in the future; Christians must suspend that belief – no matter how logical it may be in some ways and no matter how many intelligent and ethical people, including Christians, have believed it in the past.

Since notions about resurrection were somewhat novel and difficult to believe even early on, it is highly likely that many Christians in the first few centuries retained a level of belief in reincarnation. Orphism, for instance, which had origins in the sixth century BCE but appears to have been revived in the early Christian era, was such a strand; Orphic ideas and mysteries later became connected with Pythagoreanism, which in turn influenced the Christian notion of the wise and holy man.[346] If some Christian groups saw Jesus as a highly evolved human being – perhaps as a reincarnated soul who had lived previous lives as Moses and others – who suffered and died but then was able to come back to physical life in a different way, we have evidence for the retention of the belief in reincarnation in some strands of early Christianity.

The Graeco-Roman world out of which Christianity emerged was comprised of a wide range of beliefs, practices, and rituals around death and the afterlife; the literature that has survived, some of which makes up the New Testament, hints at this diversity but is only the tip of the iceberg. The New Testament canon and the writings of the church fathers was the literature of the theological victors, primarily those that eschewed reincarnation and notions of a positive afterlife experience for most souls. On the other hand, archaeological, epigraphical and some literary evidence attests to the existence of occult and magic, astrology, forms of witchcraft and other nature-based religions, superstition, and belief in reunions with favorite deities. Common people in these Mediterranean cultures, many of whom were slaves, worshipped a constellation of deities who promised life after death and eternal heavenly banquets. Evidence for practitioners casting spells on lovers or enemies attests to extensive belief in the ability of supernatural beings to aid with everyday problems. The healing miracles of Jesus, as found in the Gospels, would not have seemed especially unusual in the culture: standard medical treatments by the god Asklepios, the goddess Hygeia, and by various kinds of healers involved "miracles" on a fairly regular basis. For the new Christ-cult to be successful, pagans would have craved the same kinds of benefits from the new religion – if not even better – in order to convert.

Therefore, discussions of the soul among elites would not have had much impact on the lower echelons of the population, at least not immediately. For various sociological and political reasons, beliefs and practices developed in one way among elites and church leaders and in other ways among lower-status persons, until such time as Christianity became the established religion of the empire and all inhabitants were compelled to act and believe in the approved manner. For our purposes in discerning which early (and current) Christian notions mesh with the paranormal evidence, let us look briefly at some of the concepts and practices around immortality and the afterlife that developed in Christianity over time.

The healing miracles of Jesus, as we have noted, are widely viewed by moderns, including New Testament scholars, as fictional stories told in the early church for various reasons. The so-called miracles defy natural law so must have been preserved in the literature to help the struggling new sect to survive. For instance, the church needed to portray Jesus as at least as powerful as other wonder-workers in the ancient world. As we have seen with the paranormal literature, however – postmortem Doyle, mediums such as Hancock, Assante and Home, NDEs, and the SOPHIA Research Program at the University of Arizona – miraculous healings, and healings done in concert with spiritual laws that can be accessed by modern practitioners, can indeed be real and even in accord with physical laws. Thus it is entirely possible – logically and scientifically – that many of the healings that Jesus and his followers performed were accomplished by appealing to spiritual laws, and the Gospel stories of healing miracles may thus indeed be true accounts.

As mentioned above, Jesus' resurrection is similarly viewed by moderns as impossible, merely a story (albeit a powerful one) that came about because of visions of believers living in an oppressed social context. However, in view of the Life Readings of Edgar Cayce and what we know from other sources – NDEs, EVPs, and the work of accomplished mediums – about the barrier between the physical world and the "other side," it is possible to view Jesus' resurrection as an actual physical event. It is also possible, as we will see in Chapter 6, that all human beings have the capability of overcoming death in much the same way.[347] We will discuss resurrection more below as we dialogue with modern commentators.

The notion of Purgatory developed over time because some souls that were not thought to be good enough for heaven but not bad enough for hell needed a place to go after death until they were "worthy" of heaven; by the Middle Ages, the notion of Purgatory in the West had taken such firm hold that the church was granting indulgences in large numbers – for a price – to believers who wanted to help their deceased loved ones out of that in-between stage.[348] What we have seen in the paranormal literature is that there do appear to be various levels or planes to which souls "go" at death. Souls that are "stuck," in haunting situations, for instance, might be viewed as residing in a Purgatory of sorts. Kelsey, the Episcopal priest writing in the 1970s, speaks of Purgatory as a place or condition where souls can be given a fresh start. He states, "The real difference [between hell and Purgatory] is that in hell I feel caught and do not know that I can get out, while in purgatory I know that I am free to work toward a destiny far more magnificent than we in this world can imagine."[349] This idea dovetails with what psychics, mediums and others have realized when it comes to praying for the souls of the deceased: some souls who are on planes closest to the physical world can be aided by the prayers of the living. Thus the notions of Purgatory and indulgences appear not to be so much a matter of petitioning the church or the Pope, or of monetary transactions, but rather of prayers and love toward the deceased.

We touched briefly above on the issue of sin and forgiveness, and we shall discuss this more in Appendix II. For now, however, it should be noted that the concepts of justice, evil and what happens to "bad" souls at death is very important to moderns. In the United States, one of the few advanced nations that still retains the use of the death penalty in many jurisdictions, murder and violence are a fact of life, and the cry for justice is heard on almost a daily basis. Many self-avowed Christians, witnessing horrendous violence, murder and serial killing, appeal to the Christian notions of judgment and hell to support the death penalty. It can be extremely difficult for victims, survivors and many others in our culture to imagine their good and just God sending any evil soul anywhere but eternal damnation; it makes logical sense to many that putting a hardened criminal to death protects others, serves justice, saves taxpayer money, and is a deterrent.

The paranormal evidence suggests a different scenario. One basic point that comes through time and again is that no human being should take the life of another (except in self-defense); no person should end the life journey of another before its time is up. The law of karma and cause and effect is such that a murderer or other person who vilely wrongs another will have to "pay" for that in some way, either in the current incarnation or another one. Also, as we have seen, such disturbed, violent souls appear to go to a dark, dreary place at death until they begin to realize that there is a better way. In the case of medium Noreen Renier, for instance, and other mediums who assist law enforcement in solving crimes, the deceased victims often work with the living in bringing about the arrest of perpetrators. The paranormal literature further shows that we, not a God figure, judge ourselves and our own actions after death, so murderers will ultimately need to confront their own actions. Interestingly, there is also evidence that killers and their victims sometimes reconcile on the other side.

There are some indications in the paranormal literature that argue against the use of the death penalty. However, there are other important points to be made around the issue of justice and punishment. For one, as many victims' family members attest, grieving and holding onto anger and revenge against a perpetrator or someone who has wronged them can be very debilitating; some courageous family members of victims profess to forgiving the perpetrator, but at the very least acknowledging with some assurance both that their deceased loved one is at peace and that the perpetrator will eventually have to atone – due to the law of cause and effect – can be very liberating. In addition, afterlife research strongly suggests that there is a reason for the evil deed; in some cases, the death of an innocent person is the working-out (often in a pre-birth decision) of that soul's karma.

At a more societal level, we in the US might consider the underlying nature of our culture and how that might contribute to violence in the first place: the US is by far the most violent nation, with the highest incarceration rate, of any of the advanced Western nations,[350] and it might behoove us to ask why. Are we lacking a crucial spiritual undergirding at this point in our history because the basics of Christianity – which disavow reincarnation, self-judgment and the law of cause and effect – combine counterproductively with the secular denial of a joyful and loving afterlife and the related "Protestant work ethic" that equates earned wealth and happiness with hard work? In other words, if the Western principles we have inherited, from Christianity and elsewhere, which do not truly provide a constructive spiritual undergirding for many citizens who then resort to violence to have their needs met, and if the paranormal evidence might provide an antidote to this spiritual malaise, it might behoove us to take them more seriously. We will explore specific suggestions for disseminating paranormal wisdom in Chapter 7.

The Christian notion of the soul's "eternal rest" at death, as asserted especially during the burial service – "Rest eternal grant to him, O Lord: And let light perpetual shine upon him"[351] – is another idea that bears scrutiny in light of the paranormal evidence. Eternal rest too has its roots in the dualistic orthodox notion we have been discussing. To the modern mind, the idea of eternal rest after death sounds utterly boring and unappealing, although some people who have had very difficult lives might take comfort in the idea of a long sleep – at least for awhile.[352] The paranormal evidence, however, overwhelmingly shows that, for most souls at least, following a short "rest" period, the afterlife is anything but restful and boring. Souls are always busy, generally serving others in some way and growing spiritually. From EVPs and NDEs to OOBEs, Cayce, Doyle, past and present mediums, and dreams, the evidence lands definitively on the side of souls "doing" in heaven what they need to be doing – and are joyful in the process.

Christianity has a long history of mysticism that is only now being rediscovered by the church. Mysticism, from the Greek μυστικός, can be defined as "an immediate knowledge of God attained in this present life through personal religious experience. . . The surest proof adduced by the mystics themselves for the genuineness of their experience is its effect, viz. its fruit in such things as an increase of humility, charity and love of suffering." Among the famous mystics of the Christian tradition are Clement of Alexandria, Hildegard of

Bingen, Francis of Assisi, and Julian of Norwich, all considered saints of the church.[353]

While the writings and visions of the traditional, and even modern, mystics differ, many of the insights they glean from their sublime experiences have parallels in the paranormal literature. The descriptions of the afterlife from NDEers, for instance, come very close, if not identical, to many of the mystics' descriptions of heaven. Similar depictions of the afterlife are witnessed by people who have been regressed to past lives, by the majority of psychics and mediums, by Monroe's OOBEs, by the testimony of postmortem Doyle, and by the Life Readings of Edgar Cayce. While some of the traditional Christian mystical literature can seem utterly fantastic and impossible, each account should be assessed in a balanced way for its worth as legitimate witness to what most of us can expect when we cross the threshold of death.

There is a final strand of human experience, even beyond that of Christians, that can also be brought into this discussion, and that is the relationship between dreams and the afterlife and heavenly realms. In the Hebrew Bible, there are numerous stories and references to dreams, mostly in the context of prophecy and warnings. An angel of God appears in a dream to Jacob, and God himself appears to Abimilech and to Laban in dreams (Gen. 20 and 31). The Lord appears in a dream to King Solomon in 1 Kings 3, where a lengthy conversation takes place. God asks Solomon what he wants, and Solomon responds in a way that pleases God: "Give thy servant [Solomon], therefore, a heart with skill to listen, so that he may govern thy people justly and distinguish good from evil."[354]

The best-known examples of significant dream communication in the New Testament are the stories of angels appearing to Joseph in two dreams, as found in Matthew 1 and 2. In the first, the angel tells Joseph of the significance of Mary's pre-marital pregnancy, and in the second, the spiritual being warns Joseph to take Mary and Jesus into Egypt, away from Herod's murderous madness.

In the paranormal literature, especially the OOBE evidence and consciousness studies, God and angels are not usually "met" in dreams, but it is during the night's sleep that deceased loved ones are often most able to make their presence known to the living and relay important messages. As Assante points out, "Untold numbers of encounters [with the deceased] occur in dreams while we are asleep. The dead use dreams to reach us more than any other means, because dreams are the natural crossroads of inner and outer realities. In dreams, the dead have more latitude, and we have less resistance."[355] Monroe believes that we leave our bodies and travel to the "other side" every night in our dreams,[356] and this belief is paralleled in Eastern teachings, as described by Chopra: "[W]e all yearn for these other planes [of existence] so much that we travel to them at night in our sleep. Then the astral body actually leaves the physical body, remaining attached by a filament that brings it back again."[357] Dreams connect our physical bodies with our consciousness, which survives bodily death, and thus put us in touch with wisdom and knowledge not generally accessible to us in our waking states. Once again, therefore, we can see how some traditional religious beliefs can be respected and taken seriously when viewed in the context of the paranormal evidence.

As we shall see in Appendix II, a number of Christian tenets, as summarized in the Apostles' Creed, have virtually no credence when compared to the paranormal material. Since Christian beliefs are so pervasive and influential in Western culture, despite the overwhelmingly secular nature of that culture in many ways, we will discuss more thoroughly in Chapter 7 how the insights from afterlife and paranormal research and belief, along with the wisdom of our ancestors from the Neolithic era on, can help individuals and society in significant ways.

Spiritualism

As we have seen in Chapter 2, a number of researchers who conducted experiments on paranormal phenomena in the nineteenth century were influenced by Spiritualism, a religious movement that still exists today. Skeptical, and sometimes hostile, scientists disparaged their Spiritualist colleagues, maintaining their materialistic, Post-Enlightenment opinion that religion and science are incompatible. In a number of cases in those early days of investigation, the pro-paranormal researchers were supported and even revered by the general public while roundly criticized by fellow scientists and intellectuals.

Arthur Conan Doyle's *The History of Spiritualism* in two volumes is the earliest definitive work on the founding and development of Spiritualism. Doyle traces its birth to Emanuel Swedenborg, a man of many talents and interests: a military engineer, a zoologist, anatomist, financier, political economist and "a profound Biblical student who had sucked in theology with his mother's milk." Swedenborg's psychic development did not take shape until he was 55 years old, yet his impact on paranormal investigation was pivotal. His insights into what we might expect "on the other side" came via visions,[358] and much of what he saw and experienced significantly parallels the findings of psychics, mediums and investigators of our own day.

Swedenborg perceived in his visions that the afterlife was comprised of many spheres that represented "various shades of luminosity and happiness, each of us going to that for which our spiritual condition has fitted us." He learned that both angels and devils existed but "were all human beings who had lived on earth and who were either undeveloped souls, as devils, or highly developed souls, as angels." His visions showed him that we do not change significantly as persons when we cross over, that old or diseased people are invigorated at death, and that there is no eternal punishment.[359]

Continuing with Doyle's *History*, further significant revelations appeared on the scene in the person of Andrew Jackson Davis (1826-1910), a poor and uneducated man who nevertheless cultivated many psychic gifts and convinced people – including a Professor George Bush of the University of New York and possibly Edgar Allan Poe – of his gifts' validity.[360] Doyle notes that Davis, while in trance, surpassed Swedenborg in some of his revelations: his vision moved beyond our present universe, which dissolved "once more into the fire-mist from which it had consolidated, and then consolidate once more to form the stage on which a higher evolution could take place. . . This process he saw renew itself innumerable times, covering trillions of years, and ever working towards refinement and purification." Davis also experienced the assistance of spirit guides, who did not control him or desire to be worshipped but were present to help and act as companions on the spiritual journey.[361]

While today few of us know the name Davis, Doyle speculated that, because the uneducated seer tapped into many of Swedenborg's revelations without knowing anything about him, then went beyond Swedenborg's understandings, "the power which controlled Davis was actually Swedenborg".[362]

Doyle next traced, in two chapters, the story of the Fox sisters, pointing out that most Spiritualists put the birth of the movement at March 31, 1848. It was on that date, in Hydesville, New York, that a series of rappings, knockings and dialogues between family members, neighbors and spiritual entities came to a head. Young sisters Margaret/Margaretta/Maggie (1833-1893) and Catharine/Cathie/Kate

Fox (1837-1892) were at the center of the events, which were detailed in a signed statement by their mother, Margaret Fox, on April 11, 1848.[363]

Even before the Fox family had taken possession of the house a few years earlier, unexplained noises had frequently been heard by the occupants, especially at night. On the evening of March 31st, the rapping phenomenon became so pronounced that neighbors were called in as witnesses. Kate, on a childish whim, began asking the spirits yes-and-no questions, which were answered intelligently. Over time, the information that emerged from the "conversations" indicated that the spirit was a man who had been murdered and buried in the home. While an initial round of digging did not reveal any evidence, it was reported in the *Boston Journal* in 1904 that a skeleton had indeed been found in the walls "and clears [the Fox sisters] from the only shadow of doubt held concerning their sincerity in the discovery of spirit communication." The *Boston Journal* article continued, "The finding of the bones practically corroborates the sworn statement made by Margaret Fox, April 11, 1848."[364]

Doyle continued to describe in detail the history and careers not only of Maggie and Kate Fox but also of their much older sister Leah (1814-1890). All three became well-known as mediums, earning the respect and confidence of a wide range of educated observers and noted business and religious leaders, on the one hand, and widespread criticism and accusations of fraud on the other; both respect for and criticism of the Fox sisters continue to this day.[365] In contrast to other commentators on the Fox sisters who hold the skeptical view, Doyle concluded that they were genuine and that there was little if any fraud or deception in any of them when it came to their psychic gifts.[366]

Under the pressures of alcoholism, money, and her Roman Catholic husband, the Arctic explorer Dr. Elisha Kane,[367] Maggie denounced her psychic gifts in a public forum in New York, with her signed confession appearing in the *New York World* on October 21, 1888; a similar statement against Spiritualism by Kate had appeared in the *New York Herald* on October 9, 1888. Problems had been brewing for quite some time leading up to this, however, as Kate and Maggie had a falling-out with Leah, who was attempting to take Kate's children away from her.[368] While the Wikipedia article on the Fox sisters says almost nothing about the subsequent retraction of the confessions, Doyle explains in detail that the sisters realized too late that they were being exploited by people who wanted to make money from their repudiations of Spiritualism. In *Light* only a month after the repudiations, in November 1888, a letter was published from Kate that read in part, "So many people come to me to ask me about this exposure of Maggie's [of Spiritualism] that I have to deny myself to them." A year later, Maggie granted an interview that was witnessed by, among others, the long-time US minister to Portugal, J.L. O'Sullivan. In this interview in New York City, Maggie expressed her support of Spiritualism and related that she was influenced by people hoping to make money from destroying the movement. She stated, "Would to God that I could undo the injustice I did the cause of Spiritualism when, under the strong psychological influence of persons inimical to it, I gave expression to utterances that had no foundation in fact. . . . [M]y belief in Spiritualism has undergone no change. When I made those dreadful statements I was not responsible for my words." Also in the interview, which was transcribed then signed by her on November 16, 1889, and offered to the public, she avowed to eschew séances and devote herself "entirely to platform work." She further made it clear that Kate was in complete sympathy with her.[369] Sadly, Kate and Maggie both died in poverty a few years after this controversy erupted.

Today, Spiritualism survives in the US under the auspices of the National Spiritualist Association of Churches, based in Lily Dale,

New York. Members' authority derives "from the progressed souls of the etheric planes who, through mediums, bring their knowledge to earth in order to free humanity from out-dated creeds and superstitions." Spiritualists teach that communication is possible between souls on earth and those residing in the so-called Etheric Planes. Further, they hold to the theory of evolution, believe that Jesus is a great teacher, and maintain that we create our own heaven and hell, that our main purpose on earth is to progress spiritually, and that love of one another is the basis of right living.[370] While Spiritualists do not believe per se in reincarnation, Doyle did, and his postmortem testimony bolsters his stance on the issue while in the physical world.[371]

Responses to Current Thoughts on the Paranormal and the Afterlife

Now that we have examined afterlife beliefs of our prehistoric ancestors, ancient and modern Jews and Christians, and Spiritualists, we will turn to an examination of the afterlife and paranormal opinions of some professionals in the field of religion.

As someone who has been involved on at least a weekly basis with mainline Christian denominations for 60 years, and as someone who holds two degrees in theology, I have known dozens of priests, deacons, bishops, spiritual directors, and religious (monks and nuns), most of whom I greatly respect. I have colleagues who are Jewish and Muslim, as well as colleagues in religion who have no particular faith tradition or who are confirmed atheists or agnostics. The sincere compassion, dedication, courage, and pastoral abilities of religion professionals, their long years of training, and their education are much more worthy of the esteem than our culture often gives them and more valuable than the salaries they are often paid.

Interestingly, many of these devout professionals, even progressive ones, hold so firmly to standard Western beliefs about the afterlife that they shun information about the paranormal and what happens to us after death. Some of this stance is due to our overall Post-Enlightenment culture, as we have seen, as well as their training in colleges and seminaries. Scholars of religion, as well as a number of religion writers in the popular press, may address paranormal phenomena and issues around the afterlife but then often dismiss them. I will begin by noting a sampling of this scholarly material and dialoguing with it, and we will conclude with some observations about the paranormal in the context of religious leaders and communities.

In *The Life of the World to Come: Near-Death Experience and Christian Hope*, long-time Smith College professor Carol Zaleski examines death, immortality, near-death experiences, the Life Review, and the afterlife in the context of the daily cycle of prayers in Christian convents and monasteries, including Lauds, Vespers and Compline. While her book is a beautiful treatment of a range of topics and contains many important insights, Zaleski nevertheless partially dismisses NDEs by calling them "a visionary encounter with death," an encounter that is symbolic and in the domain of the imagination.[372] She also concludes that death is a mystery and that we must primarily trust that souls abide in the precepts of eternal love and security.[373]

More recently Zaleski has written on immortality in her column for the *Christian Century*. The venerable bi-weekly, a generally progressive publication that has been in circulation since 1884, frequently publishes pieces like Zaleski's on the afterlife, heaven, and eternity, which we shall see.

In the November 28, 2012, issue, Zaleski treated Eben Alexander's *Proof of Heaven*, commenting that "[w]e are in a curious and puzzling situation, therefore, in which the hope for immortality is criticized in some circles as unbiblical and sub-Christian, yet affirmed in others as a matter of established empirical fact." She categorizes Alexander's story as "a glimpse, not a proof" and urges readers to have a "healthy skepticism" and to "turn to the deeper reasons for belief in the promise of eternal life." In her article she offers helpful descriptions of different conceptions of the soul – Christian, Platonic, New Age, Jewish, Muslim[374] – but basically discounts the possibility that what Alexander experienced is real, despite the fact that his experience is parallel to millions of experiences around the world and a true offering of hope for humanity. Interestingly, the one letter that *Christian Century* printed in response to Zaleski's article (in the January 9, 2013, issue) makes this very point; the writer, Owen Norment, states, "Too often theologians ignore or reject [material emerging now about NDEs] outright."

Rodney Clapp, in a *Christian Century* column entitled "Life after life after death" in the May 30, 2012, edition, begins by outlining the "standard view of life after death" that focuses on the dualism of body and soul: the body dies and the soul either goes to heaven or hell. Clapp analyzes a selection of Hebrew and New Testament texts and speaks of a new/old view whereby the church should focus more on "resurrected bodies" than on the individual soul. He acknowledges that the "recent cascade" of books on the subject, directed primarily to the church, might bring hope to the daily lives of people in the pews.[375]

Clapp also had heaven on his mind approximately one month later. Writing in the June 27, 2012, issue of *Christian Century*, he asked a burning question for many of us: "will there be pets in heaven?" He again turns to scripture, specifically 2 Peter 3:13, which speaks of a new heaven and a new earth. Clapp also cites Isaiah 11:6-9, the utopian "peaceable kingdom" passage about wolves living with lambs and so on. He admits that none of these Biblical allusions are particularly helpful in answering the pet question, then argues that all dogs (to take that example) "are very much alike" and thus not as individual as us human beings. Clapp postulates that we might commune with animals in the afterlife but that the animals will be "perfect representations of the species" rather than particular pets that we have known on earth. He concludes on a hopeful note, that the new creation will include animals and will be wondrous.[376] However, he is obviously unfamiliar with the paranormal literature – especially the EVP evidence and the readings of psychics and mediums – that shows that individual animals do survive death, with their personalities intact.

Like Clapp and Zaleski, Sarah Kenyon Lischer of Wake Forest University takes up the issue of proof of heaven in the August 7, 2013, issue of *Christian Century*. Echoing Zaleski in November 2012, Lischer comments primarily on Eben Alexander's book, stating that she only read it grudgingly after friends urged her to. While her initial response to the book was positive, she came to feel that she will be disappointed and bored if heaven is the way Alexander portrays it. She imagines "a different heaven, one in which our relationship with God becomes perfected – not homogenized" and asserts that, for Christians, Alexander's message "doesn't add anything to the witness of the Gospels." She asks in conclusion, similarly to Zaleski, "Why search for proof [of heaven] when we have the assurance of the unseen?"[377] It is unfortunate that Lischer does not take her friends' enthusiasm more seriously or consider for very long that perhaps they are onto something. She does not consider that perhaps what Alexander is offering – along with all the others around the world who have had NDEs – is not only extremely important and valid pastorally but can also be supported by a vast array of facts and documentation.

Craig Wilson of *USA Today* also takes a negative, even disparaging, stance on the explosion of recent books on NDEs. Writing in *Christian Century* in the March 20, 2013, issue, Wilson chalks up the rash of these books and people's excitement about them as readers' search for comfort and "something reassuring." He uses very pejorative language in his piece, which seems oddly out of place in *Christian Century*, a venerable journal with a wide and intelligent readership: "Heaven is hot. . . Just ask any bookseller in America." "Folks have been going to heaven with amazing regularity lately." "Three of these tales have ascended to heavenly heights on *USA Today's* best-seller list recently." "Can you hear the publishing angels singing?"[378] As is the case with the other writers cited above, Wilson (and apparently the highly-respectable editors of *Christian Century*) are woefully unfamiliar with the history of paranormal research, the science that is being conducted in universities today on paranormal activity, the consistent validity of the insights of psychics and mediums, and the compassionate pastoral and ethical uses that can be made of the material.

Interestingly, in the August 22, 2012, edition of *Christian Century*, a short article appeared announcing that the John Templeton Foundation has granted the University of California Riverside a three-year $5 million grant "to research beliefs and traditions about an afterlife and how those ideas affect humans." The research focuses on a number of topics we have been discussing: NDEs, free will, heaven, hell, and reincarnation. A Templeton press release from March 2013 used a tone often used by deniers and skeptics, however, when describing the public's response to the announcement of the grant. The *Los Angeles Times* article, written by Larry Gordon, began this way: "Announcements of a well-funded research project at a major university often elicit, welcome or not, professional and amateur advice. But those messages usually don't recount a dead cat's spirit flitting into the afterlife." Later, author Gordon recounts that the grant's principal investigator, philosophy professor John Martin Fischer, and his colleagues "won't be chasing the most kooky tips, hunting ghosts or attending séances to chat with the dead."[379]

While Fischer is a highly respected "expert on such heady issues as free will and death's meaning" and vows to respect all religions, Gordon and possibly even Fischer himself, an atheist, already betray their skeptical stance toward religious and other beliefs in an afterlife. Gordon states that the Templeton research is following close on the heels of the popularity of Alexander's *Proof of Heaven*. Gordon comments that "Critics contend he was just hallucinatory. Oliver Sacks, the neurologist and author, wrote in the *Atlantic* magazine that such hallucinations can have spiritual meaning but 'cannot provide evidence for the existence of any metaphysical beings or places. They provide evidence only of the brain's power to create them.'" Gordon also quotes renowned University of Chicago philosopher Martha Nussbaum: "I do not think the prospects for finding evidence of a life after death are high (unfortunately!)." As for Fischer himself, he and his wife are avoiding discussing death with their three children, choosing instead to focus on health; believing death to be "a scary thought," Fischer and his wife's goals are to live "as long as possible in a healthy and productive way and figure out how to accept death gracefully when it comes."[380] It is hoped that Fischer, Gordon, Nussbaum, Sacks and others interested in the question of immortality will keep an open enough mind to take seriously whatever evidence emerges to ensure that they present the material fairly to an inquisitive public; one also hopes that, if they change their minds, they admit it publicly, as so many other skeptics have done in the past.

Moving from *Christian Century* and the work of the Templeton Foundation to another progressive publication, this one from the Westar Institute (the parent organization of the Jesus Seminar), *The Fourth R* also occasionally publishes articles on the afterlife and related topics.[381] These too present the intelligent lay public with interesting, articulate viewpoints on a wide range of topics, yet hardly any of them address the enormous body of evidence about the survival of the soul after death found in the science and from NDEs, psychics and mediums, and OOBEs.

In the March-April 2013 edition of *The Fourth R*, Pieter F. Craffert took a neuroanthropological approach to the issue of Jesus' resurrection, citing ritual practices of the Sisala clan in Ghana. Craffert reports that an anthropologist named Bruce Grindal witnessed a significant event in October 1967, when "the corpse of a dead drummer start[ed] to shake, then rise to its feet, spinning and dancing . . . and eventually pick[ing] up the drumsticks and begin[ning] to play. The Sisala members were fully convinced that the drummer had been raised from the dead." Grindal experienced an alternate state of consciousness (ASC) during this event, which became very significant in his life and work. The drummer's resurrection was understood "as a local interpretation of the events."[382]

Craffert then went on to analyze this event in light of Jesus' resurrection, arguing that "belief in a resurrected Jesus [is] a consensual reality:" "just as in the case of death divination for the Sisala, Jesus' bodily resurrection is and was real for his followers."[383] Thus in this way, argues Craffert, it is possible that "Jesus raised his body from the dead."[384]

As might be expected, Craffert's article invited controversy. In the same issue, *The Fourth R* published a harsh response from Professor Robert M. Price of the Center for Inquiry Institute. Price, a prolific writer and editor, draws on respected New Testament scholarship in his critique, and there is much to be said for literary and sociological treatments of the Graeco-Roman world in which Christianity developed. But in a manner that is typical of afterlife deniers and of many scholars at the otherwise progressive end of the spectrum, Price concludes dismissively with "by now we should have learned not to take [ancient gospel writers' and others'] word that they are genuine accounts of events experienced by anyone, ever."[385] If

Price is familiar with any of the paranormal literature, he ignores it here.

In concluding this chapter, I will now dialogue more specifically with priests, Christian counselors, spiritual directors, scholars of religion and churchgoers on our topic. For the most part, as we have seen from writers published in *Christian Century* and *The Fourth R*, religion professionals are generally on the side of the skeptics when it comes to dealing with the paranormal phenomena current in today's cultures. There are some valid reasons for this ambivalence. One is the conviction that faithful people should focus on life in the physical world – the social justice goal – and leave the soul's fate to God. The Christian faith stance underlies this position: the Christian's stated belief that Jesus' death and resurrection have "conquered" death seem to forestall much further discussion or contemplation of the matter. If we think of death at all in a Christian context, we cling to the ideas we have discussed above, including what might happen to "evil" souls.

Priests, scholars and other religious leaders, perhaps unwittingly, also fall into the "science" trap. It is understandable that religion professionals, marginalized especially among intellectuals, would also want to bolster their creeds and beliefs as much as possible with established "proofs" and not be considered living in an unscientific, intangible world of ghosts, demons, angels and spirits.

In addition, constraints emerge from the very training that religious leaders have had and the various denominational polities they must uphold. In the Christian context, for instance, when a candidate for the priesthood, or a person entering a religious order, embarks on his or her vocation, s/he must take vows to uphold the beliefs and practices of his/her denomination or order, as well as to obey one's superiors. Christian ordinands affirm that Jesus Christ is their Lord and Savior; Episcopal and other priests and deacons promise to obey their bishops; and monks and nuns take on the vows of chastity, poverty and obedience. Christian church leaders affirm that the Bible – Holy Scripture – contains "all things necessary to salvation."[386] Nearly every week, Christian priests (and laypeople) recite the Apostles' or Nicene Creed, with their archaic language and counter-rational faith statements.

In the academy, professors of religion find themselves in a similar bind. Their constraints center around the need for respect from their colleagues in Western institutions of higher education, the oftentimes uphill battle to show that their work is relevant to the academy, students and the larger world, and the problem, especially in public institutions, of not appearing to proselytize, a concern related to perceived First Amendment limitations. As we have seen from the examples of the nineteenth-century paranormal pioneers, today's investigators who undertake this kind of research can often expect to lose a great deal of respect, and even their livelihoods, from their skeptical colleagues and superiors.

It comes as no surprise, then, that priests, other Christian leaders and religion scholars give almost no automatic support for any deviation from standard platitudes and centuries-old traditions. Religious leaders who explore paranormal phenomena, NDEs, OOBEs, and the witness of psychics and mediums must do so "under the radar" and very carefully, even in fairly progressive contexts. Pastorally affirming to a bereaved person, especially one whose loved one has died young and/or tragically, that the deceased "lives in the light of God," is one thing, but suggesting that the person can connect with the deceased by means of a séance, spirit circle, psychic, dreams, EVP, ITC or some other method could border on professional suicide.[387]

My hope in presenting the evidence in this book is that bishops, priests, deacons, rabbis, monks, nuns, spiritual directors, religion scholars and lay leaders – at the highest levels of religious organizations and the academy – will find not only answers, solace and comfort from this material but also some usable, available tools for pastoral and teaching purposes. This is not to say that every sermon, every remembrance given at a funeral or every college lecture must describe the heavenly spheres or what the deceased might be experiencing "on the other side," because we simply do not know in any individual case and one must always deal sympathetically and pastorally with those who are grieving. What it might mean, however, is that paranormal phenomena and the scientific evidence that are very much available in the twenty-first century can be included as part of the pastoral arsenal, part of the training offered in divinity and theological schools, and part of religion courses; I will offer specific suggestions in Chapter 7.

Awareness of what is available is paramount. As I hope is apparent, with television, the Internet, and technology, the evidence for paranormal phenomena is pervasive in our culture if we know where to look. Many Americans, no matter what their backgrounds, are exposed to this material in a way that has never before been possible. It is unfortunate that, when seekers start to ask ultimate life questions and sense the validity of a real individual afterlife, they are often met by skepticism in the form of religious leaders in religious circles and educators who hold to Post-Enlightenment materialism. These seekers are thus not being served and remain removed from a significant sphere of life – religion or spirituality – that should be able to help them. Mainstream religion will continue to become less and less relevant in the modern Western world, and college students and young people will be deprived of tools that can assist them as they mature, if religious and academic leaders do not embrace the life-affirming, reliable paranormal material. Conversely, seekers *can* be helped at very deep levels if religious communities can incorporate paranormal evidence and discussions of the afterlife into their services, theology and programming. Thus synagogues, churches, convents, monasteries, retreat centers and schools have an extraordinary opportunity to become communities of hope, communities that not only incorporate comforting afterlife notions but also ways to link those notions with tools for living better lives on earth.

The best that Christianity and the West at large have to offer has always done this – from the love teachings of Jesus and other revered persons to concern for the poor and oppressed to the striving for social justice to the offering of places for contemplation and mystical experiences. To become too a locus for the linking of ethical, principled earthly living with a heavenly existence of indescribable beauty, joy, peace and spiritual growth would be a true gift to a hurting world.

Chapter 6: Themes and Findings

- *"I would hold out to all a hope beautiful and true beyond compare. I would assure them of progression to be won by desiring and striving after beauty, love and wisdom."* – Arthur Conan Doyle postmortem
- *"The place I went was real. Real in a way that makes the life we're living here and now completely dreamlike by comparison."* – Eben Alexander
- *"People are put in our path at a particular time because they have a lesson to teach us or because we have one to teach them. We are always in the right place at the right time... Each lesson we learn contributes to our soul's growth."* – Chip Coffey
- *[The bonding we identify as love] "is the major energy base for our intellect... It incorporates both pain and pleasure; it is the union of opposites to create a whole."* – As reported to Robert A. Monroe

The material on the paranormal and the afterlife – whether it comes from scientific investigations, psychics and mediums, near-death experiences (NDEs), or out-of-body experiences (OOBEs) – begins to point in certain directions. There are a number of themes that recur in two or more of these types of phenomena; we have met these themes earlier in discussing the paranormal scene today, the history of paranormal research, and the practices of our Western forebears. Here we will trace these themes and examine the overlaps and deviations between the findings from paranormal research and Western, primarily Christian, religious tenets. Appendix III summarizes these themes and the evidence that supports them.

Survival of Our Basic Selves

One of the most common and basic findings from the paranormal material is that, when we die, our basic personality survives. Electronic Voice Phenomena (EVPs) and other evidence captured by electronic instruments show that the voices and images that come through are similar, if not identical, to what they were in the physical world. Theresa Caputo, Chip Coffey, John Edward, Maureen Hancock, Phil Jordan, Noreen Renier, James Van Praagh, Nancy Orlen Weber, and other mediums channel definitive, identifiable character traits of the deceased, in addition to mundane details of survivors' lives that only they could know. Average people all over the world have dreams and visions of loved ones who have crossed over, and those spirits are immediately identifiable to those in the physical world. People who have experienced NDEs "meet" their deceased relatives on the other side and dialogue with them; NDEers who do not necessarily recognize spirits whom they meet in spirit later identify them from photos as relatives who crossed over before the NDEer was born or when very young. Clients of paranormal investigators who are haunted by an entity unrelated and unknown to them can pick the spirit being out of a photo line-up of historical photos resulting from research of the home or area.[388]

Evidence from OOBEs further confirms the survival of our basic selves. People near death and people who are under duress and in excruciating pain who experience OOBEs retain their personalities during the experience. Willful OOBEs, sometimes called astral travel, have been reported, as have been cases of dreams of living persons who are visible to other living persons.[389] In the Introduction to Monroe's *Journeys Out of the Body*, Charles Tart notes characteristics of many OOBEs:

> [T]he experience of an OOBE is usually one of the most profound experiences of a person's life, and radically alters his

beliefs. This is usually expressed as, 'I no longer *believe* in survival of death or an immortal soul, I *know* that I will survive death.' The person . . . knows that he possesses some kind of soul that will survive bodily death. . . . Considering the importance of the idea of the soul to most of our religions, and the importance of religion in people's lives, it seems incredible that science could have swept this problem under the rug so easily.[390]

Interestingly, Monroe did not find evidence for Biblical ideas about God or heaven in his 12 years of journeys, but the survival of souls, selves and personalities was irrefutable. He closely documented what he called the Second Body of each of us – a "body" that survives death and has the same personality and character as in the Here-Now[391] or Earth Life System[392] – and several places to which he ventured, especially Locale II[393]. Monroe notes,

> It is not known from the experiments to date whether everyone who dies automatically "goes" to Locale II. Also, there is no present evidential material to indicate that the presence of a human personality in Locale II is permanent. It may be that, like an eddy or vortex, we gradually lose energy and eventually dissipate into the Locale II medium once we leave Locale I (Here-Now). It is conceivable that the result of this process would grant recognition of immortality in that we survive the grave, but not forever. Perhaps the stronger the formation of personality, the longer the "life" in this different state of being. Thus it could be that survival is both reality and illusion.[394]

The supposition of some religions that our personalities are ultimately subsumed into a universal consciousness, seemingly without individual identity, is addressed by Arthur Conan Doyle in his communications after his bodily death. He revealed, through his medium, "[E]very religion is linked to one or another of the different planes of life we are illuminating. . . Spiritualism . . . is largely confined to the seven astral planes of life. . . . ¶ Buddhism is linked with the third sphere of heavenly life. . . . [T]he ultimate goal of all is to attain that condition of consciousness where the personality dwindles and is absorbed, and the individuality becomes so at one with the Universal that, in losing itself, it becomes the very pulse of God."[395]

When Doyle first passed from this world to the next, he experienced a number of things that he relayed through his medium. This too speaks to the issue of personality and how our individuality relates to the infinite reality: "There are no trimmings on a man when he has passed the Second Death; only pure spirit remains. . . One thing only was I conscious of – and that was the Allness, the infinitude, the wonder of God's love. In that supreme moment I knew no such thing as separateness of existence. Personality had died, but individuality was reborn."[396] Thus the individual survives but ultimately becomes one with the universe.

Eben Alexander addresses this reality in another way in *Proof of Heaven*. While in his week-long coma, when there was no brain function and he actually was not aware of who he was, he learned that "the greatest clue to the reality of the spiritual realm is this *profound mystery* of our conscious existence. . . . We – each of us – are intricately, irremovably connected to the larger universe. It is our true home."[397] Alexander further related that the angel figure, or Girl on the Butterfly Wing, who was guiding him throughout his journey, whom he did not recognize, turned out to be his long-deceased birth sister. "I had seen her heavenly self . . . . [T]here was no mistaking her, no mistaking the loving smile, the confident and infinitely comforting look, the sparkling blue eyes."[398]

These testimonies speak to the issue of the expansion of consciousness that many – perhaps most – human beings experience when they cross over. Our personalities survive, but we are often able to know and understand more fully. This expansion sometimes starts as a person is dying a natural death: "they experience a kind of 'keenness' of their senses, especially that of hearing and sight."[399]

This sometimes becomes the Life Review described by many who have had NDEs, where the spirit of the dying individual becomes acutely aware of all the good and harm s/he has done in his/her earthly life. Jeffrey Long, author of *Evidence of the Afterlife*, found from the monumental Near-Death Experience Research Foundation (NDERF) study that 22.5 percent of NDE survivors had experienced a review of past life events. Significantly, over 21 percent of those stated that they judged themselves – they were not judged by another being – and witnessed the effect of their life choices and decisions; many also experienced the actual feelings of others with whom they had interacted years earlier.[400]

Thus the survival of our individual personalities is closely linked to the "judgment" we experience at death. As Doyle also affirmed almost 85 years ago, there is no final judgment per se from a God apart from ourselves: "*At the last trump* – but this does not mean at the end of the world, as our Christian friends are wont to believe. It means at the end of the soul's world of matter."[401] The issue of self-judgment is important in that it challenges the Christian belief of God as Almighty Judge: "Over here we do not judge *anyone*; with broader vision we do not see a God vindictive or cruel, but an infinite love, a divine and compassionate intelligence."[402]

If our basic selves survive, does this include the basic selves of young children and babies, whose personalities have not been fully formed yet or who cannot yet speak? What about aborted fetuses and those that have been miscarried? The comforting, astonishing evidence shows that unborn fetuses, pre-verbal babies, and young children not only survive and "look down" on their parents and other relatives but also grow, mature, provide reasons why they died young and help those left behind in this world. Maureen Hancock, Tom and Lisa Butler, James Van Praagh, Chip Coffey, Ryan Buell and Michelle Belanger give examples in their books, and Theresa Caputo does the same in episodes of *Long Island Medium*. Young children are encountered by the *Ghost Hunters* and *Ghost Adventures* teams as well.

- Tom and Lisa Butler of the American Association of Electronic Voice Phenomena (AA-EVP) describe an EVP whereby a boy that had been miscarried spoke several times through a tape recorder: "Grandpa" (when there were no grandchildren in the family) came through several times. "Why don't you ask him [his name]?" came through from the deceased grandmother, and "Evan" in a young boy's voice was recorded in response to the grandmother's question.[403]
- Long, in *Evidence of the Afterlife*, recounts the NDEs of several children, including one, Sandra, who lost consciousness at the age of five. During her experience, she first encountered a friend who told her to go home at once; she went back into her body and woke up to her relieved parents, only to be told that that friend had died of a heart attack the day after she had entered the hospital. Also during her coma, Sandra met a girl she did not recognize and, after recovering, began drawing a picture of her. Her parents, so shaken that they had to leave the room, then explained to her that the girl she had encountered and whose picture she was drawing was a sister Sandra never knew about who had been struck by a car and died before Sandra was born.[404]
- AA-EVP member Martha Copeland's daughter Cathy died in a car accident. Martha is able to connect with Cathy via EVPs that are captured in tape recordings, on voice mail and via

computer. Martha has gleaned evidence that Cathy's pet dogs and a pet rat are both on the other side with Cathy.[405] A spirit team associated with AA-EVP, which communicates via EVPs and delivers messages to people whose loved ones are on the other side, record bi-weekly in so-called Big Circle recording sessions. Martha and Cathy form part of this circle.[406]

- Psychic Maureen Hancock's 19-year-old nephew Sean died suddenly when a car he was working on fell down and crushed him. While the family was devastated by the loss, Sean came through to Hancock indicating that his "contract" for life on earth was only for 19 years; he has become one of her spirit guides.[407]

Another vexing question related to the survival of our basic personalities is that of abortion. Do we not murder a person when an abortion is carried out, as many maintain? Psychic James Van Praagh has gleaned important wisdom on abortion from his spirit guides. A new spirit being born into the physical world is linked to its earthly mother "and picks up everything that is around and within the mother's aura. Once life is set in motion, nature takes charge and fulfills what it knows to do." Sometimes an event in the mother's life or psyche ends the pregnancy through miscarriage; the soul then waits for another opportunity to grow." Van Praagh has learned that abortions often occur for the mother's spiritual growth. In fact, "[b]efore incarnating, a spirit will set up a situation like having an abortion to work through lessons of self-worth, guilt, failure, and love of self." Because of these spiritual conditions, there does not seem to be any karmic ill effect on a woman who has an abortion.[408]

We have mentioned above that pets' souls also survive death. We do reunite with our pets in the afterlife, as many people hope and sense. Mediums such as Theresa Caputo and Maureen Hancock channel animal spirits to their owners, and there is a great deal of EVP evidence for postmortem animal communication. EVPs and animal images captured by Tom and Lisa Butler, Martha Copeland, and many others provide evidence that spirits care for animals, not only our pets, who die suddenly or are killed.[409] Investigator Anabela Cardoso in Portugal has reported on experiences with animal communications, including domestic animals speaking in the languages of their owners.[410] Monroe encountered many animal spirits in his journeys out-of-body.[411]

Lisa Butler describes how she was devastated over the fate of animals and livestock that perished in a major flood in the Midwest a number of years ago. She contacted entities on the other side who assured her that the "animals also survive." Entities on the other side, they were told, rescue the animals and help them cross over. For awhile after the tragedy, the Butlers continued to contact the entities to find out how the animals were faring and finally, after a week, received a frustrated reply, "Stop with the animals! They are all right!" This brings home the lesson that those on the other side have human limits and should be treated with the same respect we should treat one another.[412]

Our personalities on earth are often heavily influenced by physical and mental ailments. The paranormal evidence shows that such problems often completely dissipate at the time of the death transition. An EVP researcher named Clara Laughlin received clear messages from her husband Tom, who had died of a heart attack in an ICU in 1981. Tom's voice came through in a May 2, 1983, recording, saying, "I was sick on earth. No more. No longer sick."[413] The researcher Hans-Otto König learned in a recording in Germany, "Damage to the material body has no influence on the astral body."[414] White Eagle teachings, associated with the findings from Doyle, provide the same wisdom: "You ask if those who suffer lose their handicap when they pass from the physical body. We answer, yes, most certainly."[415] This confirms, of course, that cremation and other extreme damage to our bodies do not negatively affect our spirit bodies.

Dementia and Alzheimer's disease usually disappear on the other side, as do the effects of comas and mental illness. In many cases, those that suffer with these ailments hear and understand what is said to them while in the physical world, even if they do not react, so our expressions of love, forgiveness and concern become very important after they cross over. EVP and mediumistic messages that address the guilt feelings of some caregivers implore survivors not to worry that they did not do enough for their loved one or that they were not present at the death. Entities on the other side assure survivors that they could not do anything further and that they were not meant to be present when the loved one passed over. It is vital to both parties, then, that the love and care be expressed.

When a departed spirit communicates through a psychic or instruments and seems to be still in agony, pain or mental confusion, there is often a reason. Perhaps s/he does not realize that s/he has died and can now be released. Some souls are afraid to cross over completely due to their religious beliefs about being judged, while others who believe in a time of Final Judgment feel they cannot progress to a higher plane because they are not experiencing this cosmic salvation event. In other cases, "some entities have remained near the physical locale because another discarnate entity that they are close to refuses to move on" (e.g., family members, soldiers).[416] Higher spirits indicate that such "stuck" or lost spirits are vibrating at a different frequency, closer to the earth plane, and that they need to look for the light that can assist them. As we shall see below in a discussion of the power of prayer, some spirits can be helped more by those of us still in the physical world, because of the vibrations, than they can be by the spirits on the other side.[417]

The evidence from mediums, EVPs, NDEs, OOBEs, postmortem Doyle and spirit circles – gatherings of like-minded "helper" entities on the other side – show that spirits, complete with the character traits and personalities that defined them in the physical world, are around us all the time. Depending, apparently, upon their missions and callings on the other side and upon which astral, mental or heavenly plane they exist, they know what their loved ones are doing (and even thinking), and are often aiding or influencing them even if they do not realize it.[418] Spirits do not appear to spy on us, however, and generally do not intrude[419] (hauntings, of course, are exceptions).

The survival of our basic personalities and character traits thus has a bearing on religious, especially Christian, tenets in several ways. First, if our basic personalities go with us to the afterlife, rather than transform automatically to pure angelic beings as many might assume (or hope), it behooves us to attempt to become the best people we can possibly be while still in this life. As we will discuss more fully below with regard to reincarnation, the way we live our lives in the physical world affects what we will become and experience on the other side – just as the lives we lived in the past affect the lives we have chosen to live now. Postmortem Doyle reported on different planes of existence in the afterlife, as we have seen and will explore in more detail below. These levels, as noted through his medium, have a direct bearing on our conduct in this world and our spiritual growth: "For that particular astral, mental, or celestial plane to which he is destined he lays the foundation in this physical world, the result being that he attains to lesser or fuller degrees of astral life, of mental, and of celestial life according to the aspiration and growth of his soul whilst on earth."[420]

Second, if most of us will experience an expanded consciousness at death, as mentioned above, it follows that we might wish to start expanding our consciousness and learn and grow spiritually now. If we become aware in our physical lives that much of our basic selves will continue after we die, and that the soul might journey to many levels in some confusion at first, it makes sense to develop spiritually as much as possible to be prepared for entering the larger life. The traditional religious admonition to live well (spiritually) so that one will die well is borne out by the paranormal evidence.

The survival of fetuses, babies, children and animals, and the evidence that their consciousness expands just as adult human beings' do, further supports the notion that we are all ultimately One, that there is purpose and meaning in the universe, and that love and compassion truly do extend to "the least of these." When we extend love and concern to others, it matters – to them and to our own spiritual growth as well.

The "Heavenly" Realms and Angels

Judaism and Christianity have long-standing traditions of the heavenly realms, home not only of God but also of angels. In the ancient imagination, heaven was above the earth. The English word "angel" is derived from the Greek word angelos, meaning "messenger." One of the most well-known stories of angels in scripture, which bridges Judaism and Christianity, is of the angel Gabriel visiting the Jewish girl Mary to announce the coming of Jesus.[421]

Post-Enlightenment, and certainly in our age when human beings have ventured into outer space and even landed on the moon, it is difficult for moderns to believe in a heaven "up there." It is also hard to believe in angels and other non-human spirits: they often just seem too contrived and fantastic. The paranormal evidence, however, demonstrates the existence of "heaven" – if not an actual physical place, then a place or condition in a different dimension. There are various levels in this realm, and on at least some of them, spirits of the deceased build dream houses, live in gorgeous settings, and congregate with others. Colors are vivid and different from what we experience on earth. Spirits are happy and busy. We reunite joyfully with those who have gone before us (and those who come after us), but we do not necessarily gather *continually* with loved ones, and that is as it should be as we journey on our individual paths of spiritual growth.

Also in these realms, the evidence shows that there are angels – advanced souls who have never incarnated into human bodies – who truly come to our assistance on earth. Our "guardian angels" can be these beings or the spirits of our loved ones who have predeceased us. Any number of medical and other miracles can be attributed to these beings, as attested by mediums, EVPs, Monroe's OOBEs and other evidence.

Jeffrey Long, from the NDERF study, found definite evidence for a heavenly realm and guardian angels. In the survey, respondents were asked, "Did you seem to encounter a mystical being or presence" during their NDE? 49.9 percent responded, "Definite being, or voice clearly of mystical or otherworldly origin;" another 9.8 percent responded, "Unidentifiable voice." Respondents described these beings as angels, "filled with love, joy, patience, [and] compassion;" they were often glowing or comprised of bright light without discernible features.[422]

Eben Alexander, referred to above, is one of the most recent survivors of an NDE to describe both heaven and angels. Speaking in terms of the Core, Alexander describes a "place" of indescribable beauty where vital lessons are learned. He reported three teachings: "You are loved and cherished. You have nothing to fear. There is nothing you can do wrong." Unconditional love, he discovered, was at the base of all existence.[423]

Psychics and mediums such as Van Praagh, Coffey, Caputo and Hancock also channel spirits who serve as guardian angels and guides and who describe places of peace, joy and comfort. Hancock, for instance, says that spirits have indicated to her that they "create their heaven to be whatever they feel comfortable with" – being near the ocean, hiking in the mountains, and the like.[424]

Robert Monroe's OOBEs were more mixed than those of most NDE survivors in that he found more negativity, but he did witness some of the beauty, joy and peace in the other locales he visited, and he was assisted at times by beings unknown to him.

Probably the most explicit, vivid and extensive reporting on the nature of heaven and of angelic beings is the postmortem testimony of Arthur Conan Doyle, on which we have touched above. He learned a great deal about the different astral planes and spheres where spirit beings reside and communicated this wisdom through his medium. The "fifth astral plane," for instance, is characterized by ". . . brighter conditions [than lower planes], a desire to do something for the fellow next door. . . . Earth conditions tend to reproduce themselves. We gather in public worship, we dwell in houses not beautiful, somewhat dilapidated, and occasionally not exactly salubrious."[425] In the so-called fourth sphere, "Now things are decidedly better. . . Families dwell together, we see the homes described in many spiritualistic books, the lakes, rivers, mountains, flowers and animals. . . On this plane the soul attains to mental and spiritual development. . ."[426]

Doyle confirmed that there is an "angel world apart from the human race, apart from the human chain of evolution, formed of souls never incarnated in a human body, souls advanced through a process of natural development, souls in close contact with inner laws of creative service. ¶ Of such are the angels of music."[427] Monroe experienced much the same and learned that some nonhuman intelligences "apparently are from the same galaxy as we are. Others seem to be from other energy systems and times. There are even those that suggest the possibility that they once were human."[428]

Doyle has more to say about heaven and what souls experience when they first pass over:

> After passing through the "death" of the astral body, when the man discards his astral vehicle and enters the heavenly life, we there find a condition of at-one-ment – attunement – a condition wherein the soul is conscious only of the one vibratory note of love and service. In this sphere the soul is cognizant mainly of the great cosmic powers. ¶ In speaking of that Second Death through which we all pass after experiencing a period of unconsciousness – which may last for minutes, hours, days, or even years – a period of quiescence of consciousness, we said that the spirit then wakes to life rich, vivid, renewed. . . ¶ [T]he soul passes not through every mental plane, but migrates to the one particular mental plane to which he is attuned.[429]

Commenting further on this mental plane of the afterlife, Doyle tells us, "The mental plane is very powerful, and on it it becomes necessary for the soul to use the mental faculties, which become unloosed as it enters this plane of existence. A delicate balance must be attained between the mental and the spiritual before the soul wakes to the celestial. For a period it would seem the soul must grow in quietude. . . . ¶ In the celestial world the work of creation commences. . . . Almost having become angelic, he dwells amongst angelic beings."[430]

When it comes to meeting Jesus or experiencing "God" in the afterlife, the vastly different experiences of people who have had NDEs further suggest that there are surprises in store – most of them probably good, if not indescribably wonderful. Some near-death survivors do report meeting Jesus, even if they have not been particularly religious in their previous lives, while others who may have been very devout do not necessarily report meeting Jesus. Further, the experience of "God" tends to be one of indescribable immensity and love, both intensely personal and truly universal and eternal.

These testimonies confirm the true existence of "heaven," however one might want to describe or term it. Therefore, while many oppressed peoples the world over, suffering terribly in this life, have had only heaven to look forward to, we can take comfort in the fact that their hopes were almost certainly realized and, in fact, that their suffering on earth had a purpose (however difficult that is for us to comprehend). For those of us, on the other hand, who are fairly comfortable, well off and fortunate, living our lives in joy and gratitude helps us prepare for the joys ahead, and acceptance of our "lot" – of our suffering and challenges – is essential: we have in fact chosen this path for reasons that will one day become clear to us.

The Power of Prayer

Prayer – both corporate and individual – is at the heart of Christian practice and ritual, as it is in other traditions as well. Recent surveys in the US find that over 50% of the adult population prays daily.[431] Some studies have been conducted testing the theory that patients in hospitals who are prayed for recover more quickly than those who are not prayed for.[432] While there is no substantial scientific proof, patients anecdotally report that they feel the positive benefits of prayer.[433]

Cynics question the efficacy of prayer: what does it matter? How is it possible that people thinking about someone, or congregations lifting up their hearts and voices in prayer, can have a positive effect on a desired outcome?

The paranormal evidence sheds light on why prayer is beneficial and should continue to be practiced, not only because of a possible positive outcome to the person or situation being prayed for but also on the person or persons doing the praying. There are at least two reasons for this. At one level, as shown by the paranormal evidence, spirits on the other side communicate through thought and not language. At another level, our individual karma and spiritual growth are at stake: positive thoughts that we direct toward others are beneficial to us in our spiritual development.

Doyle speaks of prayer in conjunction with family reunions in the afterlife. He reports through his medium, "[F]amilies meet and exchange experiences, meet in wonderful love and happiness and peace." In this context, Doyle speaks of vast open-air cathedrals, "where they praise God by song and love and prayer, in gratitude, in profound thankfulness."[434]

Van Praagh, among other mediums, has learned through his spirit guides and trance states that in the heavenly existence "[e]very thought a spirit has is made visible and appears as its own unique light radiating from within." Spirits at this higher level experience complete cognition; thoughts are not hidden but rather become the main vehicle of communication.[435]

Alexander discovered the same thing through his coma, and Monroe through his OOBEs, and the power of thought – of prayer – is closely related to the fact that time on the other side is different than time in the physical world. An associate of Alexander's was able to communicate with him telepathically during his unconscious state because time does not behave the same as on the other side: "A moment can seem like a lifetime, and one or several lifetimes can seem like a moment."[436] Similarly, Monroe discovered that time is non-existent; there is no cyclical separation, and communication was instantaneous. "[T]hought is the wellspring of existence. . . . As you think, so you are."[437] As psychic Michelle Belanger puts it, the spirits' "method of communication bears more in common with telepathy . . .

More often than not, spirit communication is just this barrage of images and sensations."[438]

Obviously it is not easy as we exist in the physical world to affect physical or environmental change just by thought or prayer. It is also not always easy for entities on the other side to get through to us; sometimes the one who has crossed over *has* tried to communicate with loved ones but cannot pierce the veil. The evidence suggests, however, that prayer, positive thoughts, and meditation are never wasted and, in cosmic terms, do have ultimate power and influence. We will come back to the issue of prayer and thought in Chapter 7.

Evil, Purgatory and Hell

The problem of evil and the question of why tragic things happen to good people are topics that human beings have struggled with since the dawn of time. If God is so good and omnipotent, as we are taught in the Christian faith, why does he allow such things to happen – greed, exploitation, violence, murder? Victims of rape and incest, and the relatives of murder victims, suffer terribly, often for the rest of their lives, from the evil inflicted upon them and their loved ones. Often their only hopes are that their perpetrator will be punished eternally and that they themselves will see their departed loved ones after death. In certain parts of the US, and among many in the population, there is a visceral need for capital punishment: death to the perpetrator is viewed as the only possible justice.

In the Roman Catholic tradition, there is a long-standing belief in Purgatory, "the huge area between Heaven and Hell, . . . the place where everything from minor faults to serious sin are purged. It's a gray area just as there are gray areas in all aspects of existence."[439] While there is no mention of Purgatory in the Christian creeds (Apostles' or Nicene), there is certainly mention of hell: Jesus descends there for three days. The Psalms speak of hell, thanking God for sparing the petitioner or asking God for deliverance,[440] and the Christian tradition has a centuries-old theme of evildoers being cast into outer darkness forever – "wailing and gnashing of teeth." [441] Children throughout the ages have long been disciplined through fear, being told to behave and obey in order to avoid going to hell at death.

The paranormal evidence suggests that these concepts are only part of the reality. While the evidence does indicate the existence of evil and some level of punishment or justice for those who commit truly wicked deeds on earth, the vast majority of the paranormal material focuses on "normal" people, most of whom are quite good overall. Furthermore, the "end result" of our existence is union with the Divine – who is Love – and this fate holds true for *all* souls. As we have seen above in relation to other themes and which we will explore further below, the spiritual journey is about growth, love, service, reincarnation and learning from past lives.

For now, let us consider the fortunes of certain souls whom we might consider evil – those who commit murder, serial killers, rapists, child molesters, violent psychopaths, arsonists, those who harm and torture animals and/or human beings, unscrupulous individuals who abuse their power and/or wealth, and others who victimize their fellow beings in any way.

There is little evidence in the paranormal literature of people who noticeably communicate from Purgatory or hell. According to Doyle, spirit circles, EVPs, and psychics and mediums, many of the *victims* of evildoers reside in a beautiful place and are at peace, while there is another "place" where evil spirits exist after physical death. Is this Purgatory? It seems logical to assume that some evil spirits do abide there for some length of time. According to Michael H. Brown, a journalist writing from a Roman Catholic perspective, spirits generally reside in Purgatory for 30-40 years.[442] While Brown also asserts that most of us go first to Purgatory, other paranormal testimony suggests a very different scenario: loved ones communicate via mediums and EVPs only a few hours, days, weeks, months or years after passing over. Doyle in fact reports that "Souls go [to Summerland[443]] and inhabit an astral body. They do not at once become greatly wise or spiritual. Rest and refreshment after the toils of their earth life is the first necessity. This they obtain, and they remain in the astral world while time slips past." "Great things are not demanded of those living in the restful Summerland."[444]

Purgatory appears to be one of the levels of the afterlife that is visited by some spirits, and for differing lengths of "time," and not others. Episcopal priest Morton Kelsey describes Purgatory as "a place of redemption and renewal where we are transformed and grow more and more into children of God."[445] Postmortem Doyle reports that "even the Master Jesus himself descended into a condition of uncertainty and what is described as 'Hades', the sphere of the disquieted spirits. So, too, must every man on leaving the earth pass through that belt of the disquieted souls of men."[446] These observations, then, can help us answer the question of what happens to the spirits of truly evil persons.

Evil entities are often encountered by investigators from the Paranormal Research Society, The Atlantic Paranormal Society, the *Ghost Adventures* team, and others; the work of Ed and Lorraine Warren and their nephew John Zaffis pointedly attests to the existence of evil. Doyle, through his medium, asserted that ". . . unprincipled spirits can manipulate astral thought-forces to suit their own mischievous purposes."[447] EVPs record hateful words and phrases from the other side that do the same; evil beings truly menace both places and people. Many beings still appear to reside, as ghosts, in their homes, in theaters, prisons, and hospitals and on battlefields over 200 years after their death. It seems that being "stuck" is a form of Purgatory and that such souls dwell there for a generation or more.

Further postmortem evidence from Doyle provides descriptions of evil and the places where evildoers go when they pass over, at least temporarily:

[W]hat of those [places] of a slower, of a lower vibration; perhaps even lower than this earth? These are not pleasant places, for they are peopled by humans whose lives have attuned them to such planes. They are grey, misty, dark-November-fog places, good to get out of. That is why they exist; to spur their folk to get away, by their own spiritual efforts.[448]

He who has lived a life gross, material, sensual, or selfish, finds himself in "queer street" [in trouble]. . . . He passes onward, through the underworlds. Every step towards salvation must be earned.[449]

The lowest astral plane consists of a land of desire, burning and persistent desire, the which the man has fostered during his life on earth. Those who migrate thither are such as hold neither affection nor love for any creature save self. . . . In the greyness are seen stunted trees and vegetation, while forms of men live and dwell in mists damp and thick, being themselves clothed in grey; being in fact so wrapped up in themselves, in self-centredness as to create about themselves environments unpleasantly cold and repellent.[450]

Monroe also gleaned evidence about evil and "hell" through his OOBEs. "It is easy to conclude that a momentary penetration of this nearby layer would bring 'demons' and 'devils' to mind as the chief inhabitants. They seem subhuman, yet have an evident ability to act and think independently. . . ¶ In these worlds where thoughts are not only things, but are everything, including you, your poison or perfection is of your own making. If you are remorseless killer, you may end up in that part of Locale II where all are of the same design. This truly would be hell for such people, for there would be no innocent, defenseless victims. ¶ Project this outward, and you can begin to perceive the myriad variations. Your destination in the heaven or hell of Locale II seems to be grounded completely within the framework of your deepest *constant* (and perhaps non-conscious) motivations, emotions, and personality drives. The most consistent and strongest of these act as your 'homing' device when you enter this realm."[451]

Medium Van Praagh too has learned about the lower places from his spirit guides. "This lower region vibrates at a much slower rate than the upper regions. Here the light is dim and fades almost to a faint darkness. . . A pungent and unpleasant odor pervades it. . . ¶ Spirits in such a dark realm harbor mental attitudes of hate, malice, and the need for control over others" and include "murderers, rapists, thieves, swindlers, cheaters, assassins, or anyone who has harmed another human being. . . A soul remains in this darkened hole until all of its lowest desires are lived out."[452]

Monroe similarly reports on the nature of the gray areas. "There are, however, more positive prospects to report regarding heaven and hell. If they exist, they are somewhere in Locale II. ¶ In non-physical trips to Locale II, often there is a 'layer' or area which one must pass through. . . It seems to be the part of Locale II closest to Here-Now, and in some way most related. It is a gray-black hungry ocean where the slightest motion attracts nibbling and tormenting beings."[453]

What becomes abundantly clear from these reports is that we possess free will to do good or evil; we constantly make these choices. At the same time, we are also predestined for union with God: "Whilst that soul has been given a degree of freewill choice whereby to accept or reject good or evil, so also it can never break its link with the great Soul, God. To God there is always an upward pull. . . . ¶ The magnetic force of the divine intelligence must ever hold him on the path of eternal progression... Thus no man can escape his destiny, which is ultimate perfection, ultimate *return* to the God of his creation."[454]

Legitimate questions might then be raised about the relationship between psychics, mediums and other paranormal techniques and the solving of crimes, especially violent crimes and murder. In the television shows *Sensing Murder* and *Psychic Detectives*, Laurie Campbell and Pam Coronado, Noreen Renier, Phil Jordan, Nancy Orlen Weber and others assist police in several jurisdictions; some of the young people featured in *Psychic Kids* similarly aid law enforcement in solving crimes and missing persons cases. Tom and Lisa Butler offer an example of a murder in Vienna, as reported in a 1987 edition of a publication of the Spiritualist Association of Great Britain. The voice of the female victim was heard saying a name on a tape recorder. Police at first laughed at the evidence but later found a man by that name who ultimately confessed to the crime and was sentenced to life in prison.[455]

As we saw in Chapter 2, Noreen Renier is one of the most prominent psychics aiding law enforcement in solving violent crimes. She has been able to "see" features of perpetrators that can be sketched by police artists to aid in the identification. When she channels the final moments of a murder victim's life, she acutely feels their pain; when she shifts to "being" the murderer, she takes on his or her rage and malice. The readings often exhaust her.[456]

As Renier and many other psychics and law enforcement officials insist, their methods and work are only one tool in finding answers to the mysteries they investigate; it is extremely rare for paranormal evidence to be the sole tool in solving a crime and, to date, such evidence is not accepted in courts of law.

Deniers and cynics repeatedly point out that many crimes go unsolved despite clues offered by psychics and paranormal investigations. Based on the evidence we have seen about victims who have crossed over, there are a number of possible reasons why they might not be able to help investigators on this side. In some cases, the victim may not know s/he is dead and thus cannot help in the search. While that may seem hard to believe, this is not particularly uncommon, especially in the case of sudden death or of children.[457] Relatedly, the victim may not know his/her assailant and can only give vague clues to the medium.

It is also the case that a message that comes through from the other side may be false; because our basic personalities survive, people whose motives are not always pure also exist on the other side and could well be fabricating something or outright lying. There is a great deal of evidence for impressionable people in the physical world attempting to channel spirits only to connect with unscrupulous ones. The medium or EVP/ITC investigator who wishes to help solve crimes thus needs to be collaborating with trustworthy spirit guides with whom they have established a good relationship.[458]

Another stumbling block in a criminal investigation that attempts to use paranormal techniques is that the victim may well have moved on beyond the crime, feels that solving it is no longer a priority as the spirit moves on in his/her growth, and therefore does not need or desire to come through to the medium or investigator. The evidence strongly suggests that issues of justice may be different on the other side than they are for us. As Doyle pointed out through his medium, "a large percentage of those in the spirit world entertain no desire whatever to return to the earth plane. . . It is not for everyone to seek or try to force communication between the so-called dead and the living."[459] This does not, of course, mean that we in the physical world should not strive for justice, try to solve crime or attempt to connect with souls who have crossed over.

Renier has also experienced incidents where she was channeling the strong emotions of the victim's families, which can throw off a reading.⁴⁶⁰ In one interesting case involving a horse that was murdered, she could only channel images of the people who were involved with the horse: the horse did not experience fear of the person who shot him or of the gun, so Renier instead focused on the bullets that killed the horse, which led to the identity of the shooter.⁴⁶¹

All of this speaks to the need for further research and the possibility of invaluable assistance between the "living" and the "dead." Can the psychic gifts of children and young adults be encouraged and nurtured, rather than ignored or punished, in the service of crime-fighting? This is one of the goals and missions of the *Psychic Kids* television show and the professionals on the show who maintain private practices helping such children and their families.

Further, can we imagine law enforcement officials across the country and around the world forming a network of psychic investigators who in turn cultivate their own crime-fighting spirit circles? Can law enforcement be trained in "intuitive techniques"?⁴⁶² Law enforcement officials have begun taking psychics and their clues seriously, as we have seen with Noreen Renier. Tom Shamshak, former police chief in Spencer and Winthrop, Massachusetts, contributed to four episodes of *Psychic Kids* and later founded a group of psychics, the Cold Case Collaborative, which explores the possibility of using psychic abilities in conjunction with traditional police procedures to solve crimes.⁴⁶³ A website devoted to the stories of police professionals attesting to the efficacy and validity of using psychics and mediums to solve crimes can be found at http://www.victorzammit.com/articles/psychicdetectives.html.⁴⁶⁴

Can we also possibly imagine the families of victims even helping to solve their loved ones' murders by listening to their own intuition and signs from the other side?

As we come to the close of our discussion of evil we encounter the issue of non-human evildoers such as demons. Psychics and paranormal investigators disagree on the nature and even existence of demons. For some, a demon is a fallen angel, an angel's evil counterpart.[465] Others acknowledge that demonic possession is a real possibility in some cases but that "the demonic lives in the deep psyche of our minds. The attack is more psychological than physical."[466] There is also the theory that "[s]mall particles of evil [are] scattered throughout the universe" and are far outnumbered by the good particles.[467]

If demons and evil spirits exist in some form, how much damage can they do to people in the physical world? Can they injure or kill people? Monroe's stories suggest that entities on the other side may not always know they are touching someone as forcefully as they are. He recounts an incident in 1963 where he astrally visited a businesswoman acquaintance of his, R.W. He ventured out of his body, went to her beach cottage where she was sitting in her kitchen with two young women, and reached out to pinch her (she had previously promised to remember that he would try to contact her in spirit). Monroe thought he was only pinching her slightly, but she not only let out a loud yelp but also subsequently showed him the bruise he had made.[468] This incident suggests that an entity that scratches someone and leaves a mark or even draws blood may merely wish to get someone's attention and does not really intend to do harm. On the other hand, some spirits (including demons) really do intend harm.

Can evil spirits that are "stuck," then, be released by prayer? Viewers of the paranormal television shows can see episodes in which exorcisms or cleansings are performed in haunted locations. Many of these rituals, which often include prayer and imploring to God, Jesus, saints or other positive spiritual beings, do successfully reduce disturbing occurrences. The stuck spirits are encouraged to "go toward the light," and the heaviness of the atmosphere often does diminish and even disappears. Thus the evidence for evil events and cleansings coincides well with Christian theology about evil and redemption, whether or not we speak specifically of other-worldly demons. Psychics, mediums, healers and paranormal investigators surround themselves with protective rituals, practices, and prayers in order to reduce the possibility of being harmed or being channels of harm to others.

What, then, in the overall "agenda" of the universe is the relationship between good and evil? The paranormal evidence points in the direction of the vast preponderance of good in this world and the next and of the fact that evil *needs* to exist in order for us to see and to know the good. In the words of postmortem Doyle,

> [T]hese conditions of intelligence – or, if you will, "light" and "darkness" – work and evolve side by side, and are the actual complement one of the other. ¶ . . . Always men have conceived that good must oppose evil. Again, nothing is farther from the truth. "Evil" stands always as the complement to the condition you call "good", so without evil good could not be. . . ."[469] Further, *"that which you call "evil" is also of God; the universal Intelligence which man calls God contains both good and evil!"*. . . ¶ We must live and strain and strive, all and each of us, for a perfect balance, so that darkness shall never overcome the light; but rather that good and evil together shall, not as masters but as our servants, work out in us the perfect law with perfect precision.[470]

Doyle further attested that good and evil "are not so opposed as appearance warrants. . . ¶ Might we not then describe the angels of darkness as the individualized powers of evil, as great destructive forces which consume that which is unwanted. . .? . . . Appearing to destroy, actually they do not destroy; though we have said they consume, rather they *transmute*."[471]

EVP testimony further supports this view. Luxembourg investigators Maggy Harsch-Fischbach and her husband Jules Harsch used radio systems to communicate with the other side. Their spirit contact, a higher being who asked to be called Technician, provided these insights in late 1986:

> The grief and suffering people bear and have to go through is a part of their inner self. Some of it is through their own action or initiated by higher forces in order to activate the learning process that leads to recognition, improvement, and perfection. . . It is all closely connected and tied in with free will and choice of the individual, which God's power has granted to each of us as a great gift. . . . Without free will and choice, there is no recognition of truth which comes from within. Therefore, blind obedience is not what higher powers want. . . God prefers the seeker and those who question.[472]

Spiritual Growth, Reincarnation and Pre-Birth Decisions

One of the prevailing themes that emerges from the paranormal evidence, as we have seen, is that we human beings are not just physical bodies but also spiritual souls. If there is another level of existence "on the other side" and if those on the other side can often pierce the veil and communicate with us, as the evidence significantly suggests, it follows that souls might (even must) grow in spirit – and that spiritual growth is or should be one of the primary goals of our earthly existence. This certainly resonates with devout and sincere Christians and others who feel that there is more to life than our material goals and trappings.

Most strands of Christianity, however, do not officially condone a belief in reincarnation or the rebirth of souls over and over again on earth. As Noel Langley has described in his work on Edgar Cayce, the notion of reincarnation was respected in many circles in the ancient world until certain church fathers and Byzantine rulers removed most vestiges of the doctrine. The story of how this respect came to be overturned is complex and convoluted.

According to Langley, Origen (185-254 CE), a major early Christian theologian, states in several of his writings his strong belief in reincarnation. In *Contra Celsum*, Origen supports Pythagoras and Plato on the issue: "Is it not more in conformity with reason that every soul, for certain mysterious reasons. . . is introduced into a body according to its desserts and former actions?" And in *De Principiis*, Origen says, "Every soul . . . comes into this world strengthened by the victories or weakened by the defeats of its previous life. . . ."[473]

Another influential church father, Clement of Alexandria (150-220 CE), maintains in *Exhortations to the Pagans* that we "were in being long before the foundation of the world."[474] And St. Gregory (257-332 CE) asserted that "it is absolutely necessary that the soul should be healed and purified, and if this does not take place during its life on earth, it must be accomplished in future lives."[475]

What happened to reincarnation in Christian thought, then? Why did the church come to condemn it, and what replaces it? Langley traces the change to the abuse of power exerted by the Emperor Justinian and his wife Theodora. Justinian "summoned the Fifth Ecumenical Congress of Constantinople in 553 A.D. to condemn the Platonically inspired writings of Origen." As we noted in Chapter 5, Plato, followed by Origen and many others, shared a firm belief in reincarnation,[476] which was referred to as "metempsychosis" in some sources; Jewish Kabbalah writings also held to the notion of reincarnation.[477] Theodora, a very devious woman, became a convert to the controversial doctrine espoused by the Monophysites, a sect that contended that Jesus' physical body was wholly divine. This doctrine completely rejected the teachings of Origen, which included the argument that Jesus was both human and divine. While the Chalcedonian Decree of 451 CE protected the teachings of Origen, and while Justinian supported this decree, Theodora and the Monophysites set about expunging all Biblical references to reincarnation. Theodora's motive seems to have been to bolster her megalomaniacal hope for "instant apotheosis upon departing this life."[478]

Langley goes on to explain other machinations of Theodora, which probably included having two Popes killed. Langley states, "Theodora, having contrived the murder of two Popes, expected to instill their successor Virgilius with her own mania for exterminating all traces of the Chalcedonian Decree and its division of Christ into two separate entities, human and divine. She failed."[479] However, after her death, Justinian remained under her influence. In 531, the same year as the Chalcedonian Decree, he issued the Three Chapters Edict, a little-known ruling that was recognized by Pope Virgilius and the four Popes who followed him. This Edict was ostensibly an attack on Origen and all theologies that depended on his writings, but was apparently never really ratified by the entire church body. During the period when it was believed that the church was condemning Origen, most references to reincarnation were apparently deleted from Gospel manuscripts: "Justinian's deletions and alterations of the Gospels would have been completed in very short order, and so would the elimination of all and any evidence of the vandalism."[480] It appears that the church never scrutinized the workings of the Fifth Ecumenical Council to examine what was actually enacted, which had the effect of the church – both West and East after the split of 1054 – coming to accept Origen, for the most part. What was not realized, or what was suppressed, was that Origen's writings included support for reincarnation. Langley, quoting Head and Cranston in *Reincarnation, An East-West Anthology*, concludes: ". . . during the many centuries when the Church believed it had condemned Origen, it was mistaken. ¶ However, one disastrous result of the mistake still persists; namely, the exclusion from the Christian creed of the teaching of the preexistence of the soul, and, by implication, reincarnation."[481]

This history of the abuse of power in high places in the church, along with a desire on many theologians' and clerics' parts even today to turn a blind eye to the universal law of cause and effect, help explain why the church looks at the afterlife the way it does. Denying reincarnation enables Christians (and, consequently, Westerners) to believe that they will not have to pay for their misdeeds but will rather be completely redeemed at death and united with God. The denial or reincarnation and the immortality of the soul also helps instill in some modern Westerners, perhaps especially intellectuals, the fear (perhaps subconscious) of total annihilation at death, a fear that has wide-ranging ethical and societal consequences.

The rediscovery of the expurgation of reincarnation in scripture strongly suggests that the time is ripe to reexamine afterlife beliefs, as we have done here. The paranormal literature unites spiritual growth with reincarnation and the law of cause and effect. Scientific research and techniques, the work of psychics and mediums, and evidence from NDEs and OOBEs all point in this direction.

Dr. Ian Stevenson, whom we met in Chapter 4, studied stories of reincarnation and past lives from a scientific perspective for most of his career, publishing the influential four-volume collection, *Cases of the Reincarnation Type*, between 1975 and 1983. Many psychics and mediums glean evidence from their spirit guides about past lives of their clients and have undergone past life regressions themselves. Monroe encountered many of his previous selves in his OOBEs.

EVPs also provide evidence for reincarnation. Sarah Estep, founder of the AA-EVP, has been told by spirits on the other side that she and they knew each other in past lives. Estep connected with a spirit who identified himself as Jeffrey, who said that they were brother and sister in eighteenth-century Philadelphia. Estep conducted research and found evidence that this might well have been the case.[482] Another researcher, Carol, recorded voices addressing her as Kathy. At first Carol thought she was picking up messages for someone else, but further experiments and some contacts with living German investigators revealed that the voice belonged to a German spirit who had had a sister in a previous life named Catharina. When Carol asked the voice if she was Kathy in a past life, the spirits replied, "You ARE her!"[483]

Among the most explicit discussions of reincarnation comes from the postmortem testimonies of Arthur Conan Doyle. When someone dies and

> is freed from the prison of flesh he will automatically migrate to that particular plane in the different worlds for which he has fitted himself... ¶ When people express loathing of the thought of reincarnation, it is indicative of a closed mentality... When one reviews life and examines closely the long experience inevitable before man draws near to spiritual completion, one recognizes not only the necessity for reincarnation, but the tremendous importance of the smallest detail of life. ¶ In the world of spirit all is law, order, and harmony.... [M]an's thoughts, his creations, become like his angels of good or evil. When he views his life from a higher plane of existence, he well realizes the disaster of those mental creatures of gloom and depression and selfishness which were and are his children.[484]

A more recent accounting of reincarnation comes from Dr. Brian Weiss in *Many Lives, Many Masters* and other works. Weiss, a renowned psychiatrist, recounts his experiences conducting past-life regressions on his patient Catherine. His work with Catherine and other patients supports Stevenson's, Cayce's and others' findings: that we live many lives on earth and grow through them; that we keep meeting the same souls time and again for the purpose of spiritual growth; and that tapping into our past lives can greatly ameliorate problems we are encountering in our present incarnations, including physical ailments. In addition to recounting past lives, Weiss – through Catherine – encountered "Masters," higher-level beings who imparted great wisdom. This too supports findings throughout the paranormal literature.[485]

Massachusetts-based psychic and healer Maureen Hancock also hears from her spirit guides that we repeatedly return to earth to work through challenges in order for our souls to grow; "we have a set of goals to help us reach our highest vibrational level."[486]

Postmortem Doyle reported that not all spirits reincarnate: "[W]hilst souls do continually return to the earth, there are still many who refrain.. . . ¶ If you could apprehend with the clairvoyant eye, you would be astounded to see radiating from the earth plane innumerable 'spirals' of colour and light, pulsing upward and onward. All these 'spirals' represent man's varying paths of progression. . . [E]veryone is not expected to advance along the same pathway."[487] Assante has found the same truth in her years of channeling spirits and using her mediumistic gifts.[488]

If we live many lives on earth, who is making the decisions regarding our next incarnation? While there is evidence that Masters or higher-level beings influence the date, time and manner of someone's death – e.g., people who experience NDEs are sometimes told they have a choice as to whether to return to their bodies, while others are "commanded" to return for certain reasons – the decision seems generally to be made by our own souls in conjunction with the higher beings or consciousness. That is, decisions are made before we are born, and our higher selves know at least the basic outlines of what we will face. In the words of postmortem Doyle, through his medium, it is in the 'waiting halls of heaven' where the soul "waits until the call comes or he accepts the order to descend, to take another dip into earth life."[489]

This scenario is further affirmed by Monroe through his OOBEs: The conscious mind is "a modulator of a master or driving force. Who is the master? Call it supermind, soul, greater self – the label isn't important. ¶ It is important to know that the conscious mind automatically responds to commands of the master without question. In the physical state, we seem only dimly aware of this. In the Second State, it is a natural occurrence. The supermind knows unquestionably what is 'right,' and problems result only when the conscious mind stubbornly refuses to recognize this superior knowledge."[490]

Edgar Cayce, in doing Life Readings of hundreds of people, also encountered the issue of pre-birth decisions. In the words of Noel Langley, "However sore the straits may be in which you find yourself, you put yourself there by your own previous indifferences to the laws [of cause and effect]. Whatever laws you broke, you broke of your own free will, the free will given you in the beginning by your Maker. You alone chose to be where you are at this moment."[491] For example, "The murderer who shed innocent blood in one life will balance the scale in another by symbolically shedding his own. More than one case of leukemia [in Cayce's Life Readings] was directly attributed to this reckoning."[492]

The issue of pre-birth decisions raises the issue of mass tragedies, a phenomenon described by Van Praagh as Group Karma: "people decide to die together [in a bombing, a plane crash, or a natural disaster] to burn off karmic debt. . . . [T]hese kinds of tragedies are all a part of our spiritual destiny on earth." Due to the suddenness of this type of death, "spirits may stay at the scene and wander around to try to figure out what happened to them." Some entities believe that they have not really died. "In tragedies of this proportion, individual souls usually need assistance and comfort to make the spiritual readjustment to the afterlife." When the spirits realize they have crossed over, spirit guides or deceased family members begin to assist them in the transition.[493]

Assante has a different but related perspective on this. Simultaneous deaths are completely bound up with choice, "for all causes of fatality." "If more than one person is involved, individual decisions combine to form agreements. . . For those who elect to die in group or mass events, altruism is often the reason, whereby forfeiting the body is believed to serve a greater good. Past lives also play a role, as do general life decisions made prior to conception."[494]

Generally speaking, there is a wide gap of earthly years between incarnations.[495] In some instances, however, there is a need for a quicker re-entry into physical form. Stevenson reported a case from the Tlingit Indian clan in Alaska whereby a man who died in 1946 was reincarnated 18 months later as his own great-nephew.[496] More recently, Theresa Caputo has uncovered examples of deceased young children coming back as a later child of the same parents, as shown in episodes of *Long Island Medium*. It is possible that many baby boomers were in their most recent earthly existence victims of the Holocaust,[497] and my own personal theory is that many innocent victims of murder today or young people who die tragically were sadistic soldiers or wartime leaders from World War II.

While the notions of reincarnation and pre-birth decisions can be extremely difficult and painful for some people to recognize, they can provide possible answers to the hard questions of life and can lead us on paths of growth and spiritual maturity. We live many lives on earth, we decide on these lives – in conjunction with higher wisdom – before we are born, and there are real consequences to our actions, both good and bad, as we live each life. We have often traveled in those lives with many of the same souls in order to work issues out and grow spiritually. Pre-birth decisions and reincarnation thus go hand-in-hand and matter a great deal to our present lives.

Suicide

As we can see, pre-birth decisions determine what happens to us in this lifetime. Does this also apply to people who take their own lives? While it seems possible that someone might make a pre-birth decision to commit suicide, the paranormal evidence is fairly consistent in maintaining that suicide is not usually a good choice. At the same time, many people who do take their own lives report from the other side that they are at peace and growing, that they remain in the presence of their loved ones, and that they realize they made a mistake. While Christian belief condemns suicide, maintaining that such souls are forever damned, and while Christian practice has often denied these persons a Christian burial, these stances are refuted by the paranormal evidence. Those who commit suicide, like all other souls who have departed this world, need love, compassion and understanding.

Van Praagh has learned through his spirit guides that "the 'problems' that cause this act [of suicide] are still very much a part of its mental and emotional mindset." Spirits often have a great sense of remorse for their action and experience depression. If such souls were mentally and/or emotionally ill in their earthly state, they need to receive compassion and understanding both from spirits on the other side and from loved ones in the physical world. Eventually, says Van Praagh, "these souls will become aware of their higher spiritual natures and will begin to seek a way out of their situations. . . . Above all, these spirits must learn how to forgive themselves."[498]

SIDEBAR: SUICIDE STORY FROM A MEDIUM

Michelle Belanger recounts an explicit, graphic encounter with the very angry spirit of a woman who, unknown to Belanger until later, had just killed herself in a hotel room. Working the late shift at the hotel, Belanger began to sense an angry and impatient presence; it was "having a very bad day." Soon there followed a flood of sensations and messages from the other side, leaving Belanger with a number of impressions: the spirit was that of a middle-aged woman, with a sense of weariness, and of short stature with dyed blond hair. Belanger also detected a slight southern accent.

Belanger sensed that the spirit was asking, angrily, "Why? Why am I still here?" Belanger realized she was dealing with a suicide, while at the same time the woman was beginning to realize that nothing had been resolved by taking her own life. Belanger began trying to counsel the woman, telling her she needed to make peace with her problems if she was going to move on. However, the spirit "was hearing none of it." For the rest of the night, the spirit interfered with Belanger's work at the desk, using her energy to attack the hotel's computer three times as Belanger tried to complete the nightly audit. Belanger reports that they "fought back and forth for most of the night." The ghost finally departed around 5:00 a.m.

When Belanger's manager arrived shortly thereafter to start his shift, Belanger was seething because of all the interruptions. When she finally calmed down, she shocked the manager by asking him, "So, when were you going to tell me about the chick who killed herself?" Guiltily, he asked who told her, since everyone had been sworn to secrecy. When Belanger revealed that the woman had "spent half the night up here making my life miserable," the manager paled and found the registration card. It showed that a woman from West Virginia had checked in, and he confirmed Belanger's impression that she was short and blond. As far as Belanger knew, the woman never returned in spirit to the hotel, and she hoped that the woman was finally able to move on.[499]

SIDEBAR: SUICIDE STORY FROM A PARANORMAL INVESTIGATION

Ryan Buell and his colleagues from the Paranormal Research Society experienced a suicide situation in an episode entitled "Requiem." As recounted in *Paranormal State*, the team traveled to Morris, Pennsylvania, to investigate incidents experienced by a college student, Kristy. Jim, the previous owner of the house in which she lived with her parents when not at college, had shot himself in the barn when he learned he had Alzheimer's disease. Kristy did not feel comfortable in the barn and had felt a "black hand" passing across her neck. Her mother had also heard a noise in the barn, "turned and saw a black blur, followed by what sounded like a gasp, or some sort of labored breathing." Buell reports that he too felt that there was something "uneven" and not quite right about the barn.

The team set up elaborate equipment in the house and barn to investigate over the course of two days. The case of Jim became intertwined with that of a young boy, Walter, who had died on the property years before at the age of 11. Chip Coffey and another medium, Patti, were brought in to assist with the investigation. Coffey was more in tune with Walter, who seemed to back away from him every time Coffey approached him mentally, but Patti was the one who had an experience seemingly related to Jim, although her knowledge of him was minimal. She was in a truck outdoors during Dead Time (early morning, usually around 3:00 a.m.) when a thunderstorm came up. She saw a man holding onto the trunk of a swaying tree and later accurately described Jim, as the team knew from photographs. She reported that she psychically sensed him saying, "I did a bad thing. I did a bad thing," suggesting that he felt guilty about having taken his own life.

Buell consulted with a neuroscientist about Alzheimer's and, hearing that someone with the disease might continue to worry about it after death, spoke to Jim during Dead Time and told him he could stop worrying about Alzheimer's on the other side.

During the second day on the case, Coffey announced that Jim was planning to appear in the barn and that Jim was telling him, "Just watch." Suddenly four of the team's cameras malfunctioned one after the other. "First it was Kristy's bedroom, then the kitchen area where Walter died, a second camera in Kristy's bedroom, then the barn." Buell further reports, "The cameras didn't simply go black. Each image dimmed, as if the camera were losing power. Everything got darker until the screen was suddenly tinted a bloody red. Then, it blacked out for half a second. Three to five seconds later the cameras all returned to normal." The team ruled out natural explanations and still has no idea how this might have occurred.

In order to honor Jim's remains, some of which were still buried on the property and unable to be recovered, Buell arranged for a memorial guard to perform a military service on Jim's behalf. The paranormal activity on the property stopped thereafter. Similarly, Buell gathered people around to pray for Walter's soul and deposited blessed medallions. Kristy then reported that she felt much better at the house and, although occasionally she feels Walter's spirit when she returns home from school, does not feel afraid.[500]

NDEs experienced by people who attempt suicide further affirm that attempting to take one's own life is generally a mistake and that the afterlife is a positive and hopeful "place." Such NDEers report a spiritual rebirth after their return to the physical world.[501]

Similarly, Anne Puryear recounts the tremendous sorrow and desperation her 15-year-old son Stephen experienced on the other side after he hanged himself. Stephen realized almost immediately that he did the wrong thing and tried desperately to get back into his physical body. He called out repeatedly to his loved ones and was sickened and hysterical that none could hear or respond to him. He was accompanied by a "sweet lady," an angelic being, who helped him understand what was happening to him. He asked her to guide him back to his body, which disgusted him in its messy hair and strange skin. Stephen reported to his mother through her trances and automatic writing, "I went over and tried to squeeze into my body, but I kept slipping out." He finally managed to move into his body, but it did not respond. He begged the lady to help him, but she said, "You can't stay in your body anymore. You will have to stay here with me." He argued and screamed to no avail until eventually he rested, and the spirits assisted him in moving on and dictating the book to his mother in order to help others avoid making the same mistake he did.[502]

Assante's experiences with departed souls are slightly different and demonstrate the myriad of nuances around suicide. The terminally ill, for instance, may choose assisted suicide; they "are generally well primed for the consequences and have little trouble on the other side." Someone who chooses to sacrifice his or her life on behalf of another, similarly, "dies in the exalted awareness of the fundamental oneness of humanity, a great advantage to anyone in passing over." In cultures such as ancient Rome and Japan, with the tradition of hara-kiri to preserve honor, suicides also do not experience a great deal of shame when they cross over, due to the communal support and approval.[503]

These stories demonstrate a number of truths in conjunction with our survival after death and the fact that our basic personalities survive. First, they confirm that spirits operate through energy, as evidenced through computer and other electronic interference; second, that spirits can and should be spoken to with love and/or firmness; third, that suicide does not always solve one's problems from the physical world; and finally, that our honoring the dead and praying for their souls are efficacious acts.

Jesus' Resurrection and Our Own

Christians in particular may be interested in what the paranormal literature has to say about the issue of Jesus' resurrection. Historical and theological scholarship on this issue is vast, as we have seen in Chapter 5, with theories ranging from literalism (Jesus really died, was buried, returned to earth in some recognizable form for a few weeks, then ascended in spirit to heaven) to an understanding that something remarkable (but ultimately explainable) happened to Jesus' earliest followers but we will never know exactly what.

Frank J. Tipler, in *The Physics of Immortality*, maintains that physics "will permit the resurrection to eternal life of everyone who has lived, is living, and will live." Outlining the Omega Point Theory, Tipler postulates that, as the universe is defined as "the totality of all that exists," so is God, and thus "definitely a God Who exists mainly at the end of time." Science, specifically physics, and religion come together logically and rationally in Tipler's theory. [504] About Jesus' resurrection, however, Tipler remains unconvinced, on exegetical grounds, that Jesus' body actually changed: "I conclude that similarities of Jesus' resurrection body with the resurrection body predicted by the Omega Point Theory is just a coincidence."[505]

In contrast, however, the White Eagle teachings associated with postmortem Doyle and the Life Readings of Edgar Cayce maintain that Jesus' resurrection was an actual event due to his advanced nature and his early education in Egypt and India. According to the White Eagle teachings, "Jesus raised his body from the dead; his life had been such that the very atoms of his body were spiritualized. In that state of purification of the physical form he vanished, when the time came, from the sight of his disciples. . . [T]his can be done by all who have attained to the required degree of initiation into spiritual life."[506] Cayce's readings show that Jesus' early training helped him hone physical, mental and spiritual skills that readied him for his ministry, his suffering and his death. Jesus was able to appear to the disciples, to be touched by them and to eat and drink with them after the crucifixion due to "regeneration, re-creation of the atoms and cells of the body."[507]

The ability to "defeat death" is supported by testimony from both Eastern and Western sources. People have been known to be buried alive, then adjust their breathing, pulse rates and other physiological functions and stay alive. There are examples, for instance, of Indian yogis existing "in a state of very deep and controlled meditation" for upwards of 30 years. In British Cameroon in 1932, an entire village, trying to avoid paying taxes, was found to be "asleep, with their vital functions suspended," in eight feet of water.[508] It therefore does not seem to be entirely out of the question that Jesus himself had these abilities and escaped death, at least for awhile.

Love: The Ultimate Purpose and Goal

As should be evident from our discussion, one of the basic, most consistent and most hopeful themes that emerges from the paranormal material is the primacy of Love. Even Monroe, whose reporting of his OOBEs tends to be more clinical and business-like than those of the psychics, mediums, scientific investigators, Cayce, Doyle, and those who have had NDEs, speaks of love:

Most important, you are not alone [in Locale II]. With you, beside you, interlocked in you are others. They do not have names, nor are you aware of them as shapes, but you know them and you are bonded to them with a great single knowledge. They are exactly like you, they are you, and like you, they are Home. You feel with them, like gentle waves of electricity passing between you, a completeness of love. . . You give and receive as an automatic action, with no deliberate effort. It is not something you need or that needs you. The 'reaching out' is gone. The interchange flows naturally. You are unaware of differences in sex, you yourself as a part of the whole are both male and female, positive and negative, electron and proton.[509]

Love pervades all of existence. Love is eternal and casts out fear. Love is God. Love is the ultimate destiny of all souls. In this afterlife of love, the soul cannot but be compelled and to desire to serve and grow.

In Chapter 7, we will show how the examination of paranormal evidence of all kinds is not only comforting as we seek to know the fate of our departed loved ones but also a vitally important tool in the healing of a hurting world.

Chapter 7: Ethics and Comfort

- *"The ultimate mission of all of the after-death communication activities is for people to grow in spiritual maturity... With that understanding of their eternal natures, they will change their outlook on life and their behavior."* – R. Craig Hogan
- *"... [W]hen a person crosses over, their first task on the Other Side is to reflect on the life they've led here and understand why they made the choices they did, see how their actions affected others, and realize what they still need to work on while on the Other Side."* – John Edward
- *"For many Christians Medjugorje awakened the almost forgotten conviction that God, Christ and the Virgin are real beings who are near us, converse with us and guide our lives at a personal and collective level."* – René Laurentin and Henri Joyeux
- *"There can be no drive or urge for the soul [against its will]".... [In life celestial] "There is a harmony, a divine music.... The soul finds a supreme joy in service, in self-giving."* – Arthur Conan Doyle postmortem

Building on Chapter 6, where we investigated traditional Jewish, Christian and Western themes that are both supported and challenged by the evidence gleaned from paranormal experiences and research, we can begin to draw important life lessons that inexorably link our current and past lives in the physical world with our lives on the other side. While this goal is nothing new to mystics and philosophers, the paranormal evidence provides more clarity on the nature of "heaven" and the "why's" of tragedy, suffering and hardship. The evidence supports in more tangible ways than mysticism, philosophy, or psychology what Christians mean by hope, the resurrection and eternal life, allowing us to deepen our faith that "all will be well" and providing us with additional tools and insights to bolster our life's journey.

Why Am I Here?

The paranormal evidence shows that all of us, as we approach adolescence and adulthood (if not before), should ponder this most basic of existential questions: "Why am I here – on earth, in this life?" The primary answer to the question is "to grow spiritually and return to our origins in Divine Love." This challenges not only each of us as individuals but also churches, other religious institutions and even our secular communities to be capable enablers of such searches and growth. Not only are there countless means at our disposal to grow spiritually – corporate worship, meditation, contemplative and centering prayer, retreat centers, spiritual direction and companionship, psychotherapy, psychoanalysis, centuries of religious and spiritual writings – but also a constant, though sometimes subtle, hunger among people of all ages and conditions for spiritual "food."

The paranormal evidence reminds us that it is our own karma that is being worked out every minute of every day. Whatever we ourselves can do to grow spiritually is a step in the right direction, and some of these steps might include finding ways to disseminate the wisdom of spiritual growth to those who may be the farthest from it in this life – violent criminals, prisoners, gang members, drug dealers, unethical business leaders, unscrupulous politicians, and those who are cruel to animals. Outreach that taps into the paranormal evidence might include the following:

- Because it is a locale of suffering, healing and often death, a hospital can train its staff about near-death experiences, the scientific evidence for the survival of the soul after death, the validity of psychics and mediums, and reincarnation. It can

then create literature and programs on these topics to offer to patients and their families and to the wider community. There should be no religious proselytism either toward staff or toward patients, but rather an offering of a different way of looking at life.
- Mental health professions such as psychology, counseling, pastoral counseling and social work – because these practitioners are often at the front lines of illness and suffering – can incorporate evidence from paranormal investigation into their curricula, teachings and practices. Counselors can in turn find ways to offer this information to their clients, as appropriate.
- Churches and other religious communities, as locales for spiritual nurture and growth, can support clergy who validate parishioners' paranormal experiences and present the paranormal evidence through sermons, literature, workshops, programs and retreats.
- A prison, a setting for those have committed horrendous acts, as well as for those who guard them, can make paranormal literature and information available to inmates and staff.
- Members of the law enforcement community can be more receptive to working with reputable mediums and psychics to solve crimes and find missing persons. Law enforcement can create a database to store the contact information of practitioners in their local community.
- A university or college, site of the acquisition of knowledge, could support scientific research on paranormal phenomena, in ways similar to the Universities of Virginia and Arizona and those in Europe, offering credit-bearing courses to

students as well as lectures, programs and workshops to the community.
- Grammar, middle and high schools, with their missions of teaching and nurturing our young, can make available to children and teenagers age-appropriate resources on the paranormal and related phenomena. As we have seen, young children are often much more aware than adults of unusual happenings, "ghosts," angels and visions of the deceased, and their experiences should be appropriately validated by the adults around them. Youth should also be warned about the dangers of "experimenting" with beings on the other side, since we are all potentially susceptible to spirits who do not necessarily want the best for us. Making legitimate materials available can also counteract the misleading and even dangerous information that youth are daily exposed to through the Internet and the media.
- Employers in all sectors in our capitalist society can train its top managers about NDEs, the scientific evidence for the survival of the soul after death, the validity of psychics and mediums, and reincarnation. The purpose would be to inform workers' ethical behavior, including ways in which the company or organization can best serve the wider community in which it thrives.
- A mayor, city council or town manager can partner with churches, synagogues, hospitals, schools, libraries and companies to present programs and workshops to the public about the evidence in order to reach the public.
- Journalists, the media, Wikipedia authors and editors, and others who have far-reaching influence via the written word can work to ensure that their powerful words are beneficial,

positive and fact-based, not biased, harsh or vicious. The search for truth and the uncovering of fraud can be done without personal attacks on well-meaning people or skewed, deceptive attacks on paranormal phenomena.
- A town library could ensure that books and materials – including online materials – that deal positively with the paranormal are available.

The main point of these initiatives would not be to "convert" people to a particular brand of religion or way of behaving but rather to provide the information to the general public as a service, much like public health information is now widely available. The efforts to make available these materials serve several purposes: they plant seeds that can be enormously helpful to individuals as they ponder the question "Why am I here?"; they are potentially very beneficial to society; they provide a corrective to the oftentimes limited materialistic Post-Enlightenment mindset in which we live; and they positively impact the karma of those making the efforts.

Obviously many people in our society will continue to ignore the "why am I here" question or decide that they live to exploit others, become wealthy, enjoy life's pleasures, or accumulate material goods. The paranormal evidence is overwhelming that such souls may not readily adjust to the heavenly realms when they cross over and will almost certainly need to keep returning to earth in different incarnations until they purge themselves of their materialistic thoughts, words and actions. Those of us who may be exploited or injured by such people, by the same token, are also being tested or are learning lessons – probably due to the nature of our own past lives – and thus need to understand how best, for our own karma, to respond to the negative treatment.

This Side and That Side

As we have seen, there is ample evidence for clear and constructive communication between those of us on this, the physical, side of existence and those on the other side. There are ways in which spirits can help us and ways in which we can assist souls in their journeys in spirit.

Spirits help us already in many ways; it is just for us to be more fully aware of their assistance.[510] Beings on the other side aid us through our intuitions and brainstorms as well as through our dreams. Guardian angels save us from mishaps and injury, and plant helpful ideas in our minds. We can cultivate ways to tap into these interventions.

Spirit circles have formed all over the world to provide comfort and support to those who have lost loved ones; spirits assist psychics and mediums in helping their clients know why someone has left this world suddenly, tragically and seemingly without purpose; and spirit guides have bridged many gaps between deceased souls and loved ones, whether through channeling, automatic writing, EVPs, dreams, or other means.

As we have seen in Chapter 4, specific kinds of spirit circles or groups of experts and professionals have joined with groups and individuals on earth to communicate at certain times for particular purposes. While in the physical world, Doyle encountered this phenomenon through experiences with his "Home Circle." He recounts a female spirit conversing with him about her life on the other side – her work, her living situation, the general joyous and productive atmosphere. At one point she reports, "I am one of those who are working for the cause [of Spiritualism] on this side hand-and-glove with you."[511]

Doyle also relates information from "The Case of Lester Coltman," a young scientist who began to communicate from the other side shortly after he crossed over. Coltman reported that he was working in a laboratory that was "primarily concerned with the study of the vapours and fluids forming the barrier which, we feel, by dint of profound study and experiment we may be able to pierce," leading the way to communication between earth and "heaven." Coltman explained that "many good souls working in my laboratory" lived a short distance away and were directed by a "dear old Chinaman," Coltman's assistant.[512]

Support for people grieving the loss of a loved one can be found, for instance, in the Big Circle of the Association TransCommunication. The Big Circle, a worldwide group recording session, consists of persons who have lost someone dear to them and who gather their energies together every other Thursday evening to connect with spirits on the other side. The group came about at the impetus of those in the spirit world. The sessions generally start with a brief meditation to focus attention on the spirit one wishes to contact, followed by the participants recording for approximately five minutes. As we have seen, energy is the key: when positive energies are combined for a singular purpose, the communication between this side and the other side is made more possible. The Association site features a number of articles describing participants' connecting with their loved ones in spirit.[513]

Even before the death by suicide of her teenage son Stephen, author Anne Puryear was in communication with three spirit guides. She learned over time, through trial and error, how to receive vital and trustworthy guidance from these beings on the other side. After Stephen's death, the guides provided her with answers and comfort about Stephen's life on the other side – that he was working on how to communicate better with Anne and that he was reviewing his earthly life. When Anne asked her guides why they did not warn her that Stephen was about to take his own life, the guides affirmed that they had tried to do this but that Anne was undergoing too much stress in her life and not recording her dreams, so they were not able to get through.[514] As we have seen in our study, these types of communications are witnessed by many psychic practitioners, NDEers, and current and past researchers.

The postmortem testimony of Doyle and other sources provide evidence for the great potential for spirits to aid in physical healing of disease and conditions. Among the many pieces of wisdom that Doyle communicated through his medium in the 1930s was information and advice on the treatment of disease. Doyle maintained that all disease was linked to the lack of harmony between the physical and the psychic body. Some conditions can and should be treated in traditional ways, with drugs, herbs and other current therapies, while others should be dealt with more spiritually. Doyle asserted that "all life – all human life – can be divided into rays of certain vibration." This vibration is expressed by color, so the health care provider should determine "the ray/colour to which his patient vibrates." In this way, the provider can see where the weaknesses are in the patient and thus how to treat him or her. Doyle, through his medium, declared that all diseases are ultimately curable.[515]

Using this model, then, the health care provider should be in touch and in sync with the theories of rays, colors, and vibrations and with psychic and spiritual truths. These observations from the 1930s parallel those of mediums, psychics and others more recently, such as Maureen Hancock and Reiki practitioners, who use their psychic gifts in healing therapies. As many traditional religions teach, the body is a vessel for the spirit and should be treated with care. Even though the physical body will eventually decay or be destroyed, our lives in them remain vitally important.

Finally, we have seen through the range of paranormal evidence how thought is the prevailing means of communication on the other side. This concept addresses skeptics' and deniers' criticisms about why in some cases people who have had an NDE, or those who are reached through mediums, are vague about how they learned something: the entities in spirit do not "speak" through "language," and our normal senses of sight and hearing are not used; rather, communication takes place as thought, telepathy or thought transference.[516] A fairly good analogy would be what we experience many nights in our dreams.

Mediums such as Caputo, Hancock and Renier call upon positive spirits in prayer or by invocation before they conduct readings. As Van Praagh, the renowned medium, says, prayer is a form of thought and "one of the greatest tools we possess. Through prayer, we can transcend the physical by connecting our minds to our hearts. We direct our thoughts and desires to the one force, the one source that is all of life. . . The optimum way to pray is selflessly. Praying for others . . . directs energy away from the egocentric self and redirects this energy to others. In giving to others, we truly give to ourselves."[517] Van Praagh's wisdom echoes millennia of mystics and sages, in both East and West, who have long said much the same thing.

Paranormal investigators as well often recite prayers to mitigate damage, injury and negativity from "stuck" spirits and demonic forces in haunted locations (regardless of who or what demons may be or where they might originate), and of course exorcisms are conducted almost exclusively by prayers and rituals.

Prayers for the deceased, then, are never wasted, and much of the evidence, especially from psychics and mediums, demonstrates that our loved ones on the other side know about and greatly appreciate benevolent actions, words and memorials that are carried out in their memory. Prayers for the "faithful departed," as practiced in Christianity, generally have as their purpose to aid Christian souls, and a Roman Catholic belief is that souls need assistance in escaping

Purgatory.[518] However, we have seen that the concept of Purgatory is not quite legitimate for many deceased: most souls appear to experience great joy and peace on the other side, even as they learn what they still might need to accomplish in their spiritual journey.[519]

Some religious communities have as part of their mission to pray not only for needy individuals but also "for all the souls in the world." This is the case with the Cistercian order of St. Joseph's Abbey in Spencer, Massachusetts. The monks "pray for the dead all the time: at the end of every office, at the end of every meal, and during mass." These monks believe "that unless we all go to heaven, no one will."[520]

Whether or not a religious community believes explicitly that souls go to hell or Purgatory, it might consider putting in place something similar to what the monks of St. Joseph's do: find ways to pray collectively and generically, perhaps in special liturgies, for the souls of those who are "stuck" in lower planes in the afterlife or who have committed evil acts on earth, for the purpose of helping them on their spiritual journey. It is certainly not harmful for individuals to pray for such souls.

Interestingly, spirits on the other side are also helped by our explorations of their "world" and what they "do" after they have left the physical world. "Some [spirits] have been waiting for decades to tell you of their undying love, to inspire, encourage, reassure, counsel, and warn. To assuage your grief and bring solace and comfort. To seek forgiveness or to forgive."[521] Our acts of reaching out to them, as well as our prayers, are far from harmful, superstitious or gullible: they enhance our lives and their journeys.

Fear and Hope: "All Will be Well"

As should be clear from our discussion, there is little reason for most of us, if we are generally good and well-meaning people, to fear death. Those who believe that everything goes – and stays – black and dark when we die may experience a sort of nothingness for a time, but the evidence consistently points to an experience of unfathomable love, peace, joy, acceptance, forgiveness – and the survival of our basic personalities. People who have been anxious that "heaven" might be boring – who bridle at the thought of playing the harp for all eternity – should not have any level of boredom on the other side. Those who are afraid of pain can be comforted by the countless reports of painless, and sometimes even joyful, transitions at bodily death. Those who are inconsolable over the death of a beloved pet or animals killed by evil persons or acts of nature should take great comfort from the evidence that animals too survive, and that pets reunite with their owners. Those who feel guilty over deeds they have committed against their fellow human beings will most likely need to confront these deeds, but the evidence shows that the Life Review is generally gentle, loving and forgiving.[522]

Once we are able to rid ourselves of the fear of death, many possibilities open to us to live our lives abundantly and lovingly. For one, we can come to a peaceful, abiding knowledge that what we do here is vitally important; even if our good efforts seem futile at times, they do have positive effects in our own spiritual development and in the universe. This should help us understand that focusing on our spiritual life and growth here, which often seems slow and plodding or even naïve and "anti-scientific," results in good karma and also a peaceful, joyful and purposeful journey on the other side. We can further abide in the assurance that this life, although often quite wretched and in some instances way too short, is not all there is and that, in fact, we have chosen this life to help us grow spiritually. The wretched and painful things, in fact, are part of our growth.

If this sounds familiar from traditional religious training, the best of parenting, the best of citizenship, and the best of therapy, that is not surprising. The paranormal evidence does not presume to offer a different ethic or way of life. Rather, it confirms Doyle's assertion that belief systems and ways of life, such as Spiritualism, which assert the existence of the soul and the afterlife, are completely compatible with the best of all religions, and that they are highly logical and rational. "Spiritualism makes a universal appeal. There is only one school of thought to which it is absolutely irreconcilable . . . materialism."[523] Doyle's statement is confirmed, 100 years later, by today's testimonies – NDEs, psychics and mediums, dreams, after-death communications – all of which point in the direction of a spiritual life and spiritual growth.

Word to the Wise

While it is probably clear that I disagree with many of the comments made by deniers of paranormal phenomena and skeptics who doubt the survival of the soul after death, it is not my place to condemn them outright. There is much to be said for being skeptical, and many of the deniers do view themselves as skeptics – they have not yet encountered the definitive proof they need that would convince them that there is more to existence than this current life. As someone trained in New Testament studies and early church history, I routinely question established precepts and traditional authority. Similarly in politics and with social justice issues: debate is normal and essential, and there are few definitive, once-for-all answers. We are incredibly fortunate in the United States to live in a nation that values and upholds free speech, and with the dawn of the Internet and other "democratizing" media, millions of people can exercise their free speech rights to express skepticism of anything they want.

For myself, I try to keep an open mind, about nearly everything. For several decades, I only sporadically thought about reincarnation after I devoured in my 20s almost a dozen Edgar Cayce books that have reincarnation as their foundation. Christianity does not officially support reincarnation, and it is not a particularly common topic for casual conversation, but it has long simmered in the back of my mind. Now, however, I can view it in an entirely different light, with many more sources of information to inform my thinking. There is probably much for me to learn about reincarnation, so I still keep my mind open, but for now I am a firm believer in it, in the ways I have outlined.

Consciousness studies, quantum mechanics and other scientific areas are bolstering paranormal evidence on many fronts (whether those researchers always intend to or not).[524] The evidence we have been examining strongly suggests something important when it comes to science, the paranormal, the afterlife, death and so on. That is, what we in the physical world currently see (or dismiss) as being "beyond the veil" or non-existent, depending on one's stance, will one day be known as part and parcel of scientific and natural understandings. Two hundred years ago the human race did not know about electricity or germs, but they were there in nature (and one can postulate that spirits on the other side probably did know about them). We human beings needed to advance sufficiently before we had the intellectual capacity and tools to comprehend the physical, natural principles of electricity and microbiology. Our sophisticated scientists in some fields today (and some of us non-scientists intelligent enough to understand the concepts) can grasp even more advanced physical and natural concepts – such as consciousness and quantum mechanics – which have presumably "been there" all along. It thus seems to be only a matter of time (another ineffable concept!) before we in our physical selves will attain a point in our development where the physical and the spiritual "meet." I believe we are on our way in this direction – that mystics and people with psychic and mediumistic gifts, for instance, are already leading the way.

My main advice to strenuous deniers, therefore, especially those who harshly devalue and malign those of us who do take the evidence seriously and attempt to live ethical lives based, at least in part, on it, is to keep an open mind, to seek facts, and to acknowledge facts when they are revealed. I am unsure as to what critics' motivations are for their condemnations, so I cannot specifically address motivation, but I would merely say that keeping an open mind and compassionately contemplating the experiences of others might be beneficial to skeptics' own education, growth and possibly even happiness.

Some Possible Benefits to Grasping the Law of Cause and Effect
    I have come to the conclusion that two millennia of Christians, and Westerners who have inherited the basics of the Christian religion, have lost a great deal by disavowing reincarnation, karma and the law of cause and effect. The Emperor Justinian, the Empress Theodora, and the church officials who supported them in their war against reincarnation did the world a great disservice. Many of our problems in the West can be traced to our underlying materialistic belief that this physical world is all there is and that we only live one life on earth.
    It is this basic materialistic stance, it seems, that is at the basis of Mary Roach's hysterically funny and well-written, but basically skeptical, book *Spook*.[525] In a year of journalistic research, Roach explored many facets of paranormal investigation – NDEs, ectoplasm, EVPs, reincarnation, psychics – by interviewing luminaries in the field, traveling around the globe, exploring original documents, and looking back in history. She unearthed a large number of facts and tidbits but seemed almost completely bound by materialistic questions, maintaining among other things that "[d]ead people never to seem to address the obvious – the things you'd think they'd be bursting to talk about, and the things all of us not-yet-dead are madly

curious about. Such as: Hey, where are you now? What do you do all day?" Etc.[526] She takes issue with the fact that Doyle and physicist Sir Oliver Lodge both became converts to Spiritualism because they lost sons in World War I, and she has problems with answers that mediums sometimes receive from spirits on the other side.[527]

    As I hope is apparent from the evidence we have examined, the end-all and be-all of human existence cannot be found in material or physical concerns, even though they are important in many ways and part of the larger picture. Roach, like other skeptics and deniers, does not seem to understand that the landscape (as it were) changes to some extent on the other side – and thus so do the priorities of most entities. The question of "where they are" has been addressed fairly clearly in our examination: spirits are here with us, only in another "dimension," in another form. What they "do" all day is a rather moot question: time is different on the other side, first of all, and "doing," "being" and "thinking" all overlap. As we have seen time and again, mediums receive seemingly mundane bits of information for their sitters precisely so that the sitter knows that it is the spirit of their loved one – and only that personality – coming through, and that the medium's knowledge cannot come from any other source (ESP, the Internet, and so on). The fact that people who lose loved ones become attracted to the paranormal, Spiritualism and spiritual issues should not be viewed suspiciously, or that somehow the grieving one is being "duped" by an irrational belief system, but rather that we sense that our love for the deceased did not die with our loved one and we are compelled to stay in touch with that love.[528]

    In dealing with issues of the afterlife and the paranormal, then, we must turn our attention away from our normal physical existence and toward the spiritual dimension. The spiritual includes the larger, more universal perspective on fairness and justice – that of karma, reincarnation, and the law of cause and effect. If we enlarge our perspective and begin thinking in terms of the law of cause and effect – the universal supposition that this life is only one of many, that we reap what we sow, and that we must resolve our problems either here or in another incarnation on earth – we can begin to imagine very different scenarios in our collective and personal lives.

- If we acknowledged reincarnation, we would know why a place immediately seemed very familiar to us and why we felt that we knew a new acquaintance our whole lives. We *have* known that person – that soul – and been in relation with him or her before.
- If we lived our lives under the law of karma, we would be much less apt to cheat, defraud or harm a neighbor or colleague, knowing that our unsavory actions will have to be repaid.
- If we acknowledged reincarnation, we would know that we must live by our finer instincts rather than stoop to greed, self-aggrandizement and rampant materialism; we would know that these goals will almost certainly need to be confronted in another incarnation on earth. We would, alternatively, realize that pursuit of spiritual growth is not just for rabbis, imams, monks, nuns, clergy and other religious "professionals" but for each of us.
- A life under the law of cause and effect would help us move more quickly through the grief of separation and loss. We would know that physical death is only one stage in our endless spiritual pilgrimage and that we will meet our loved ones again – and again – throughout eternity.
- If we acknowledged reincarnation, we would understand the "why" of tragedy: the death of a supposed innocent in this world is most likely the playing-out of a karmic debt, and the

death of a group of people in the same cataclysmic event is almost certainly an example of group karma – they have made a pre-birth decision, for whatever reason, to cross over together. Disease is not always a result of actions in a previous lifetime, but many occurrences of disease and serious, chronic illness may be.

- If we lived by the certitude of karma, we would take comfort in the fact that our good, positive words and deeds, no matter how seemingly insignificant, worthless or repaid with evil, are never lost or useless. No good is wasted under the law of cause and effect.
- If we realized the truth of reincarnation, we would understand that it is not luck or fate that matches or pairs us with someone as a life partner: it is planned, and for a reason.
- If we acknowledged the truth of reincarnation, we might be better able to deal with the pain of not attaining a certain dream in this life, such as being married or having children. We would know that we most likely had had these experiences in previous lives, that we might be able to access them through therapy or regression, and that there are reasons for our current state of affairs.

In short, if religious communities and even our wider culture began acknowledging the truth of reincarnation and its corollary, karma, we might well see an enhancement of our society's ability to meet more people's deep emotional, psychological and spiritual needs. But we will never know if we do not try.

Love and Service

As we draw our investigation to a close, let us return to one of the roots of Western culture, the life and teachings of the Jew Paul who launched, for better or worse, what came to be known as Christianity.[529]

One of the most powerful passages in the New Testament is 1 Corinthians 12:4-12, St. Paul's discussion of spiritual gifts – what each person contributes to the good of his or her community:

> Now there are diversities of gifts, but the same Spirit. And there are differences of administrations, but the same Lord. And there are diversities of operations, but it is the same which worketh all in all. But the manifestation of the Spirit is given to every [human being] to profit withal. For to one is given by the Spirit the word of wisdom; to another the word of knowledge by the same Spirit; to another faith by the same Spirit; to another the gifts or healing by the same Spirit; to another the working of miracles; to another prophecy; to another discerning of spirits; to another divers kinds of tongues; to another the interpretation of tongues; but all these worketh that one and the selfsame Spirit, dividing to every [human being] severally as he will. For as the body is one, and hath many members, and all the members of that one body, being many, are one body: so also is Christ.[530]

St. Paul, writing to the nascent Christ-centered gathering of Jews in Corinth in the first century, was saying that there are a myriad of ways to serve the community. For the community itself to be whole and unified, all gifts must be contributed and used. We can extrapolate to our own situation today, not only referring to Christians and the church but also to any community in which we find ourselves – town, workplace, nation, world: if we want that community to function well, on behalf of all its members, we must each offer and use whatever our gifts and talents we may possess. As we have seen through the paranormal evidence, each of us brings to our lives not only these different talents and strengths but also weaknesses and shortcomings that we must work out and work on in order to grow spiritually. Using our gifts, talents and strengths in the service of our communities is what we are called to do in our lives on earth – for others and for our own karma.

Another of St. Paul's powerful passages, also in 1 Corinthians, is often heard at Christian weddings, those primary social and religious rituals celebrating love. It too is worth quoting at some length:

If I speak in the tongues of men and of angels, but have not love, I am a noisy gong or a clanging cymbal. And if I have prophetic powers, and understand all mysteries and all knowledge, and if I have all faith, so as to remove mountains, but have not love, I am nothing. If I give away all I have, and if I deliver my body to be burned, but have not love, I gain nothing. Love is patient and kind; love is not jealous or boastful; it is not arrogant or rude. Love does not insist on its own way; it is not irritable or resentful; it does not rejoice at wrong, but rejoices in the right. Love bears all things, believes all things, hopes all things, endures all things. Love never ends; as for prophecy, it will pass away; as for tongues, they will cease; as for knowledge, it will pass away. For our knowledge is imperfect and our prophecy is imperfect; but when the perfect comes, the imperfect will pass away. When I was a child, I spoke like a child, I thought like a child, I reasoned like a child; when I became a man, I gave up childish ways. For now we see in a mirror dimly, but then face to face. Now I know in part; then I shall understand fully, even as I have been fully understood. So faith, hope, love abide, these three; but the greatest of these is love.[531]

Here Paul moves beyond the gifts he spoke of earlier, not negating the gifts and our service to community but rather moving to the ultimate: everything in existence revolves around love. Love is the end-all and be-all, love is eternal, love does not die, love is at the base of all gifts.

Of course, love – romantic, filial, "brotherly" – is not the sole possession of Christianity; it is the subject of sages worldwide throughout the ages, an abiding universal truth, transcending all races, nationalities, religions and social systems. The social and hard sciences might try to "explain" love through hormones, evolutionary survival, childrearing, chemistry, and other means – and these are not entirely incorrect – but most human beings know instinctively that love is much more than biology and psychology.

The paranormal literature attests to the truth of love's eternal and essential nature at every turn. The energy experienced by NDEers and OOBEers is that of an abiding love that pervades all things; these people emerge from their experiences with the fruits of love described by Paul – patience, kindness, joy, hope. Those who try to find words to describe the "God" or Being they encounter through an NDE or OOBE use the concept of love. The visionaries of Medjugorje were permeated with love in the person of the Virgin Mary. Psychics and mediums bring messages of love, joy, peace and forgiveness from spirits of the deceased to those they have left behind on earth. Evidence from EVPs and ITCs do the same. The testimonies of the postmortem Arthur Conan Doyle and young Stephen, Anne Puryear's son, assure us repeatedly that love is the nature of the afterlife, of "heaven."

Those of us around the world who live lives full of love and opportunities for service do not necessarily need to know intellectually about the nature of the afterlife, the reality of reincarnation, or the law of cause and effect. Obviously many saints and martyrs throughout human existence have lived their lives without such knowledge; they have certainly tapped into this wisdom from other perspectives. However, a conscious, persistent recognition of the truths of the paranormal evidence, the survival of the individual soul after death, the nature of heaven, the law of cause and effect, and reincarnation provides the modern, Post-Enlightenment, Western mind with more than mere faith; the paranormal evidence from the legitimate, rational sources we have examined gives us the kinds of information and solace we need to live our lives fully and without fear in this world, at this time in human history, no matter where we are in our life journey.

This is not to say that our lives are easy; in fact, the evidence shows that life in a material, physical body is very challenging for most of us. But an understanding of the complete interconnectedness of this world and the next, in the comforting context of love, gives us a more concrete base from which to deal with these challenges. We can thus go far beyond standard religious and philosophical explanations for life's difficulties than just "your suffering is God's will" or other harmful platitudes.

My hope for the reader is that you will more fully explore on your own the many paranormal and related resources that are now available. Most of us desire assurance that our lives will continue after we "cross over" and that we will meet deceased loved ones again on the other side. If we also use this comfort in conjunction with the exploration of spiritual growth on this side, the use of our individual gifts to serve our communities, and the realization of the eternal nature of love, we will witness a wonderfully transformed self and society. In the words of Tom and Lisa Butler, "there is no death and there are no dead." This is an extraordinary promise to us all.

Appendix I: Short Biographies of Nineteenth-Century Paranormal Researchers and Renowned Supporters

Barrett, William Fletcher (1844-1925). British physicist and parapsychologist; experimented with mesmerism and thought transference. Born in Jamaica and educated in England, Barrett studied chemistry and physics and, in 1873, became Professor of Experimental Physics at the Royal College of Science for Ireland. Among other things, he discovered Stalloy (Permaloy), "a silicon-iron alloy used in electrical engineering."[532]

Barrett became interested in the paranormal in the 1860s and began investigating poltergeists and thought transference in the 1870s.[533] He used the same exacting tests that he was trained to use in his other experiments, including taking constant measures to prevent cheating.[534] His research led to publications in the prestigious journal *Nature*, his involvement with Spiritualism, and his co-founding of SPR with Henry Sidgwick (see below) in 1882. He then helped found the ASPR in 1884, thanks to an invitation by William James (see below),[535] and was its president in 1904. His publications on the paranormal included *On the threshold of a new world of thought: an examination of the phenomena of spiritualism* in 1908; *Psychical Research* in 1911; *Deathbed Visions* in 1926; and *On the threshold of the unseen* in 1917.[536]

Despite encountering fraud in some of his explorations,[537] he encouraged his fellow scientists to continue to investigate paranormal phenomena. He repeated "throughout his long career" that "sooner or later psychical research will demonstrate to the educated world, not only the existence of a soul in man, but also the existence of a soul in Nature."[538]

Clemens, Samuel/Mark Twain (1835-1910). American writer (*Tom Sawyer* and *Huckleberry Finn*). While Clemens is not a paranormal investigator per se, his involvement with the Societies and the other researchers, and his belief in the afterlife, justify including him here.

Clemens had been haunted for 24 years by a horrifying dream that he had had three days before his brother Henry's death. In the dream, Clemens had a terrifying vision of Henry in a casket that was balanced across two chairs; white roses and a single red rose were lying on Henry's chest. It was 1858, and Samuel and Henry were working on a paddle-wheeler on the Mississippi River as riverboat captain trainees. Samuel was at his sister's house the night of the dream, while Henry stayed on the ship, the *Pennsylvania*. The morning after the dream began as normal, when Samuel re-joined Henry on the ship, but they were again separated when Samuel was reassigned to a companion boat.[539]

Just as the *Pennsylvania* cruised south of Memphis three days later, with Samuel's boat a day behind, the boiler on the *Pennsylvania* exploded, killing or injuring 150 people. Samuel rushed to the scene where survivors, including Henry, were being treated in the local hospital. Henry died that night with Samuel at his side. The next morning, "Sam walked numbly down to a room where the bodies of the dead were awaiting burial. Henry lay in a metal casket, balanced across two chairs. ¶ As Sam Clemens stood, blinking against the memory of his dream, a volunteer nurse stepped up to the coffin and gently laid across it a bouquet of white roses with a single red bloom in their midst."[540]

Clemens, famous following the publication of *Tom Sawyer*, was drawn to the work of the SPR and joined when it first convened in 1882. In the December 1891 issue of *Harper's*, Clemens under the name of Mark Twain wrote to personally endorse the science of the supernatural, saying that the SPR "had accomplished what many said could not be done." He stated that the SPR researchers had freed people like himself to speak publicly on such subjects and noted that, earlier, his editor had discouraged him to do so, despite his fame. Twain focused his article specifically on telepathy (or "mental telegraphy") and cited a number of personal incidents that he felt were now supported by the work of SPR scientists. As might be expected, Twain's article met with controversy, and he was roundly criticized in a *Scribner's* article by Joseph Jastrow from the University of Wisconsin, who maintained that Twain's examples were mainly coincidences that could be explained away logically. Jastrow, along with Stanley Hall, a professor at Clark University in Massachusetts who had founded the *American Journal of Psychology*, hoped by their skepticism to dismantle ASPR.[541] They did not succeed, nor did they succeed in convincing Clemens/Twain that his perspective was wrong.

Crookes, William (1832-1919). British chemist and physicist; pioneer of vacuum tubes (Crookes tube, Crookes radiometer), and discoverer of thallium. Crookes, who was knighted in 1897, had a long and distinguished career in chemistry and physics. In addition to his many accomplishments, he also worked with plasmas, nuclear radioactivity, cathode rays, and helium.[542]

Drawn to Spiritualism in the 1860s, Crookes felt that "science had a duty to study preternatural phenomena associated with spiritualism." He studied a number of contemporary mediums, including Kate Fox, Florence Cook and D.D. Home, and witnessed their various abilities in the areas of rappings, levitation, and spirit writing. While roundly criticized by such skeptics as Harry Houdini, who felt that Crookes had been "hoodwinked," Crookes served as president of the SPR from 1896 to 1899[543] and became a member of other groups interested in the paranormal. Among his fellow believers in Spiritualism, until his death in 1919, were Alfred Russel Wallace and Oliver Lodge (see below). Crookes' experience was another in which his fellow scientists disparaged his work and made him go "underground" for a time.[544]

Gurney, Edmund (1847-1888). British psychologist; experimented with hypnotism and thought transference. As a young man, Gurney studied music, medicine, physics, chemistry, physiology and law. He "passed the second M.B. Cambridge examination in the science of the healing profession" in 1880, having become interested in psychical research by that time.[545] He came to William James' attention, and they became close friends. Drawn to the riveting account of Samuel Clemens' precognitive vision of his brother Henry's death (see above), Gurney and Frederic W.H. Myers (see below) began to view various paranormal phenomena as somehow related and worthy of investigation. To find evidence for "the ordinary occult," the SPR ran newspaper ads requesting readers' tales of paranormal encounters. Gurney was the one who handled the correspondence in late 1883, writing back to the informants to ask for confirmation, witnesses and documents. He estimated that he wrote approximately 1,600 letters in the space of two months, finding the stories compelling and authentic.[546] Gurney's work, and his collaboration with Myers and Frank Podmore, led to the publication in 1886 of the massive *Phantasms of the Living*, as discussed in Chapter 3.

Gurney also conducted experiments in hypnosis and telepathy, which led him and James to participate in a series of harsh letters to the editor of *Science* criticizing ASPR president Simon Newcomb.[547] Gurney's curiosity and drive also led him to investigate "hallucinations of the sane" or crisis apparitions, resulting in 5,705 answers to another survey question in 1874. Gurney's goal was to "eliminate statistical doubt" that a vision of a person who had died was due to chance or coincidence; he believed that he would need a sample ten times larger to establish this goal.[548]

Gurney was unfortunately duped by a fraudulent assistant in his telepathy research, which severely disillusioned him. He died of an overdose of chloroform in June 1888. While it was thought by some that he had committed suicide, his death was most likely an accident, since he had been prescribed chloroform for neuralgia.[549] In the early 1900s, female mediums in England and the US attested that they had received spirit messages from Gurney, as well as from Myers and Sidgwick (see below).[550]

Hodgson, Richard (1855-1905). Australian-born psychical researcher based in England; early member of SPR; exposed fraudulent mediums. Hodgson studied law but was more interested in poetry. It was his disciplined and consistent life that came to Henry Sidgwick's attention by the early 1880s. Judging Hodgson to be "a natural investigator," Sidgwick assigned him an ambitious SPR project: investigating the validity of Madame (Helena Petrovna) Blavatsky in Bombay, India.[551] Hodgson did so, thoroughly, and "concluded that her claims of psychic power were fraudulent."[552]

Hodgson was introduced to the medium Leonora Piper around 1886 and, at one point, being naturally cynical, outright accused Piper's spirit guide, Phinuit, of being a fake. Over the course of several more visits to Mrs. Piper, however, Hodgson received messages from Phinuit that stunned him. (See Chapter 3 for details.) Hodgson had Piper followed and thoroughly vetted by detectives and concluded that there was no evidence whatsoever that she was committing fraud.[553]

Hodgson then worked with Piper strenuously, carefully and systematically for several more years, publishing his findings in *Proceedings of the Society for Psychical Research* in June 1892.[554] His findings were somewhat inconclusive: while he felt that Piper's trance was genuine, her guide Phinuit was, in Hodgson's view, probably a "coping device, a subconscious way for the medium to protect herself against whatever mental battering took place in her trance state." Hodgson, along with William James, further felt at this time that the insights that resulted from Piper's trances were vague, ambiguous and pointless.[555]

However, Hodgson promised more results in the future, which was encouraging to those who believed.[556] When a close friend of his died and apparently started communicating with Hodgson through Piper, Hodgson concluded after many sittings that it was indeed his friend communicating from the other side. After Hodgson himself crossed over, he found it difficult at first to communicate but then did succeed and in fact participated in cross-correspondence exercises with Frederic Myers, Piper and several other female mediums. These stories are outlined in detail in Chapter 3.

Interestingly, the triviality of Piper's insights, which James and Hodgson initially criticized, can now be seen as having great value. As is the case with current reputable mediums, the mundane, trivial pieces of information that come through the medium to the client are the data that most convincingly show the client that his or her loved one is truly present: there is no way that such mundane observations could be discovered by research, detectives, or a Google search.[557]

Hyslop, James (1854-1920). American psychologist; professor of philosophy at several colleges between 1880 and 1891; professor of ethics and logic at Columbia University 1895-1902; secretary-treasurer of ASPR 1906-1920.[558] Hyslop met medium Leonora Piper around 1888, and it is this experience that sparked his interest in paranormal phenomena. He reported in a 1901 edition of the *Journal of the Society for Psychical Research* that he had received messages through Piper from his father, his deceased wife, and other family members. After Hodgson's death, Hyslop took the lead in examining Piper's gifts and revived the faltering ASPR.[559]

Hyslop's output on psychical research was significant – at least seven books between 1905 and 1919 (these in addition to textbooks on philosophy and ethics). He was firmly convinced of the existence of an afterlife, stating in *Life After Death* in 1918, "Any man who does not accept the existence of discarnate spirits and the proof of it is either ignorant or a moral coward."[560] He also became a convert to the Spiritualistic hypothesis.[561]

Like many other professionals who explored the afterlife and conducted paranormal research, Hyslop was roundly criticized by his colleagues, in part due to being misquoted by the press. At Columbia, Hyslop's own university, a faculty rival, James McKeen Cattell, "openly demanded that the university president order Hyslop to abandon his crusade" and may have asked the president to censor and fire Hyslop.[562]

Hyslop's longtime secretary and research assistant, Gertrude O. Tubby, seems to have had no doubt about his integrity or the truth of what he was discovering. She wrote *James H. Hyslop – X His Book* in 1929, her account of postmortem communications from Hyslop.[563]

James, William (1842-1910). American psychologist, philosopher, and leader of the pragmatist movement. James originally trained as a physician, graduating from Harvard Medical School in 1869, but his health was poor, so he could not practice. He was an instructor in physiology at Harvard from 1872 to 1876, after which he came to believe that psychology was a laboratory science, not a mental philosophy. Philosophy in turn "became an adventure in methodological invention and metaphysical discovery." He published his monumental work, *The Principles of Psychology*, in 1890, which was highly influential in the field.[564]

With that book completed, James turned his attention to the nature of God, the immortality of the soul, religious experience, and psychical research.[565] Blum's excellent book, *Ghost Hunters*, focuses on James and his work with paranormal investigation. As can be seen from his intersection with the other scientists and professionals described in this Appendix, James was a close colleague of many serious afterlife researchers.[566] In the popular mind today, it is assumed that James remained skeptical about many phenomena and believed that nothing could ultimately be proven, but other evidence supports more nuanced conclusions.

It was James who invited William Barrett to the US, begetting the ASPR;[567] it was James who had an initial positive and startling experience with Leonora Piper and then encouraged Hodgson to investigate her gifts.[568] James was a founder of the SPR and published praise for its work and the work of its principals in such publications as *Scribner's*. He lauded the *Proceedings of the SPR* as "a scientific journal [with] hard-headedness and never-sleeping suspicion of sources of error," and called the SPR's work "cautious, meticulous, and wonderfully puzzling."[569]

Toward the end of his life, James published an essay in *American Magazine* entitled "The Confidences of a Psychical Researcher." He stated that he had worked for 25 years with "some outstandingly good psychical researchers, conducting experiments, studying the literature, sitting with mediums both gifted and fraudulent." He accepted some of the phenomena as real but was also constantly baffled by them. He fretted over the sometimes dishonest and dishonorable demonstrations associated with spiritual investigation because they wasted time and prevented progress.[570] Overall, these conclusions mesh entirely with his pragmatism and common sense and are what would be expected of a man of James' character, stature and experience.

Lodge, Oliver (1851-1940). British physicist, inventor and writer; worked in the area of wireless telegraphy; Christian Spiritualist. Lodge received degrees from the University of London and became professor of physics and mathematics at University

College, Liverpool, in 1881. In 1900 he was appointed the first principal of newly-established Birmingham University, where he worked until his retirement in 1919. He received a number of honors throughout his career, including knighthood in 1902. He and his wife had 12 children, all of whom lived to adulthood.[571]

Lodge's scientific interests and accomplishments were widespread and his output significant, writing books on electromagnetic theory, ether, electricity, and relativity. His interest in the afterlife and communication with deceased spirits began in 1915 when one of his sons, Raymond, was killed in World War I. Lodge, like his friend Arthur Conan Doyle, became a Spiritualist. He visited mediums, especially Gladys Osborne Leonard, and became convinced, with his wife, that Raymond was communicating through Leonard. Similarly to much of the other evidence we have encountered, Lodge related that Raymond informed them "that people who had died were still the same people when they passed over;" Raymond also reported houses, trees and flowers in "heaven" and that there was no disease on the other side. *Raymond, or Life and Death*, which appeared in 1916, was the result of these readings, and it became controversial in part because Raymond also reported from the other side that soldiers who died in the war "had smoked cigars and received whisky in the spirit world."[572] As we know from other evidence, this type of occurrence is noted by others, even though it might strike us as far-fetched or odd; when people die suddenly or tragically, as Raymond did in battle, the evidence suggests that those souls are still on a plane close to earth and surrounded by familiar surroundings. Also, hauntings and other manifestations of spirits – such as odors and sounds – are often attested by reputable witnesses.[573]

Lodge joined with other investigators in examining Leonora Piper's skills, including hosting Piper and her children at his home in

Liverpool. When Piper arrived, he took extraordinary (and invasive) measures to ensure authenticity and prevent fraud. Several remarkable, inexplicable incidents took place involving a number of people. Lodge hired an investigator to check on some of the stories, and the investigator reported, "Mrs. Piper has certainly beaten me." There was no evidence of fraud.[574]

One of Lodge's lifelong stances was that science and religion were not mutually exclusive.[575] Lodge thus came to the view that Jesus' resurrection resulted from "Christ's etheric body becoming visible to his disciples after the Crucifixion."[576] This theory echoes findings from the Life Readings of Edgar Cayce and the postmortem evidence of Doyle.

Like many other respected scientists who were his contemporaries, Lodge was respected for his scientific achievements but criticized by skeptics and deniers in that same scientific community for his views on the afterlife and things spiritual. He was accused of misleading the public and of being duped. While he, along with others, may have been tricked at times by talented magicians claiming to be psychic,[577] his findings on the paranormal can indeed be supported by other investigators, perhaps even more today than in his own time.

Myers, Frederic William Henry (1843-1901). British poet, classicist, philologist, and "depth psychologist;" a founder of SPR and its president in 1900. With Frank Podmore and Edmund Gurney, he wrote the immense *Phantasms of the Living*.[578] While Myers was critical of religious viewpoints that dismissed the paranormal, he was even more critical of science, believing that it was "far too soon to declare questions of immortality and spirit off limits to rational men."[579]

Myers was involved with experiments on both Leonora Piper and Eusapia Palladino, which are described in Chapter 3 and below in the discussion of Richet. Myers was a great admirer of the medium the Rev. Stainton Moses, concluding in an obituary in the *Proceedings of the SPR* that "his life [was] one of the most noteworthy lives of our generation."[580] In October 1901, after Myers' death, E. Dawson Rogers, President of the London Spiritualist Alliance, lauded Myers and affirmed Myers' conviction "that the Spiritualistic hypothesis alone accounted for the phenomena he had himself witnessed."[581]

Perhaps the most remarkable occurrences involving Myers took place in the cross-correspondence events after his death, mentioned above in the discussion of Piper and in Chapter 3. According to Doyle, "It is at least a certainty that while he was on earth Myers had considered the project [of cross-correspondence] in a simpler form, namely, to get the same word or message through two mediums."[582] What actually transpired was much more complex and is summarized in Chapter 3.

Doyle considered Myers, along with Crookes, Lodge, Wallace, Barrett, James, Hyslop and Hodgson, to be "all in different degrees on the side of the angels"[583] when it came to supporting the precepts of Spiritualism.

Richet, Charles Robert (1850-1935). French physiologist; won the 1913 Nobel Prize for his work on anaphylaxis; president of SPR in 1905. Richet had wide-ranging interests and expertise, investigating neurochemistry, digestion, thermoregulation, aviation and breathing. He also wrote books in the areas of history, sociology, philosophy and psychology, as well as plays and poetry.[584]

Richet became interested in the Italian medium Eusapia Palladino around 1884, later conducting careful experiments on her with four researchers. In 1898, Richet wrote to Oliver Lodge with his opinion that Palladino did possess some kind of power, although it was erratic and uncontrollable. Frederic Myers agreed to meet up with Richet and Palladino in Paris to examine the medium. While Myers became convinced that Palladino was authentic – curtains in the room blew inexplicably, and cloud shapes appeared mysteriously then dissolved – Hodgson felt otherwise and wanted to list Palladino "amongst the ranks of tricksters" in the next edition of SPR's *Journal*. Henry Sidgwick, the journal's editor, made the two men compromise: Hodgson was not allowed to print any kind of list of mediums, and there would be no article supporting Palladino. Sidgwick based his decision on an earlier SPR determination that they would not have anything more to do with mediums who might be guilty of fraud.[585]

Richet published widely, for 30 years, in the areas of metaphysics, the sixth sense, mediums, ectoplasm, and related phenomena, having founded the *Annales des sciences psychiques* in 1891 and later joining SPR.[586] As noted in Chapter 3, it was Richet who coined the term "ectoplasm," and it was Richet who developed the theory of cryptethesia, whereby human beings have "an etheric body with many unknown gifts, among which a power of external manifestation in curious forms may be included." Doyle acknowledged that this theory had some merit, in that there seems to be a relationship between paranormal phenomena and the medium and that the medium may be tapping into the "outside intelligence" that gives rise to ectoplasm and other gifts. These theories are compatible with the basics of Spiritualism.[587]

Sidgwick, Henry (1838-1900). British philosopher and economist, and a founder and first president of SPR.[588] With his wife Nora (see below), he helped found Newnham College, for women only, in Cambridge in 1875 and devoted much of his energy to it and the promotion of equality for women. He was known as an excellent teacher and careful investigator in the field of political economy; he was highly influential in his work on utilitarianism and "adopted a position which may be described as ethical hedonism."[589]

In the area of psychical research, Sidgwick was not the investigator or observer that his wife Nora or his colleagues Myers and Gurney were, but he did have a knack for attracting good talent to the work, one of whom was Richard Hodgson.[590] Sidgwick was also a sympathetic listener and "became the SPR's chief diplomat, working to smooth its way to the next International Congress of Experimental Psychology" in August 1892. At the previous session of this group, as might be expected, some scientists were reluctant to have anything to do with psychical inquiry.[591] Sidgwick was able to convince organizers to allow Myers to present a paper on his work on "Experimental Induction of Hallucinations," which reported on automatic writing and visual and auditory hallucinations; he argued that hypnotism was the best way to attain repeatable results. Nora Sidgwick followed with a paper on hypnotism, citing the example of seven subjects who were able to predict results through automatic writing and other means that were not due to chance.[592]

Sidgwick, Eleanor (Nora) Mildred Balfour (1845-1936). Wife of Henry Sidgwick (1876-1900); a student at Newnham College, a women-only college that was part of Cambridge University, who served as its Vice-Principal and Principal; feminist educator; president of SPR in 1908 and one of its leading researchers.[593] At the founding of SPR, she was assigned by her husband to investigate ghosts, even though she did not believe in them.[594] Interestingly, in the 1880s Nora was a harsh critic of some of SPR's own work, specifically with mediums Kate Fox Jencken, Henry Slade and William Eglinton. She believed that there was trickery or fraud involved, which served to create a rift between SPR and some Spiritualists. Her opinions caused a storm of controversy that played out in the SPR's *Journal* and the journal *Light*.[595]

In 1892, despite her heavy responsibilities at Newnham College, Nora completed the Census of Hallucinations, a major project of SPR.

It calculated the odds of death-day apparitions of loved ones, using 17,000 reports from England (see Chapter 3 for details).[596] Nora also became involved in the cross-correspondence experiments with Frederic Myers after he crossed over (see Chapter 3) and finally became convinced that communication between the living and dead was possible.[597]

Wallace, Alfred Russel (1823-1913). British naturalist, explorer, geographer, anthropologist and biologist; published a paper with Charles Darwin on the theory of evolution through natural selection; advocate of Spiritualism. During his long life, Wallace won numerous awards in his many fields. As a social reformer, he opposed eugenics and colonialism, considered himself a socialist, supported women's suffrage, published papers arguing against militarism and the arms race, and critiqued environmental damaged caused by capitalism.[598]

In the area of paranormal research, Wallace was particularly drawn to hypnotism. Early in his career he used some of his students at the University of Leicester as experimental subjects and had some success, although, as might be expected, he met with criticism from the scientific establishment. He began work in Spiritualism in 1893 (perhaps having been attracted to it as early as 1865) and concluded that phenomena demonstrated at séances were most likely legitimate and connected to a natural reality. He was "convinced that at least some séance phenomena were genuine, no matter how many accusations of fraud sceptics made or how much evidence of trickery was produced."[599]

In 1875, Wallace published *On Miracles and Modern Spiritualism*, which was revised in 1901.[600] In the book, he reported on three spirit photography sessions in which he participated. In spirit photography, a popular manifestation of psychic phenomena in the post-Civil War era, a figure appears in the negative that is not a living subject in the photographic session. In all three of his sessions, to control for authenticity, Wallace chose his own position in the photography studio and witnessed all the plates being developed. He testified that an unmistakable image of his deceased mother came through in two of the three sittings.[601] In a session with a medium, Wallace had an experience with ectoplasm, which he described as a "white patch" that gradually formed into a "cloudy pillar."[602]

Wallace remains one of the many illustrious intellectuals of the nineteenth century to courageously conduct psychical research, adhere to Spiritualism, and suffer the professional consequences of his work.

Appendix II: The Apostles' Creed Analyzed from a Paranormal Perspective

A number of tenets of the Christian faith focus on some aspect of what moderns might consider otherworldly: the existence of God, the resurrection and ascension to heaven of Jesus the Christ, the concept of eternal life, and the notion of the Holy Spirit. The Lord's Prayer or "Our Father" is addressed to God, petitions to saints presuppose that saints still live in some ways and hear and respond to pleas for help, and visions of the Virgin Mary throughout the world affirm for believers her continuing life in another sphere.

The Apostles' Creed, which developed in the early church in the West and was first mentioned in documents around 390 CE, provides a succinct summary of the Christian faith. It is used by many Christian denominations at baptism and in the daily office[603] so can be considered a viable barometer of traditional Christian principles even today. Since Christianity has greatly influenced Western culture, for better or worse, an analysis of the Creed can assist us to see how these basic Christian and Western beliefs mesh or disagree with findings from the paranormal evidence.

> I believe in God, the Father almighty,
> creator of heaven and earth.
> I believe in Jesus Christ, God's only Son, our Lord,
> who was conceived by the Holy Spirit,
> born of the Virgin Mary,
> suffered under Pontius Pilate,
> was crucified, died, and was buried;
> he descended into hell.
> On the third day he rose again;
> he ascended into heaven,
> he is seated at the right hand of the Father,

> and he will come to judge the living and the dead.
> I believe in the Holy Spirit,
> the holy catholic Church,
> the communion of saints,
> the forgiveness of sins,
> the resurrection of the body,
> and the life everlasting. Amen.

I believe in God, the Father almighty

There is little in the paranormal evidence about a specific God-like figure. However, when entities speak or appear through EVPs, NDEs, OOBEs, and psychics and mediums, the sense of immense, overwhelming energy and love is sometimes described as or equated with "God." The divine presence, at most of the "levels" or "planes" of the other side for which we have testimony, is gender-neutral and permeated with joy, happiness, and bliss, and entities have a great desire to perform loving service. We can conclude that a traditional "Father Almighty" image is not widely supported by the paranormal evidence.

Creator of heaven and earth

If there is no Father Almighty per se, a discussion of the concept of creation is almost moot. The evidence from the other side points to an existence that has no beginning and no end and where the past, present and future all flow together.[604]

If we cannot point to a Creator but we can see earth all around us, can we even legitimately ask the question as to "who" created earth?

As for heaven, if most of us think of heaven as a locale of everlasting joy, bliss, love, and reunion with departed loved ones, the evidence shows that this is for the most part true. Those who have had NDEs, those who have heard from departed loved ones via mediums, visions or dreams, the reincarnation literature, the Life Readings of Edgar Cayce and the postmortem communications of Arthur Conan Doyle and the teenager Stephen all testify to the beauty and reality of "heaven." Other evidence points to the existence of different levels or planes of existence, some of them not very pleasant yet necessary for spiritual growth. Heaven appears to be a reality at death for almost all ordinary people, including many who commit suicide, and a consistent lesson seems to be that souls travel to the plane or place that they need to be.

The paranormal and afterlife literature suggests a vast, complex, generally wondrous existence of "worlds" that entail both what we can see with our physical eyes (the visible) and what we can or will be able to perceive with our supernatural "eyes" and other senses (the invisible). Some planes on the other side closely resemble earthly locations, while others are vastly more beautiful or significantly unappealing (yet familiar) or even extraterrestrial. Things "invisible" that have been "created" by "God," then, are real and can be accessed through dreams, mystical experiences, NDEs, OOBEs, and channeling through psychics and mediums.

I believe in Jesus Christ, God's only Son, our Lord

The figure of Jesus appears in some, though not all, experiences as described in the paranormal literature. Interestingly, many devout Christians who have had NDEs do not encounter Jesus himself, while others who may only have a passing interest or connection with Jesus in their earthly life have had experiences with him, some of which completely transform the rest of their earthly lives. Colton Burpo, for instance, "met" Jesus on the other side and affirmed pointedly that "Jesus really loves the children."[605] Burpo was raised in a fundamentalist Christian household so was familiar with Jesus at four years of age when he had his NDE.

The postmortem testimony of Doyle speaks on many occasions of the example and importance of Jesus the Christ, the Christ consciousness, and Jesus as the quintessential model for living. However, Doyle learned, once on the other side, that people should not *worship* Jesus the man so much as to strive for the Christ consciousness in our own lives.[606] Doyle further supplemented references to Jesus and Christ with appeals to the wisdom of other faith traditions such as Buddhism and Native American belief systems.[607] Specific belief in Jesus as found in more fundamentalist brands of Christianity is not, it appears, absolutely necessary for any kind of "salvation" but rather one important means of spiritual guidance and growth.[608] Even though Cayce was himself a fundamentalist in his "waking" state, his Life Readings while in trance decidedly contradict the judgmentalism that is often part of fundamentalist teachings: "The only God the sleeping Edgar Cayce knew was a loving God of infinite mercy, who has already forgiven us all."[609]

Who was conceived by the Holy Spirit

In Christian teachings, the Holy Spirit is the entity that came over Jesus' mother Mary to impregnate her (e.g., Matthew 1:18, 20), as well as what Jesus the Christ leaves to his followers as a comforter and advocate (Acts 1:8, 2:4).There is little in the paranormal literature about the Holy Spirit per se. If, however, we understand the Holy Spirit in terms of the overall nature of "the other side" as a "place" of Divine Love, the concepts of Jesus being conceived in that love and of the spiritual power that gives courage to believers resonate.

Born of the Virgin Mary

The Virgin Birth is one of the most difficult church doctrines for moderns to accept. We know that it is biologically impossible for human beings and other mammals to be conceived without both sperm and egg, although parthenogenesis has been shown to occur in other species.⁶¹⁰ What might be more palatable for us in the Post-Enlightenment age is recent scholarly evidence that the historical mother of Jesus, whether her name was Mary, Maria, Miriam, or something similar, was either raped by or had a relationship with a Roman soldier that resulted in the conception of Jesus.⁶¹¹ Later in the process of compiling the gospels and other literature in the first Christian centuries, when Greeks, Romans and other ancients realized that Jesus was significant and when the resurrection event had become important to early Christians, Jesus came to be viewed similarly to other divine beings – sons of gods, as it were. Jesus became equated with figures such as Alexander the Great, Augustus, Elijah and Moses, many of whom were viewed as part divine.⁶¹² In the ancient imagination, it was not, then, a significant leap to develop stories about Mary's holiness and special upbringing as well; apocryphal literature such as the *Protevangelium [Infancy Gospel] of James* presents elaborate stories of Mary's history as a pure, unblemished girl and woman who was worthy to bear a divine man.⁶¹³

Edgar Cayce conducted many Life Readings of clients that involved Jesus and Mary; the readings revealed that many of his clients had lived previous lives as Jesus' and Mary's contemporaries.⁶¹⁴ However Jesus was conceived biologically, he obviously had a real mother, and it is entirely within the realm of possibility that she was a good parent who instilled certain traits in Jesus the boy and laid a strong foundation for Jesus as a highly-evolved spiritual man.

Cayce's readings that attest to Mary's specialness and even holiness are supported by testimony from all over the world of her miraculous and beneficent presence in spirit. From Lourdes to Medjugorje, Mary's presence has been affirmed by thousands of witnesses, and she has often been associated with miracles. There are also testimonies from NDEers⁶¹⁵ and mystics, past and present, who have been touched, led and comforted by Mary, the quintessential female comforter, mother and even goddess.

Suffered under Pontius Pilate

This creedal statement may be one of the few that moderns can believe fully because it is supported by historical evidence. As far as can be determined from New Testament scholarship, Jesus suffered crucifixion in the Roman manner, and Pontius Pilate was the procurator (or governor) in Jerusalem at the time.[616] The primary paranormal evidence about Pontius Pilate comes from Cayce's readings. The readings parallel Luke's account that Jesus was condemned for not paying tribute to Caesar. They also affirm that Pilate's wife was well aware of Jesus and his activities and that her warning Pilate not to take Jesus' life, as recorded in Matthew 27:19, was accurate.[617]

Was crucified, died, and was buried

While there is some possibility, as per Michael Baigent et al in *Holy Blood, Holy Grail*,[618] and in Barbara Thiering, *Jesus and the Riddle of the Dead Sea Scrolls*,[619] that Jesus' crucifixion was fraudulent and that Jesus survived, the paranormal literature – especially postmortem Doyle and Cayce – asserts that Jesus did truly die in the gruesome manner of capital punishment that was Roman crucifixion. Interestingly, however, Cayce's readings also maintain that Jesus' reincarnated entity had borne the figurative cross "in each and every experience" on earth.[620]

Further, the New Testament Gospels of Matthew, Mark, Luke and John, as well as some non-canonical writings, relate the story of Jesus' burial in a tomb, also suggesting that he did truly die. Scholarship is vast on the subject of Jesus' passion and death, and there is archaeological evidence for crucifixion in the Roman Empire.[621]

He descended into hell

A number of sources in the paranormal literature, as mentioned above, testify to the existence of many layers or planes of growth on the other side, even though hell per se is neither eternal nor the fate of most souls. Ivan Cooke, in the volume relating Doyle's postmortem testimonies, offers a selection of teachings of White Eagle, who explained that Jesus did visit some of the lower planes: "Every soul must pass through such a condition, such a period of time, short or long, according to the mental condition of the man [sic] when he leaves his body. To some this is a matter of a few hours or days; to others of years. Remember, even the Master Jesus himself descended into a condition of uncertainty and what is described as 'Hades', the sphere of the disquieted spirits. So, too, must every man on leaving the earth pass through that belt of the disquieted souls of men."[622]

On the third day he rose again

Two points are important in this phrase of the Creed: the timing ("on the third day") and the action ("he rose again"). As we have seen, time is very different on the other side, so "three days" in physical terms are not necessarily three days in the spirit world. New Testament scholars, furthermore, point out that the reference to three days could well be symbolic or metaphorical. Three is a significant number not only in the Christian tradition – the Trinity, for instance (Father, Son, Holy Spirit) – but in other traditions as well. The moon's phases constitute one ancient example of a trinity – waning, waxing and full – as do the three stages of the archetypal woman's life – maiden, mother, crone.[623] In the Transfiguration story (Matthew 17, Mark 9, Luke 9), Jesus is joined by Moses and Elijah (note that Cayce asserts that Jesus is a reincarnation of both Moses and Elijah, as well as Adam, Enoch, Melchizedek, Joseph and Joshua);[624] it is three kings who visit the infant Jesus (Matthew 2); and Jesus is crucified between two men, one on each side (Matthew 27:38, Mark 15:27, Luke 23:32,

John 19:18). Therefore, "three days" can legitimately be viewed as symbolic or metaphorical in the ancient context.

While we in our science-based world tend to dismiss the notion of Jesus rising from the dead during any time frame, the White Eagle teachings related to Doyle's postmortem testimony assert that Jesus being raised from the dead not only factually took place but that similar abilities are possible for the rest of us as well: "Jesus raised his body from the dead; his life had been such that the very atoms of his body were spiritualized. In that state of purification of the physical form he vanished, when the time came, from the sight of his disciples. . . [T]his can be done by all who have attained to the required degree of initiation into spiritual life."[625]

Cayce's readings as well show that Jesus walked among his friends and others for 40 days, as recorded in the Gospels; "40 days" can also be understood symbolically as "a long time." Jesus was able to eat with his friends and be touched by them after a time because he manifested "regeneration, re-creation of the atoms and cells of the body that might, through desire, masticate material things." Jesus was able to do this because of his complete oneness with Ultimate Reality (God, Divine Love).[626]

He ascended into heaven

The paranormal literature attests strongly and consistently to the existence of "heaven" or heavens in the spiritual realm, as we have seen. As a highly-evolved spiritual being who could change the very atoms in his body, Jesus then would have been able to cross over to the other side somewhat at will. According to the Cayce readings, the Ascension event as recorded in Acts 1:9 approaches the recounting of a real event, witnessed by approximately 500 persons.[627]

He is seated at the right hand of the Father

In androcentric, monarchical cultures out of which the New Testament and the Creeds developed, the right hand was considered good and righteous, while the left was considered suspicious and evil.[628] This era was very male-dominated and hierarchical, so the image of Jesus sitting at God's right hand would have resonated with the average person. Again, though, the image must be understood as mainly metaphorical; one of the few attestations in the paranormal literature of Jesus' sitting at all is four-year-old Colton Burpo.[629] The main images of God and Jesus, as we have seen above, are those of love and energy, not male or even necessarily human.

And he will come to judge the living and the dead

While Hebrew Scripture and the New Testament both contain stories of God as judge, especially in the afterlife, the paranormal literature attests instead to self-judgment. The Life Review of those who have had NDEs, Doyle's postmortem testimonies, many cases described by mediums and psychics, and the OOBEs of Robert Monroe all speak to souls being confronted at death by their consciences. The appearances of Jesus to those in our time who have crossed over fall almost without fail on the side of mercy, love and forgiveness.

Even in the cases of evil, bad or misguided souls, it is not Jesus or God who judges their thoughts or actions; rather, these spirits appear to go to the planes where they belong – where they have sent themselves, as it were, or where they have chosen to go based on the decisions they have made while in the physical world. The literature suggests that the truly wicked go to a gray, dull place of isolation and/or a place of sleep for a period of time, until they confront themselves and can move on: "When faced with the 'judgment' – which is but the realization of *himself* – he is able to look once and for all into the deeps of himself. . . . He can go forward . . . into ever higher realms of spiritual consciousness and understanding. . . ."[630]

Many of us as well, for spiritual growth, return to the physical world via reincarnation for as long as it takes to progress spiritually, so the notion of God's judgment should be reevaluated in the face of the paranormal evidence.

I believe in the Holy Spirit

The Christian festival of Pentecost as described in Acts 2 marks the "birthday of the church," the giving of the Holy Spirit – the Comforter, the Paraclete – to the church and the people of God. The story states that "they were all filled with the Holy Spirit and began to speak in other tongues, as the Spirit gave them utterance."[631] While moderns most likely confine this tale to the realm of myth, folklore and theology, Cayce's readings link the Holy Spirit with the Christ Spirit and the Christ Consciousness. According to Cayce, the Christ Consciousness or the Holy Spirit makes one aware of the Christ Spirit, which is, in effect, the Door, the Truth and the Way.[632] Thus the miraculous gift of the Holy Spirit as related in the Creed now appears to be a factual possibility in some ways, given the evidence from the paranormal literature. It is not beyond imagining that the "tongues of fire" witnessed by the Jewish community that experienced the earthly Jesus were real at some level, or that they may have constituted visions that could be seen by many people at the same time. Nor is it impossible that, through telepathy or thought transference (the primary means of communication in the afterlife), witnesses could understand others who were speaking different languages. This is not to say that New Testament scholarship on the Pentecost event lacks value; it is still likely that the Pentecost story was overlaid with theological interpretation (not to mention the mere passage of time).

[I believe in] the holy catholic Church

"Catholic" can be defined as "universal." The Creed does not ask us to believe in the *Roman* Catholic Church but rather in the church universal. According to the Catechism of the Episcopal Church in the US, the Church "is catholic, because it proclaims the whole Faith to all people, to the end of time."[633]

From New Testament scholarship we can understand that the English word "church" is a translation of the Greek word "ecclesia," which means "assembly." Jesus was not the founder of the Christian church, as is sometimes believed. Rather, Jesus, like the majority of other people featured in the Bible, was Jewish, and Judaism in the first century was far from monolithic. There were many branches or types of Judaism – represented by the Pharisees, Sadducees, Essenes and others, as we saw in Chapter 5 – and the so-called Holy Land in which Jesus lived was subject to the Roman Empire. The early church, then, was born in Judaism and the synagogue and only became separated from that context after the fall of Jerusalem in the 70s CE. Christianity grew relatively slowly, over the span of several centuries; it was not until 313 CE that the Emperors Constantine and Licinius officially "promulgated their acceptance of Christianity into the fellowship of creeds and cults of the Empire."[634] Despite this declaration, many pagan cults continued to function and even thrive as late as the sixth century CE.

There is some evidence in the paranormal literature for modern churches being both on the right track and somewhat misguided. Postmortem Doyle, for instance, lauded the Roman Catholic and Anglican Churches for "the incense, the way the censer is used, and even the form for administration of blessing" because these rites "are practiced with deliberate intent to create and distribute power amongst the worshippers." On the other hand, Doyle criticized the non-conformist churches (which today we might consider the fundamentalist Christian groups) for having "a spiritual coldness, a lack due to complacency, and those who worship seem apt to become self-satisfied, to think themselves God's chosen and elect."[635] Chip Coffey and other mediums, including those like Coffey who are devout Roman Catholics, are often accused of consorting with the devil. However, such mediums firmly believe that their gifts are from the Divine, God or a Higher Power, not the devil.[636] Eben Alexander, like others who have had NDEs, gained a new appreciation for the church: "I didn't just believe in God; I knew God. As I hobbled to the altar to take Communion, tears streamed down my cheeks."[637]

Thus the evidence indicates that belief in and loyalty to the *church* is laudable, and even to be encouraged, but should never be to the detriment of overall spiritual growth. That is, if the church or Creeds or theology hinders true spiritual growth, it is that growth that should take precedence.

[I believe in] the communion of saints

As we have seen, some people, both past and present, are saints for all intents and purposes – people who love the Divine Being and other human beings fiercely, consistently and often self-sacrificially. Devout Christians through the ages have prayed to saints for assistance and believe that the saints have helped them. While cynics and skeptics take issue with the idea of any help coming from the beyond, the paranormal literature suggests that prayers to saints can be efficacious and that some spiritual beings that appear among us as saints were sent to earth on specific missions for the uplifting of humanity or to point us in a more charitable, loving direction.

One recent example in the paranormal literature of the existence of an early Christian saint is that of St. Stephen, the first martyr. St. Stephen was reported to have dialogued with a group of friends in 1974 in Christchurch, New Zealand. The group of witnesses to these communications included the Rev. Michael Cocks, an Anglican priest; Thomas and Olive Ashman; "a liberal Catholic priest, a Buddhist, and other curious observers." Thomas Ashman, who discovered that he had mediumistic gifts, would go into a trance, become pale, and breathe deeply, paving the way for St. Stephen's spirit to "take over." During a number of sittings, Stephen recounted his life history and his current mission on behalf of humanity. He grew up in Ancyra in today's Turkey and was 14 years old when Jesus died. Stephen's death by stoning is accurately described in Acts, according to the sittings, but the saint informed the Christchurch sitters that his death is less important than his role now as a messenger of Christ. His mission entails being "one with the Whole" and "emphasizing the positive aspects of Christian belief." On some occasions, Stephen would come through the medium speaking Greek, which the Rev. Cocks determined to be Koine, the common language spoken in the Roman Empire at the time; the use of Greek served to validate that it was an ancient figure emerging through the medium.[638]

In this example, we see evidence for a man who lived in the ancient world and gave his life for his faith then, nearly 2,000 years later, purportedly returning in spirit to transmit positive, loving messages from the other side. While the account of St. Stephen's appearances may seem far-fetched, the elements of the phenomena parallel those of other mediums: the trance itself, the fact that the medium often does not remember what is occurring while in the trance, the validation of the spirit's identity through the use of a language that is unknown to the medium, the positive, beneficent message of the spirit, the verification of certain stories related in the Bible, and the witness of many unbiased, though open-minded, observers to the trance events.

[I believe in] the forgiveness of sins

The Christian church has placed a great deal of emphasis over the centuries on forgiveness of sins. The Catechism urges Christians to repent of their sins so that they are in love and charity with their neighbors. As human beings living in corporate milieus such as the home, the workplace, the community and the church, we know on almost a daily basis the value of true sorrow for our own failings and of forgiveness of others and others' forgiveness of us: communities could not function well for very long without everyday apologies and "making up."

The church's insistence on people's wickedness and constant need for God's and others' forgiveness, however, has historically moved Western culture into the arena of "original sin," a doctrine that has arguably done more harm than good. The belief that, because Adam and Eve disobeyed God in the Garden of Eden (a purely mythological "creation" story), all babies are sinful and must be baptized soon after birth to prevent an afterlife in hell or at least Purgatory generally falls on deaf ears in modern Western culture. In fact, the tale serves to dispel people from religious participation rather than encouraging it.

New Testament scholarship has shown that the emphasis on forgiveness of the individual's sin was not one of the most important tenets in the early church. Even though St. Paul discusses human sinfulness (and maintains that Jesus died to save humankind from sin),[639] the emphasis in the West on "guilt and sin, struggle and strain" became more developed as late as Augustine.[640] Some of the earliest Christian art as well, that found in the Roman catacombs, is overwhelmingly positive and peaceful, portraying scenes of rescue and refreshment on the "other side," not judgment and punishment for sin.[641]

The paranormal literature supports this scholarly contention. As we have seen, the experience of the heavenly realms for most people for whom we have evidence – postmortem Doyle, Cayce, EVPs, NDEs, spirits who come through via psychics and mediums – are positive and non-judgmental. If anything, it is the deceased loved one asking forgiveness of those of us still on this side that emerges; the spirit seeks reconciliation with us and urges us *not* to feel so guilty for some perceived slight. For instance, many entities coming through mediums insist that a caregiver for a dying loved one not berate him-

or herself for not being at the bedside at the time of death, and there are other examples of the spirit insisting that the caregiver could do nothing more to prevent the death. Cayce's readings speak of the shedding of Jesus' blood in relation to the forgiveness of sins in this way: "For the error that man makes is the more oft against himself. . . [W]ith the breaking of the law [of love] is the making of the necessity for atonement and forgiveness. . . For through love was brought the desire to make self and his brother in at-onement."[642]

In sum, then, we are called to love and serve – and forgive – but not be consumed and burdened by guilt.

[I believe in] the resurrection of the body

As we have seen, physical bodies survive in some fashion after death: entities appear to people in the physical world in recognizable forms. It does not matter, therefore, how someone dies, whether s/he has been cremated or burned to death or has died in an explosion: the material form of our bodies becomes irrelevant, and our beings are completely transformed on the other side. James Van Praagh, for instance, often channels the spirits of people who died in the September 11, 2001, attacks on the World Trade Center, as do Chip Coffey and other mediums.[643]

And [in] the life everlasting.

The evidence from the paranormal literature is overwhelming that eternity is real, that it is full of love, joy, beauty and peace, and that we all reside in it. Postmortem Doyle asserted: "The man searching and seeking only for himself breaks every law. . . . The truly great is he who recognizes, not his own desires, but the infinite and eternal power of love. . . . [L]et all sense of self and personality fall away. . . . Such is not extinction; it is expansion."[644]

Eben Alexander expresses what so many other NDEers have discovered: "our eternal spiritual self is more real than anything we perceive in this physical realm, and has a divine connection to the infinite love of the Creator."[645]

Evidence from EVPs confirms the same reality. The communications received by Maggy Harsch-Fischbach and Jules Harsch in Luxembourg assert "that we do not die and that we continue to live beyond physical death."[646] A transcommunication group in Frankfurt, Germany, received a clear telephone message in 1987 from a paranormal investigator who had crossed over a few years earlier. The message read in part: "You will have eternal life after you pass over. . . . Do not be afraid of dying, for there is no death."[647]

Even Monroe in his OOBEs, with whom we will close, gleaned this wisdom in a profound way:

> Three times I have "gone" to a place that I cannot find words to describe accurately. . . . ¶To me, it was a place or condition of pure peace, yet exquisite emotion. It was as if you were floating in warm soft clouds where there is no up or down, where nothing exists as a separate piece of matter. The warmth is not merely around you, it is of you and through you. Your perception is dazzled and overwhelmed by the Perfect Environment. ¶ . . . This is where you belong. This is Home.[648]

Amen.

Appendix III: Comparative Chart of Attested Themes

THEME	EVPs	ITC (instruments, photos, medical tests)[649]	Psychics & Mediums[650]	OOBEs	NDEs
Abortion		√	√		
Angels, Higher Intelligences	√	√	√	√	√
Animals, survival of their souls	√	√	√	√	√
Astral Body	√	√	√	√	
Christ Consciousness			√		
Demons, unfriendly spirits	√	√	√	√	
ESP, validity of	√	√	√		√
Exorcisms, Cleansings	√	√	√		
Expanded Consciousness	√	√	√	√	√
Eternal Rest, unlikely	√	√	√	√	
Eternity, Eternal Life	√	√	√	√	√
Evil, outweighed by good		√	√		√
Extraterrestrials, existence or likelihood of	√	√	√	√	
Free will and predestination, both true	√	√	√	√	√

THEME	EVPs	ITC (instruments, photos, medical tests)	Psychics & Mediums	OOBEs	NDEs
Forgiveness, value of	√	√	√	√	
God/Divine Love	√	√	√	√	√
Going into or being in the Light	√	√	√	√	√
Group Karma			√		
Heaven, beautiful settings	√	√	√	√	√
Hell, gray areas of existence	√	√	√	√	√
Holy Spirit			√		
Homosexuality (not condemned; some cases due to past lives in opposite gender)			√		
Jesus (as friend or companion, not necessarily as Savior)		√	√		√
Joy, as a characteristic of the other side	√	√	√	√	√
Judgment, of God unlikely			√	√	√
Karma, law of cause and effect	√	√	√	√	√
Life Review, self-judgment	√	√	√	√	√

THEME	EVPs	ITC (instruments, photos, medical tests)	Psychics & Mediums	OOBEs	NDEs
Love, prevalence and power of	√	√	√	√	√
Miracles attested, New Testament and/or today		√	√	√	√
Music, existence on the other side	√	√	√	√	√
Peace, as a characteristic of the other side	√	√	√	√	√
Planes or levels of existence on the other side	√	√	√	√	√
Prayer, power of	√	√	√	√	√
Pre-birth decisions			√	√	
Purgatory, evidence against souls spending time there	√	√	√		√
Reincarnation, past lives	√	√	√	√	√
Reunion with loved ones	√	√	√	√	√
Resurrection of Jesus			√		
Saints, existence of today		√	√		

THEME	EVPs	ITC (instruments, photos, medical tests)	Psychics & Mediums	OOBEs	NDEs
Service, as essential to spiritual growth	√	√	√	√	√
Soul, survival of individual on the other side	√	√	√	√	√
Spirit Circles or Groups	√	√	√		
Suicide, survival of such souls	√		√		√
Telekinesis, validity of		√	√	√	
Thought transference, telepathy	√	√	√	√	√
Time-Place continuum, different on the other side	√	√	√	√	√
Tragic, early death, communication of these souls	√	√	√	√	√
Virgin Mary		√	√		√

Resources: Alphabetically by Author

Books and Articles

Alexander, Eben. *Proof of Heaven: A Neurosurgeon's Journey into the Afterlife.* New York: Simon and Schuster, Inc., 2012.

American Heritage Dictionary of the English Language, ed. Peter Davies. New York: Dell Publishing Co., Inc. 1970.

"American Society for Psychical Research," *Wikipedia,* http://en.wikipedia.org/wiki/American_Society_for_Psychical_Research, accessed November 14, 2013.

Asprem, Egil. "A Nice Arrangement of Heterodoxies: William McDougall and the Professionalization of Psychical Research," *Journal of the History of the Behavioral Sciences,* Vol. 46, No. 2 (Spring 2010) 123-43.

Assante, Julia. *The Last Frontier: Exploring the Afterlife and Transforming Our Fear of Death.* Novato, CA: New World Library, 2012.

"William Fletcher Barrett," *Wikipedia,* http://en.wikipedia.org/wiki/William_Fletcher_Barrett, accessed September 24, 2013.

Belanger, Michelle. *Haunting Experiences: Encounters with the Otherworldly.* Woodbury, Minnesota: Llewellyn Publications, 2009.

Blackmore, Susan, website, http://www.susanblackmore.co.uk/, accessed March 22, 2014.

Blum, Deborah. *Ghost Hunters: William James and the Search for Scientific Proof of Life After Death.* London: Penguin Press, 2006.

Bro, Harmon H. *Edgar Cayce on Dreams.* New York: Paperback Library, Inc., 1968.

Bro, Harmon H. *Edgar Cayce on Religion and Psychic Experience.* New York: Paperback Library, 1970.

Brown, Michael H. *After Life: What it's like in Heaven, Hell and Purgatory.* Milford, OH: Faith Publishing Company, 1997.

Buell, Ryan and Stefan Petrucha. *Paranormal State: My Journey into the Unknown.* New York: HarperCollins Publishers, 2010.

Burpo, Todd, with Lynn Vincent. *Heaven is for Real: A Little Boy's Astounding Story of His Trip to Heaven and Back.* Nashville: Thomas Nelson, Inc., 2010.

Butler, Lisa. "Electronic Voice Phenomena as Evidence for Life After Death," *Journal of Spirituality and Paranormal Studies.* Annual Conference 2007 Proceedings.

Butler, Lisa. "Precursor Sounds in Physical Phenomena," as published in the Summer 2002 AA-EVP NewsJournal. http://atransc.org/articles/precursor_sound.htm, accessed April 7, 2012.

Butler, Tom. "Concerns with Wikipedia," http://atransc.org/articles/concerns_with_wikipedia.htm, accessed December 27, 2012.

Butler, Tom. "Electronic Voice Phenomena: A Tool for Validating Personal Survival," *The Journal of Religion and Psychical Research*, 2002. Pp 215-26.

Butler, Tom. "Physical Processes Involved in Trans-etheric Influences," originally published in the fall 2009 ATransC NewsJournal. http://atransc.org/theory/trans-etheric_influence.htm, accessed March 25, 2012.

Butler, Tom. "What we Know about Life After Death via EVP/ITC," *Annual Conference, 2007 Proceedings,* Academy of Spirituality and Paranormal Studies, Inc., 135-47.

Butler, Tom. "Why Has There Not Been More Study of the Paranormal?" http://atransc.org/research/research_funding_nsf.htm, accessed December 27, 2012.

Butler, Tom and Lisa. "A Brief Discussion About the Safety of Communicating with the Other Side." From *Viewpoint*, Spring 2003 AA_EVP NewsJournal. http://atransc.org/articles/about_safety.htm, accessed April 7, 2012.

Butler, Tom and Lisa. "From Our Viewpoint – Proof of Survival," published in the Winter 2003 AA-EVP NewsJournal, http://atransc.org/articles/butler-survival.htm, accessed June 28, 2013.

Butler, Tom and Lisa. "The Monroe Way: Binaural synchronization induced meditative state," previously published in the Spring 2008 AA-EVP NewsJournal, http://atransc.org/articles/monroe_way.htm, accessed June 28, 2013.

Butler, Tom and Lisa. *There is No Death and There are No Dead*. Reno, NV: AA-EVP Publishing, 2008.

Cardoso, Anabela. "Brief Remarks on the Role of the Recipient in ITC." *ITC Journal*, http://atransc.org/articles/Cardoso-itc.htm, 2002; accessed June 28, 2013.

Cardoso, Anabela. "ITC Contacts with Animals?" Previously published in the August 2008 ITC Journal: www.itcjournal.org. http://aransc.org/articles/cardoso-contact_with_animals.htm, accessed April 7, 2012.

Cardoso, Anabela, David Fontana, and Ernst Senkowski. "Experiment transcript only for Visiting Hans Otto König," *AA-EVP NewsJournal*, accessed December 27, 2012; originally published in the ITC Journal, No. 24, December 2005.

Cayce, Hugh Lynn. *Venture Inward*. New York: Harper & Row, Publishers, Inc., 1964.

Chopra, Deepak. *Life After Death: The Burden of Proof*. New York: Harmony Books, 2006.

Clapp, Rodney. "Animals in the kingdom," *Christian Century* (June 27, 2012) 45.

Clapp, Rodney. "Life after life after death," *Christian Century* (May 30, 2012) 45.

Coffey, Chip. *Growing Up Psychic: My Story of Not Just Surviving but Thriving – and How Others Like Me Can, Too.* New York: Three Rivers Press, 2012.

Cooke, Ivan. *Arthur Conan Doyle's Book of the Beyond.* New Lands, England: The White Eagle Publishing Trust, 2006.

Craffert, Pieter F. "Jesus' Resurrection as a Cultural Reality," *The Fourth R*, Vol. 26, No. 2 (March-April 2013) 3-5, 10-14.

"William Crookes," *Wikipedia*, http://en.wikipedia.org/wiki/William_Crookes, accessed September 24, 2013.

Deane-Drummond, Celia, Dominic Johnson, Agustin Fuentes and Robin Lovin. "Highly evolved questions," *Christian Century* (August 7, 2013) 30-33.

"Arthur Conan Doyle," *Wikipedia*, http://en.wikipedia.org/wiki/Arthur_Conan_Doyle, accessed October 12, 2013.

Doyle, Arthur Conan. *A History of Spiritualism*, two volumes. New York: Arno Press, 1975; a facsimile of the 1924 edition.

Edison, Thomas A. "The Perfected Phonograph," *The North American Review (1821-1940)*, June 1888; 146-379; American Periodicals Series Online pg. 641.

Edward, John, with Natasha Stoynoff. *After Life: Answers from the Other Side.* New York: Princess Books, a Division of Get Psych'd, Inc., 2003.

Enns, Anthony. "Voices of the Dead: Transmission/Translation/Transgression," *Culture, Theory & Critique*, 2005, 46(1), 11-27.

"Charles Carroll Everett," *Wikipedia*, http://en.wikipedia.org/wiki/Charles_Carroll_Everett, accessed November 14, 2013.

Ferguson, Everett. *Backgrounds of Early Christianity*, 2nd ed. Grand Rapids: William B. Eerdmans Publishing Company, 1993.

Fontana, David. "ITC and its Role in Survival Research," *ITC Journal* (April 2007); http://atransc.org/articles/fontana-itc.htm, accessed April 7, 2012.

"Fox Sisters," *Wikipedia*, http://en.wikipedia.org/wiki/Fox_sisters, accessed September 24, 2013.

Furst, Jeffrey. *Edgar Cayce's Story of Jesus*. New York: Coward-McCann, Inc., 1968.

Glasson, Thomas Francis. "Heaven," in *Oxford Companion to the Bible*, eds. Bruce M. Metzger and Michael D. Coogan, 270-71. New York and Oxford: Oxford University Press, 1993.

Greyson, Bruce and Nancy Evans Bush. "Distressing Near-Death Experiences," *Psychiatry*, Vol. 55 (February 1992) 95-110.

"Edmund Gurney," *Wikipedia*, http://en.wikipedia.org/wiki/Edmund_Gurney, accessed September 24, 2013.

Gurney, Edmund, Frederic W.H. Myers and Frank Podmore. *Phantasms of the Living*, Volumes 1 and 2. A facsimile reproduction with an Introduction by Leonard R.N. Ashley. Gainesville, FL: Scholars' Facsimiles and Reprints, 1970. Originally published in London, 1886.

Hancock, Maureen. *The Medium Next Door: Adventures of a Real-Life Ghost Whisperer*. Deerfield Beach, FL: Health Communications, Inc., 2011.

Haraldsson, Erlendur. "Alleged Encounters with the Dead: The Importance of Violent Death in 337 New Cases," *The Journal of Parapsychology*, Vol. 73 (2010) 91-118.

Haraldsson, Erlendur. "Obituaries: Ian Stevenson 1918-2007," *The Journal of Parapsychology*, Vol. 71 (Spring-Fall 2007) 159-68.

Hawes, Jason and Grant Wilson, with Michael Jan Friedman. *Ghost Hunting: True Stories of Unexplained Phenomena from The Atlantic Paranormal Society.* New York: Simon & Schuster, Inc., 2007.

"Richard Hodgson (parapsychologist)," *Wikipedia,* http://en.wikipedia.org/wiki/Richard_Hodgson_(parapsychologist), accessed September 24, 2013.

Hogan, R. Craig. "Applying the Science of the Afterlife," *Journal of Spirituality and Paranormal Studies,* Vol. 32, Issue 1 (Jan. 2009) 6-23.

"Daniel Dunglas Home," *Wikipedia,* http://en.wikipedia.org/wiki/Daniel_Dunglas_Home, accessed September 24, 2013.

"James H. Hyslop," *Wikipedia,* http://en.wikipedia.org/wiki/James_H._Hyslop, accessed September 24, 2013.

James, William. "The Confidences of a 'Psychical Researcher,'" *The American Magazine,* Vol. 68 (Oct. 1909) 580-89.

Judge, Edwin A. "Pilate, Pontius," in Bruce M. Metzger and Michael D. Coogan, eds. *Oxford Companion to the Bible,* 594-95. New York and Oxford: Oxford University Press, 1993.

Kallen, Horace Meyer. "James, William," *Encyclopaedia Britannica,* Vol. 12, 883-85. Chicago: Encyclopaedia Britannica, Inc., 1963.

Kelsey, Morton T. *Afterlife: The Other Side of Dying.* New York, Ramsey and Toronto: Paulist Press, 1979.

Kripal, Jeffrey. "The Rise of the Imaginal: Psychical Research on the Horizon of Theory (Again)," *Religious Studies Review,* Vol. 33, No. 3 (July 2007) 179-91.

Lampe, Padú. "Instrumental Communication with the Dead," *The Journal of Religion and Psychical Research,* Vol. 16, No. 2 (April 1993) 143-48; copyright 2002 EBSCO Publishing.

Langley, Noel. *Edgar Cayce on Reincarnation.* New York: Warner Books, Inc., 1967.

Laurentin, René and Henri Joyeux. *Scientific and Medical Studies on the Apparitions at Medjugorje.* Dublin: Veritas Publications, 1987.

Lescarboura, Austin C. "Edison's Views on Life and Death," *Scientific American* (October 30, 1920) 446, 458-60.

Lischer, Sarah Kenyon. "Reports of heaven," *Christian Century* (August 7, 2013) 13.

Martin, Joel and William J. Birnes. *The Haunting of the Presidents: A Paranormal History of the U.S. Presidency.* Old Saybrook, CT: Konecky & Konecky, 2003.

Meier, Samuel A. "Evil," in Bruce M. Metzger and Michael D. Coogan, eds. *Oxford Companion to the Bible,* 208-09. New York and Oxford: Oxford University Press, 1993.

"Oliver Lodge," *Wikipedia,* http://en.wikipedia.org/wiki/Oliver_Lodge, accessed September 24, 2013.

Long, Jeffrey, with Paul Perry. *Evidence of the Afterlife: The Science of Near-Death Experiences.* New York: HarperCollins Publishers, 2010.

Lyons, Sean. "The Science of Reincarnation," *University of Virginia Magazine* (Winter 2013) 22-26.

MacDonald, Arthur, "The International Congress of Experimental Psychology, Held in London, August 1892," *Science,* Vol. 20, No. 511 (November 18, 1892) 288-90.

Meehl, Paul E. "Parapsychology," *Encyclopaedia Britannica,* Vol. 17, 267-69. Chicago: Encyclopaedia Britannica, Inc., 1963.

"Metempsychosis," in F.L. Cross and E.A. Livingstone, eds., *The Oxford Dictionary of the Christian Church,* 908. Oxford: Oxford University Press, 1985.

Miller, Lisa. *Heaven: Our Enduring Fascination with the Afterlife.* New York: Harper Collins Publishers, 2010.

Monroe, Robert A. *Journeys Out of the Body*. Garden City, NY: Anchor Books, 1973.

Monroe, Robert A. *Ultimate Journey*. New York: Random House, Inc., 1994.

Moody, Raymond A., Jr., with Paul Perry. *The Light Beyond*. New York: Bantam Books, 1988.

Morse, Donald R. "Apparent Apparitions in the Bible Involving Moses, Ezekiel, and Saul (Paul)," *Journal of Religion & Psychical Research*, Vol. 26 Issue 1 (2003), 32-43.

Murawski, John. "Our idea of heaven wrong, says N.T. Wright," *Christian Century* (June 13, 2012) 18.

"Frederic William Henry Myers," *Wikipedia*, http://en.wikipedia.org/wiki/Frederic_William_Henry_Myers , accessed September 24, 2013.

Myers, Frederic William Henry. *Human Personality and Its Survival of Bodily Death*. New York: Longmans, Green and Co., 1903; reprinted by arrangement with Garrett Publication, 1954.

National Spiritualist Association of Churches, "Foundation Facts Concerning Spiritualism as a Religion," pamphlet. Lily Dale, NY: National Spiritualist Association of Churches, revised April 9, 2002.

Nickels, James B. "Psychic Research in a Winnipeg Family: Reminiscences of Dr. Glen F. Hamilton," *Manitoba Historical Society Gazette*, No. 55 (June 2007) 51-60.

Olson, Roger E. Review: Jerry L. Walls, *Purgatory: The Logic of Total Transformation* (Oxford University Press), in *Christian Century* (August 8, 2012) 41-42.

"Eusapia Palladino," *Wikipedia*, http://en.wikipedia.org/wiki/Eusapia_Palladino, accessed February 14, 2014.

"Leonora Piper," *Wikipedia*, http://en.wikipedia.org/wiki/Leonora_Piper, accessed September 24, 2013.

Pitard, Wayne T. "Afterlife and Immortality: Ancient Israel," in Bruce M. Metzger and Michael D. Coogan, eds. *Oxford Companion to the Bible*, 15-16. New York and Oxford: Oxford University Press, 1993.

"Frank Podmore," *Wikipedia*, http://en.wikipedia.org/wiki/Frank_Podmore, accessed September 24, 2013.

Presi, Paolo. "Italian Research in ITC: The Interdisciplinary Laboratory For Biopsychocybernetics Research (Il Laboratorio)," originally published in *ITC Journal* (March 2000) by Anabela Cardoso; http://atransc.org/articles/presi-italian_research.htm, accessed April 7, 2012.

Price, Robert M. "A Response to Pieter Craffert," *The Fourth R*, Vol. 26, No. 2 (March-April 2013) 14.

Puryear, Anne. *Stephen Lives! My Son Stephen: His Life, Suicide, and Afterlife*. New York: Pocket Books, a division of Simon & Schuster Inc., 1992, 1996.

Radin, Dean, Marilyn Schlitz, Caroline Watt and Richard Wiseman. "Of two minds: sceptic-proponent collaboration within parapsychology," *British Journal of Psychology*, 97.3 (August 2006) 313.

Radin, Dean. Review: *Parapsychology and the Skeptics: A Scientific Argument for the Existence of ESP* by Chris Carter, in *The Journal of Parapsychology* 71 (Spring-Fall 2007) 184-85.

Read, Anne. *Edgar Cayce on Jesus and His Church*. New York: Warner Books, Inc., 1970.

Reader's Digest Association. *Life Beyond Death: Quest for the Unknown*. Pleasantville, NY, and Montreal: Reader's Digest Association, Inc., 1992.

Renier, Noreen, with Naomi Lucks. *A Mind for Murder: The Real-Life Files of a Psychic Investigator*. New York: Berkley Books, 2005.

"Charles Richet," *Wikipedia*, http://en.wikipedia.org/wiki/Charles_Richet, accessed November 14, 2013.

Roach, Mary. *Spook: Science Tackles the Afterlife*. New York: W.W. Norton & Company, Inc., 2005.

"Minot Judson Savage," *Wikipedia*, http://en.wikipedia.org/wiki/Minot_Judson_Savage, accessed November 14, 2013.

Schmidt, Helmut. "Correlation Between Mental processes and External Random Events," *Journal of Scientific Exploration*, Vol. 4, No. 2 (1990) 233-41.

Schouten, Sybo A. "Applied Parapsychology Studies of Psychics and Healers," *Journal of Scientific Exploration*, Vol. 7, No. 4 (1993) 375-401.

Segal, Alan F. *Life After Death: A History of the Afterlife in Western Religion*. New York: Doubleday, 2004.

Sheehan, Thomas. "What Comes after Christianity?" *The Fourth R*, Vol. 26, No. 5 (September-October 2013) 5-10, 26.

"Eleanor Mildred Sidgwick," *Wikipedia*, http://en.wikipedia.org/wiki/Eleanor_Mildred_Sidgwick, accessed June 7, 2014.

"Henry Sidgwick," *Wikipedia*, http://en.wikipedia.org/wiki/Henry_Sidgwick, accessed September 24, 2013.

"Society for Psychical Research," *Wikipedia*, http://en.wikipedia.org/wiki/Society_for_Psychical_Research, accessed November 14, 2013.

Sorenson, Kris. "The Intelligence Behind Taped Voice Phenomena," *The Journal of Religion and Psychical Research*, Vol. 13, No. 3 (July 1990), 129-32; copyright 2002 EBSCO Publishing.

"Spiritualism," *Wikipedia*, http://en.wikipedia.org/wiki/Spiritualism, accessed October 12, 2013.

Spong, John Shelby. *Eternal Life: A New Vision*. New York: HarperCollins Publishers, 2009.

Stearn, Jess. *The Miracle Workers: America's Psychic Consultants*. New York: Doubleday & Company, Inc., 1972.

Stevenson, Ian. "Comments on 'The Psychology of Life After Death,'" *American Psychologist* (November 1981) 1459-61.

Talbot, Michael. *Your Past Lives: A Reincarnation Handbook*. New York: Crown Publishers, 1987.

Taylor, Alfred Edward and Philip Merlan. "Plato," *Encyclopaedia Britannica*, Vol. 18, 48-63. Chicago: Encyclopaedia Britannica, Inc., 1963.

Thiering, Barbara. *Jesus and the Riddle of the Dead Sea Scrolls: Unlocking the Secrets of His Life Story*. New York: HarperCollins Publishers, 1992.

Thouless, Robert Henry. "Spiritualism," *Encyclopaedia Britannica*, Vol. 21, 240-42. Chicago: Encyclopaedia Britannica, Inc., 1963.

Tipler, Frank J. *The Physics of Immortality: Modern Cosmology, God and the Resurrection of the Dead*. New York: Doubleday, 1994.

Tymn, Michael E. "The Amazing D.D. Home," http://www.aspsi.org/feat/life_after/D_D_HOME.html, accessed March 29, 2013.

Tymn, Michael E. "An 'Interview' with Frederic W.H. Myers," *Journal of Spirituality and Paranormal Studies*, Vol. 31, No. 1 (Jan. 2008) 14-24. Accessed March 28, 2013.

Tymn, Michael E. "Comparing the Afterlife Abodes of Religion With Those of More Recent Revelation," *Journal of Religion & Psychical Research*, Vol. 26, Issue 3 (July 2003) 158-68.

Tymn, Michael E. "A *Lusitania* Victim Communicates," http://www.aspsi.org/feat/life_after/ A_LUSITANIA_VICTIM.html, accessed March 29, 2013.

Tymn, Michael E. Review: *Matthew, Tell Me About Heaven*, A Matthew Book with Suzanne Ward, in *Journal of Religion & Psychical Research*, Vol. 26, Issue 1 (January 2003) 55-56.

Tymn, Michael E. "St. Stephen Communicates," http://www.aspsi.org/feat/life_after/St. Stephen.html, accessed March 29, 2013.

Van Praagh, James. *Reaching to Heaven: A Spiritual Journey Through Life and Death*. New York: Penguin Books, 1999.

Van Praagh, James. *Unfinished Business: What the Dead Can Teach Us About Life*. New York: HarperCollins Publishers, Inc., 2009.

"Alfred Russel Wallace," *Wikipedia*, http://en.wikipedia.org/wiki/Alfred_Russel_Wallace, accessed September 24, 2013.

Weisberg, Barbara. *Talking to the Dead: Kate and Maggie Fox and the Rise of Spiritualism*. New York: HarperSanFrancisco, 2004.

Weiss, Brian L. *Many Lives, Many Masters*. New York: Simon & Schuster, Inc., 1988.

White, Sidnie Ann. "Afterlife and Immortality: Second Temple Judaism and Early Christianity," in Bruce M. Metzger and Michael D. Coogan, eds. *Oxford Companion to the Bible*, 16-17. New York and Oxford: Oxford University Press, 1993.

Wilson, Craig. "Publishers in 7th heaven with near-death memoirs," *Christian Century* (March 20, 2013) 19.

Wingert, Thomas. "Continuing a relation with the deceased: A contemporary choice for coping with grief," http://atransc.org/articles/wingert-greif_mgmt.htm, 2002, accessed December 27, 2012.

Wingert, Thomas. "The Electronic Voice Phenomena," http://atransc.org/articles/wingert-evp.htm, accessed April 7, 2012.

Zaleski, Carol. "Immortal dreams," *Christian Century* (November 28, 2012) 35.

Zaleski, Carol. *The Life of the World to Come: Near-Death Experience and Christian Hope*. New York and Oxford: Oxford University Press, 1996.

Zaleski, Carol. "Synthetic immortality," *Christian Century* (October 3, 2012) 35.

Websites (as of 4/14) and Television Shows

AA-EVP, now known as Association TransCommunication, http://atransc.org/

Eternea, http://eternea.org, "a publicly supported global non-profit research, educational and outreach organization" co-founded by Eben Alexander, MD

Fleming, Chris, http://www.aetv.com/psychic-kids/meet-hosts/

Ghost Adventures: http://www.travelchannel.com/tv-shows/ghost-adventures

Ghost Hunters: The Atlantic Paranormal Society (TAPS), http://www.the-atlantic-paranormal-society.com/

Haunted Collector: John Zaffis, http://www.syfy.com/hauntedcollector

The Journal of Parapsychology (professional guidelines), http://www.parapsych.org/section/42/ethical_and_professional_standards.aspx

Long Island Medium: Theresa Caputo, http://www.theresacaputo.com/

Mediums: We See Dead People: A & E and Biography Channel special

Monroe Institute, http://www.monroeinstitute.org/

Paranormal State: Paranormal Research Society, http://paranormalresearchsociety.org/

Psychic Detectives: http://www.tv.com/shows/psychic-detectives/

Psychic Kids: http://www.aetv.com/psychic-kids/

Sensing Murder: Laurie Campbell and Pam Coronado

Van Praagh, James, spiritual medium, http://www.vanpraagh.com

Warren, Ed and Lorraine, and New England Society for Psychic Research, http://www.warrens.net/

Weber, Nancy Orlen, psychic detective, http://www.nancyorlenweber.com/

World ITC, http://www.worlditc.org/

Resources: By Topic

Psychical Research

AA-EVP, now known as Association TransCommunication, http://atransc.org/

"American Society for Psychical Research," *Wikipedia*, http://en.wikipedia.org/wiki/American_ Society_for_Psychical_Research, accessed November 14, 2013.

Asprem, Egil. "A Nice Arrangement of Heterodoxies: William McDougall and the Professionalization of Psychical Research," *Journal of the History of the Behavioral Sciences*, Vol. 46, No. 2 (Spring 2010) 123-43.

"William Fletcher Barrett," *Wikipedia*, http://en.wikipedia.org/wiki/ William_Fletcher_Barrett, accessed September 24, 2013.

Blackmore, Susan, website, http://www.susanblackmore.co.uk/, accessed March 22, 2014.

Blum, Deborah. *Ghost Hunters: William James and the Search for Scientific Proof of Life After Death*. London: Penguin Press, 2006.

Buell, Ryan and Stefan Petrucha. *Paranormal State: My Journey into the Unknown*. New York: HarperCollins Publishers, 2010.

Butler, Lisa. "Electronic Voice Phenomena as Evidence for Life After Death," *Journal of Spirituality and Paranormal Studies*. Annual Conference 2007 Proceedings.

Butler, Lisa. "Precursor Sounds in Physical Phenomena," as published in the Summer 2002 AA-EVP NewsJournal. http://atransc.org/articles/precursor_sound.htm, accessed April 7, 2012.

Butler, Tom. "Concerns with Wikipedia," http://atransc.org/articles/ concerns_with_wikipedia.htm, accessed December 27, 2012.

Butler, Tom. "Electronic Voice Phenomena: A Tool for Validating Personal Survival," *The Journal of Religion and Psychical Research*, 2002, 215-26.

Butler, Tom. "Physical Processes Involved in Trans-etheric Influences," originally published in the fall 2009 ATransC NewsJournal. http://atransc.org/theory/trans-etheric_influence.htm, accessed March 25, 2012.

Butler, Tom. "What we Know about Life After Death via EVP/ITC," *Annual Conference, 2007 Proceedings,* Academy of Spirituality and Paranormal Studies, Inc., 135-47.

Butler, Tom. "Why Has There Not Been More Study of the Paranormal?" http://atransc.org/research/ research_funding_nsf.htm, accessed December 27, 2012.

Butler, Tom and Lisa. "A Brief Discussion About the Safety of Communicating with the Other Side." From *Viewpoint*, Spring 2003 AA_EVP NewsJournal. http://atransc.org/articles/about_safety.htm, accessed April 7, 2012.

Butler, Tom and Lisa. "From Our Viewpoint – Proof of Survival," published in the Winter 2003 AA-EVP NewsJournal, http://atransc.org/articles/butler-survival.htm, accessed June 28, 2013.

Butler, Tom and Lisa. "The Monroe Way: Binaural synchronization induced meditative state," previously published in the Spring 2008 AA-EVP NewsJournal, http://atransc.org/articles/monroe_way.htm, accessed June 28, 2013.

Butler, Tom and Lisa. *There is No Death and There are No Dead.* Reno, NV: AA-EVP Publishing, 2008.

Cardoso, Anabela. "Brief Remarks on the Role of the Recipient in ITC." *ITC Journal*, http://atransc.org/articles/Cardoso-itc.htm, 2002; accessed June 28, 2013.

Cardoso, Anabela. "ITC Contacts with Animals?" Previously published in the August 2008 ITC Journal: www.itcjournal.org. http://aransc.org/articles/cardoso-contact_with_animals.htm, accessed April 7, 2012.

Cardoso, Anabela, David Fontana, and Ernst Senkowski. "Experiment transcript only for Visiting Hans Otto König," *AA-EVP NewsJournal*, accessed December 27, 2012; originally published in the ITC Journal, No. 24, December 2005.

"William Crookes," *Wikipedia*, http://en.wikipedia.org/wiki/William_Crookes, accessed September 24, 2013.

"Arthur Conan Doyle," *Wikipedia*, http://en.wikipedia.org/wiki/Arthur_Conan_Doyle, accessed October 12, 2013.

Doyle, Arthur Conan. *A History of Spiritualism*, two volumes. New York: Arno Press, 1975; a facsimile of the 1924 edition.

Edison, Thomas A. "The Perfected Phonograph," *The North American Review (1821-1940)*, June 1888; 146-379; American Periodicals Series Online pg. 641.

Enns, Anthony. "Voices of the Dead: Transmission/Translation/Transgression," *Culture, Theory & Critique*, 2005, 46(1), 11-27.

Eternea, http://eternea.org, "a publicly supported global non-profit research, educational and outreach organization" co-founded by Eben Alexander, MD.

"Charles Carroll Everett," *Wikipedia*, http://en.wikipedia.org/wiki/Charles_Carroll_Everett, accessed November 14, 2013.

Fontana, David. "ITC and its Role in Survival Research," *ITC Journal* (April 2007); http://atransc.org/articles/fontana-itc.htm, accessed April 7, 2012.

Ghost Adventures: http://www.travelchannel.com/tv-shows/ghost-adventures

Ghost Hunters: The Atlantic Paranormal Society (TAPS), http://www.the-atlantic-paranormal-society.com/

"Edmund Gurney," *Wikipedia*, http://en.wikipedia.org/wiki/Edmund_Gurney, accessed September 24, 2013.

Gurney, Edmund, Frederic W.H. Myers and Frank Podmore. *Phantasms of the Living*, Volumes 1 and 2. A facsimile reproduction with an Introduction by Leonard R.N. Ashley. Gainesville, FL: Scholars' Facsimiles and Reprints, 1970. Originally published in London, 1886.

Haraldsson, Erlendur. "Alleged Encounters with the Dead: The Importance of Violent Death in 337 New Cases," *The Journal of Parapsychology*, Vol. 73 (2010) 91-118.

Haraldsson, Erlendur. "Obituaries: Ian Stevenson 1918-2007," *The Journal of Parapsychology*, Vol. 71 (Spring-Fall 2007) 159-68.

Haunted Collector: John Zaffis, http://www.syfy.com/hauntedcollector

Hawes, Jason and Grant Wilson, with Michael Jan Friedman. *Ghost Hunting: True Stories of Unexplained Phenomena from The Atlantic Paranormal Society*. New York: Simon & Schuster, Inc., 2007.

"Richard Hodgson (parapsychologist)," *Wikipedia*, http://en.wikipedia.org/wiki/Richard_Hodgson_(parapsychologist), accessed September 24, 2013.

Hogan, R. Craig. "Applying the Science of the Afterlife," *Journal of Spirituality and Paranormal Studies*, Vol. 32, Issue 1 (Jan. 2009) 6-23.

"James H. Hyslop," *Wikipedia*, http://en.wikipedia.org/wiki/James_H._Hyslop, accessed September 24, 2013.

James, William. "The Confidences of a 'Psychical Researcher,'" *The American Magazine*, Vol. 68 (Oct. 1909) 580-89.

The Journal of Parapsychology (professional guidelines), http://www.parapsych.org/section/42/ethical_and_professional_ standards.aspx

Kallen, Horace Meyer. "James, William," *Encyclopaedia Britannica*, Vol. 12, 883-85. Chicago: Encyclopaedia Britannica, Inc., 1963.

Kripal, Jeffrey. "The Rise of the Imaginal: Psychical Research on the Horizon of Theory (Again)," *Religious Studies Review*, Vol. 33, No. 3 (July 2007) 179-91.

Lampe, Padú. "Instrumental Communication with the Dead," *The Journal of Religion and Psychical Research*, Vol. 16, No. 2 (April 1993) 143-48; copyright 2002 EBSCO Publishing.

Laurentin, René and Henri Joyeux. *Scientific and Medical Studies on the Apparitions at Medjugorje*. Dublin: Veritas Publications, 1987.

Lescarboura, Austin C. "Edison's Views on Life and Death," *Scientific American* (October 30, 1920) 446, 458-60.

Martin, Joel and William J. Birnes. *The Haunting of the Presidents: A Paranormal History of the U.S. Presidency*. Old Saybrook, CT: Konecky & Konecky, 2003.

"Oliver Lodge," *Wikipedia*, http://en.wikipedia.org/wiki/Oliver_Lodge, accessed September 24, 2013.

Lyons, Sean. "The Science of Reincarnation," *University of Virginia Magazine* (Winter 2013) 22-26.

MacDonald, Arthur, "The International Congress of Experimental Psychology, Held in London, August 1892," *Science*, Vol. 20, No. 511 (November 18, 1892) 288-90.

Meehl, Paul E. "Parapsychology," *Encyclopaedia Britannica*, Vol. 17, 267-69. Chicago: Encyclopaedia Britannica, Inc., 1963.

"Frederic William Henry Myers," *Wikipedia*, http://en.wikipedia.org/wiki/Frederic_William_Henry_Myers , accessed September 24, 2013.

Myers, Frederic William Henry. *Human Personality and Its Survival of Bodily Death*. New York: Longmans, Green and Co., 1903; reprinted by arrangement with Garrett Publication, 1954.

Nickels, James B. "Psychic Research in a Winnipeg Family: Reminiscences of Dr. Glen F. Hamilton," *Manitoba Historical Society Gazette*, No. 55 (June 2007) 51-60.

Olson, Roger E. Review: Jerry L. Walls, *Purgatory: The Logic of Total Transformation* (Oxford University Press), *Christian Century* (August 8, 2012) 41-42.

Paranormal State: Paranormal Research Society, http://paranormalresearchsociety.org/.

"Frank Podmore," *Wikipedia*, http://en.wikipedia.org/wiki/Frank_Podmore, accessed September 24, 2013.

Presi, Paolo. "Italian Research in ITC: The Interdisciplinary Laboratory For Biopsychocybernetics Research (Il Laboratorio)," originally published in *ITC Journal* (March 2000) by Anabela Cardoso; http://atransc.org/articles/presi-italian_research.htm, accessed April 7, 2012.

Radin, Dean, Marilyn Schlitz, Caroline Watt and Richard Wiseman. "Of two minds: sceptic-proponent collaboration within parapsychology," *British Journal of Psychology*, 97.3 (August 2006) 313.

Radin, Dean. Review: *Parapsychology and the Skeptics: A Scientific Argument for the Existence of ESP* by Chris Carter, in *The Journal of Parapsychology* 71 (Spring-Fall 2007) 184-85.

Reader's Digest Association. *Life Beyond Death: Quest for the Unknown*. Pleasantville, NY, and Montreal: Reader's Digest Association, Inc., 1992.

"Charles Richet," *Wikipedia*, http://en.wikipedia.org/wiki/ Charles_Richet, accessed November 14, 2013.

"Minot Judson Savage," *Wikipedia*, http://en.wikipedia.org/wiki/Minot_Judson_Savage, accessed November 14, 2013.

Schmidt, Helmut. "Correlation Between Mental processes and External Random Events," *Journal of Scientific Exploration*, Vol. 4, No. 2 (1990) 233-41.

Schouten, Sybo A. "Applied Parapsychology Studies of Psychics and Healers," *Journal of Scientific Exploration*, Vol. 7, No. 4 (1993) 375-401.

"Eleanor Mildred Sidgwick," *Wikipedia*, http://en.wikipedia.org/wiki/ Eleanor_Mildred_Sidgwick, accessed June 7, 2014.

"Henry Sidgwick," *Wikipedia*, http://en.wikipedia.org/wiki/ Henry_Sidgwick, accessed September 24, 2013.

"Society for Psychical Research," *Wikipedia*, http://en.wikipedia.org/wiki/Society_for_Psychical_Research, accessed November 14, 2013.

Sorenson, Kris. "The Intelligence Behind Taped Voice Phenomena," *The Journal of Religion and Psychical Research*, Vol. 13, No. 3 (July 1990), 129-32; copyright 2002 EBSCO Publishing.

Stevenson, Ian. "Comments on 'The Psychology of Life After Death,'" *American Psychologist* (November 1981) 1459-61.

Tipler, Frank J. *The Physics of Immortality: Modern Cosmology, God and the Resurrection of the Dead*. New York: Doubleday, 1994.

Tymn, Michael E. "The Amazing D.D. Home," http://www.aspsi.org/feat/life_after/D_D_HOME.html, accessed March 29, 2013.

Tymn, Michael E. "An 'Interview' with Frederic W.H. Myers," *Journal of Spirituality and Paranormal Studies*, Vol. 31, No. 1 (Jan. 2008) 14-24. Accessed March 28, 2013.

"Alfred Russel Wallace," *Wikipedia*, http://en.wikipedia.org/wiki/Alfred_Russel_Wallace, accessed September 24, 2013.

Weiss, Brian L. *Many Lives, Many Masters*. New York: Simon & Schuster, Inc., 1988.

Wingert, Thomas. "Continuing a relation with the deceased: A contemporary choice for coping with grief," http://atransc.org/articles/wingert-greif_mgmt.htm, 2002, accessed December 27, 2012.

Wingert, Thomas. "The Electronic Voice Phenomena," http://atransc.org/articles/wingert-evp.htm, accessed April 7, 2012.

World ITC, http://www.worldtc.org/.

Near-Death Experiences

Alexander, Eben. *Proof of Heaven: A Neurosurgeon's Journey into the Afterlife*. New York: Simon and Schuster, Inc., 2012.

Burpo, Todd, with Lynn Vincent. *Heaven is for Real: A Little Boy's Astounding Story of His Trip to Heaven and Back*. Nashville: Thomas Nelson, Inc., 2010.

Greyson, Bruce and Nancy Evans Bush. "Distressing Near-Death Experiences," *Psychiatry*, Vol. 55 (February 1992) 95-110.

Long, Jeffrey, with Paul Perry. *Evidence of the Afterlife: The Science of Near-Death Experiences*. New York: HarperCollins Publishers, 2010.

Moody, Raymond A., Jr., with Paul Perry. *The Light Beyond*. New York: Bantam Books, 1988.

Wilson, Craig. "Publishers in 7th heaven with near-death memoirs," *Christian Century* (March 20, 2013) 19.

Zaleski, Carol. *The Life of the World to Come: Near-Death Experience and Christian Hope*. New York and Oxford: Oxford University Press, 1996.

Psychics and Mediums

Belanger, Michelle. *Haunting Experiences: Encounters with the Otherworldly*. Woodbury, Minnesota: Llewellyn Publications, 2009.

Bro, Harmon H. *Edgar Cayce on Dreams*. New York: Paperback Library, Inc., 1968.

Bro, Harmon H. *Edgar Cayce on Religion and Psychic Experience*. New York: Paperback Library, 1970.

Cayce, Hugh Lynn. *Venture Inward*. New York: Harper & Row, Publishers, Inc., 1964.

Coffey, Chip. *Growing Up Psychic: My Story of Not Just Surviving but Thriving – and How Others Like Me Can, Too*. New York: Three Rivers Press, 2012.

Cooke, Ivan. *Arthur Conan Doyle's Book of the Beyond*. New Lands, England: The White Eagle Publishing Trust, 2006.

Edward, John, with Natasha Stoynoff. *After Life: Answers from the Other Side*. New York: Princess Books, a Division of Get Psych'd, Inc., 2003.

Fleming, Chris, http://www.aetv.com/psychic-kids/meet-hosts/

"Fox Sisters," *Wikipedia*, http://en.wikipedia.org/wiki/Fox_sisters, accessed September 24, 2013.

Furst, Jeffrey. *Edgar Cayce's Story of Jesus*. New York: Coward-McCann, Inc., 1968.

Hancock, Maureen. *The Medium Next Door: Adventures of a Real-Life Ghost Whisperer.* Deerfield Beach, FL: Health Communications, Inc., 2011.

"Daniel Dunglas Home," *Wikipedia,* http://en.wikipedia.org/wiki/Daniel_Dunglas_Home, accessed September 24, 2013.

Langley, Noel. *Edgar Cayce on Reincarnation.* New York: Warner Books, Inc., 1967.

Long Island Medium: Theresa Caputo, http://www.theresacaputo.com/

Mediums: We See Dead People: A & E and Biography Channel special

"Eusapia Palladino," *Wikipedia,* http://en.wikipedia.org/wiki/Eusapia_Palladino, accessed February 14, 2014.

"Leonora Piper," *Wikipedia,* http://en.wikipedia.org/wiki/Leonora_Piper, accessed September 24, 2013.

Puryear, Anne. *Stephen Lives! My Son Stephen: His Life, Suicide, and Afterlife.* New York: Pocket Books, a division of Simon & Schuster Inc., 1992, 1996.

Psychic Detectives: http://www.tv.com/shows/psychic-detectives/

Psychic Kids: http://www.aetv.com/psychic-kids/

Read, Anne. *Edgar Cayce on Jesus and His Church.* New York: Warner Books, Inc., 1970.

Renier, Noreen, with Naomi Lucks. *A Mind for Murder: The Real-Life Files of a Psychic Investigator.* New York: Berkley Books, 2005.

Sensing Murder: Laurie Campbell and Pam Coronado

Stearn, Jess. *The Miracle Workers: America's Psychic Consultants.* New York: Doubleday & Company, Inc., 1972.

Van Praagh, James, spiritual medium, http://www.vanpraagh.com

Van Praagh, James. *Reaching to Heaven: A Spiritual Journey Through Life and Death*. New York: Penguin Books, 1999.

Van Praagh, James. *Unfinished Business: What the Dead Can Teach Us About Life*. New York: HarperCollins Publishers, Inc., 2009.

Warren, Ed and Lorraine, and New England Society for Psychic Research, http://www.warrens.net/

Weber, Nancy Orlen, psychic detective, http://www.nancyorlenweber.com/

Weisberg, Barbara. *Talking to the Dead: Kate and Maggie Fox and the Rise of Spiritualism*. New York: HarperSanFrancisco, 2004.

Out-of-Body Experiences

Monroe Institute, http://www.monroeinstitute.org/

Monroe, Robert A. *Journeys Out of the Body*. Garden City, NY: Anchor Books, 1973.

Monroe, Robert A. *Ultimate Journey*. New York: Random House, Inc., 1994.

General and Religious Topics

Assante, Julia. *The Last Frontier: Exploring the Afterlife and Transforming Our Fear of Death*. Novato, CA: New World Library, 2012.

Brown, Michael H. *After Life: What it's like in Heaven, Hell and Purgatory*. Milford, OH: Faith Publishing Company, 1997.

Chopra, Deepak. *Life After Death: The Burden of Proof*. New York: Harmony Books, 2006.

Clapp, Rodney. "Animals in the kingdom," *Christian Century* (June 27, 2012) 45.

Clapp, Rodney. "Life after life after death," *Christian Century* (May 30, 2012) 45.

Craffert, Pieter F. "Jesus' Resurrection as a Cultural Reality," *The Fourth R*, Vol. 26, No. 2 (March-April 2013) 3-5, 10-14.

Deane-Drummond, Celia, Dominic Johnson, Agustin Fuentes and Robin Lovin. "Highly evolved questions," *Christian Century* (August 7, 2013) 30-33.

Ferguson, Everett. *Backgrounds of Early Christianity*, 2nd ed. Grand Rapids: William B. Eerdmans Publishing Company, 1993.

Glasson, Thomas Francis. "Heaven," in *Oxford Companion to the Bible*, eds. Bruce M. Metzger and Michael D. Coogan, 270-71. New York and Oxford: Oxford University Press, 1993.

Judge, Edwin A. "Pilate, Pontius," in Bruce M. Metzger and Michael D. Coogan, eds. *Oxford Companion to the Bible*, 594-95. New York and Oxford: Oxford University Press, 1993.

Kelsey, Morton T. *Afterlife: The Other Side of Dying*. New York, Ramsey and Toronto: Paulist Press, 1979.

Lischer, Sarah Kenyon. "Reports of heaven," *Christian Century* (August 7, 2013) 13.

Meier, Samuel A. "Evil," in Bruce M. Metzger and Michael D. Coogan, eds. *Oxford Companion to the Bible*, 208-09. New York and Oxford: Oxford University Press, 1993.

"Metempsychosis," F.L. Cross and E.A. Livingstone, eds., *The Oxford Dictionary of the Christian Church*, 908. Oxford: Oxford University Press, 1985.

Miller, Lisa. *Heaven: Our Enduring Fascination with the Afterlife*. New York: Harper Collins Publishers, 2010.

Morse, Donald R. "Apparent Apparitions in the Bible Involving Moses, Ezekiel, and Saul (Paul)," *Journal of Religion & Psychical Research*, Vol. 26 Issue 1 (2003), 32-43.

Murawski, John. "Our idea of heaven wrong, says N.T. Wright," *Christian Century* (June 13, 2012) 18.

National Spiritualist Association of Churches, "Foundation Facts Concerning Spiritualism as a Religion," pamphlet. Lily Dale, NY: National Spiritualist Association of Churches, revised April 9, 2002.

Pitard, Wayne T. "Afterlife and Immortality: Ancient Israel," in Bruce M. Metzger and Michael D. Coogan, eds. *Oxford Companion to the Bible*, 15-16. New York and Oxford: Oxford University Press, 1993.

Price, Robert M. "A Response to Pieter Craffert," *The Fourth R*, Vol. 26, No. 2 (March-April 2013) 14.

Roach, Mary. *Spook: Science Tackles the Afterlife*. New York: W.W. Norton & Company, Inc., 2005.

Segal, Alan F. *Life After Death: A History of the Afterlife in Western Religion*. New York: Doubleday, 2004.

Sheehan, Thomas. "What Comes after Christianity?" *The Fourth R*, Vol. 26, No. 5 (September-October 2013) 5-10, 26.

"Spiritualism," *Wikipedia*, http://en.wikipedia.org/wiki/Spiritualism, accessed October 12, 2013.

Spong, John Shelby. *Eternal Life: A New Vision*. New York: HarperCollins Publishers, 2009.

Talbot, Michael. *Your Past Lives: A Reincarnation Handbook*. New York: Crown Publishers, 1987.

Taylor, Alfred Edward and Philip Merlan. "Plato," *Encyclopaedia Britannica*, Vol. 18, 48-63. Chicago: Encyclopaedia Britannica, Inc., 1963.

Thiering, Barbara. *Jesus and the Riddle of the Dead Sea Scrolls: Unlocking the Secrets of His Life Story*. New York: HarperCollins Publishers, 1992.

Thouless, Robert Henry. "Spiritualism," *Encyclopaedia Britannica*, Vol. 21, 240-42. Chicago: Encyclopaedia Britannica, Inc., 1963.

Tymn, Michael E. "Comparing the Afterlife Abodes of Religion With Those of More Recent Revelation," *Journal of Religion & Psychical Research*, Vol. 26, Issue 3 (July 2003) 158-68.

Tymn, Michael E. "A *Lusitania* Victim Communicates," http://www.aspsi.org/feat/life_after/ A_LUSITANIA_VICTIM.html, accessed March 29, 2013.

Tymn, Michael E. Review: *Matthew, Tell Me About Heaven*, A Matthew Book with Suzanne Ward, in *Journal of Religion & Psychical Research*, Vol. 26, Issue 1 (January 2003) 55-56.

Tymn, Michael E. "St. Stephen Communicates," http://www.aspsi.org/feat/life_after/St. Stephen.html, accessed March 29, 2013.

White, Sidnie Ann. "Afterlife and Immortality: Second Temple Judaism and Early Christianity," in Bruce M. Metzger and Michael D. Coogan, eds. *Oxford Companion to the Bible*, 16-17. New York and Oxford: Oxford University Press, 1993.

Zaleski, Carol. "Immortal dreams," *Christian Century* (November 28, 2012) 35.

Zaleski, Carol. "Synthetic immortality," *Christian Century* (October 3, 2012) 35.

About the Author

Valerie A. Abrahamsen holds the Master of Theological Studies and Doctor of Theology degrees in New Testament and Early Christian Origins from Harvard Divinity School. Her primary research interests are women in antiquity and New Testament archaeology, especially the site of Philippi, Greece. She is the author of *Goddess and God: A Holy Tension in the First Christian Centuries* (2006) and *Women and Worship at Philippi* (1995) and has published articles in *The Oxford Encyclopedia of the Bible and Gender Studies, The Independent Scholar, Forum, The Oxford Companion to the Bible, The Journal of Feminist Studies in Religion, Slavery in the United States: A Social, Political, and Historical Encyclopedia, A Feminist Companion to Mariology, Women in Scripture: A Dictionary of Named and Unnamed Women in the Hebrew Bible, Apocrypha, and New Testament, The Historical Encyclopedia of World Slavery, Biblical Archaeologist, The Journal of Holistic Nursing, Sisters Today, Catholic Near East Magazine, Harvard Divinity Bulletin, Macedonian Studies, Vigiliae Christianae*, and *The Journal of Higher Criticism*. Dr. Abrahamsen is a member of the Society of Biblical Literature, the Archaeological Institute of America, and the Westar Institute, and she appears in *Who's Who in America 2008, Who's Who of Biblical Studies and Archaeology* and *2000 Outstanding Scholars of the Twentieth Century*. An active Episcopalian, she is a member of St. Michael's Church in Brattleboro, Vermont, and an Associate of the Society of St. Margaret in Duxbury, Massachusetts.

Paranormal – Abrahamsen

Index

Abortion, 144, 146
Academy of Spirituality and Paranormal Studies, Inc., 97
Adam and Eve, 231
Alexander the Great, 111, 222
Alexander, Eben, 5, 9, 13, 33, 35-36, 67, 100-01, 130-32, 134, 140, 143, 151, 155, 229, 232-33
Alexander, Keith, 67
Alpha device, 89-90
American Association of Electronic Voice Phenomena (AA-EVP), 8, 57, 78, 95, 145-46, 169
American Society for Psychical Research (ASPR), 4, 41, 42-52, 56, 60, 96, 203, 205, 206, 208, 210
Angels, higher intelligences, 1, 2, 11, 24, 39, 64-65, 67, 123-24, 125, 126, 136, 143, 149, 150-54, 164, 165, 170, 178, 185, 187, 200, 213
Animals (survival of their souls), 12, 26, 39, 73, 82, 85, 86, 131-32, 146-47, 150, 152, 192
Apostles' Creed, 6, 103, 104, 116, 124, 218-33
Ashman, Thomas and Olive, 229
Assante, Julia, 36, 118, 124, 171, 173, 178
Association for Research and Enlightenment, 23
Astral body, 124, 147-48, 153, 158
Augustine, 231
Augustus, 222

AWARE Project, 66-67
Bagans, Zak, 21, 87
Baggally, W.W., 56
Baigent, Michael, 223
Baigent, Peter, 77-78
Barrett, William Fletcher, 44-45, 203, 210, 213
Begley, Patricia, 84
Beischel, Julie, 65
Belanger, Michelle, 4, 17, 22-23, 145, 155-56, 175-76
Bennett, Alan and Diana, 84-85
Bersani, Ferdinando, 80
Blackmore, Susan, 36, 68, 102
Blavatsky, Helena Petrovna, 46, 207
Blum, Deborah, 41, 209
Boden, Manfred, 84
Bogoras, Waldemar, 76-77
Boylan, Bob, 58
Boylan, Grace, 58
Brown, Michael H., 8, 157
Bryant, William Cullen, 48
Buddhism, 26, 62, 143, 221, 229
Buell, Ryan, 17-19, 90-91, 96, 100, 145, 176-77
Burpo, Colton, 9, 33, 220, 226
Butler, Lisa, 1, 8, 57, 73, 83, 95, 145, 147, 161, 202
Butler, Tom, 1, 8, 57, 73, 83, 95, 145, 147, 161, 202
Campbell, Laurie, 24-25, 27, 36, 161
Caputo, Theresa, 4, 13, 23, 31, 36, 99-100, 141, 145, 146, , 152, 173, 190
Cardoso, Anabela, 147
Carlson, Chester, 62-64, 94

Carrington, Hereward, 56
Cattell, James McKeen, 209
Cayce, Edgar, 16, 23-24, 28, 42, 119, 122, 123, 166-67, 170, 172, 179-80, 193, 212, 220, 221, 222-23, 224, 225, 227, 231-32
Chappell, Bill, 88-89
Chopra, Deepak, 8-9, 36-37, 124
Christ consciousness, 221, 227
Christian Century, 130-36
Clairvoyance, 22, 48, 63, 97
Clapp, Rodney, 131-32
Clemens, Henry, 204, 206
Clemens, Samuel (Mark Twain), 43, 203-05, 206
Clement of Alexandria, 122, 167
Cocks, Michael, 229-30
Coffey, Chip, 4, 17, 24, 90-91, 98, 140-41, 145, 152, 176-77, 228, 232
Constantine, 228
Cook, Florence, 205
Cooke, Ivan, 9, 224
Copeland, Cathy, 145-46
Copeland, Martha, 145-47
Coronado, Pam, 24-25, 27, 161
Craffert, Pieter F., 135
Crookes, William, 43, 49, 50, 71, 205-06, 213
Curie, Marie, 55
Curie, Pierre, 55
D'argonell, Oscar, 77
Darwin, Charles, 216
Davis, Andrew Jackson, 126
Dean, Larry, 84
Death penalty, 120-21
Demons, 2, 46, 67, 136, 159, 163-65, 190

Deniers, 2, 11, 14, 15, 16, 21, 30, 31, 33, 49, 67, 68-72, 86, 98-102, 133, 135-36, 161-62, 190, 193-96, 212
Dodgson, Charles L. (Lewis Carroll), 43
Doyle, Arthur Conan, 1, 9-10, 14, 40, 41, 44, 47, 56, 68, 70, 81, 100, 118, 122, 123, 125-29, 140-44, 146-47, 149, 152-53, 155, 157-58, 161-63, 165, 170-71, 179-80, 182, 187-89, 193, 196, 201, 211-14, 220-21, 223, 224-26, 228, 231, 232
Dragicevic, Ivan, 93
Duke University, 62-63
Ectoplasm, 55, 195, 214, 217
Edison, Thomas, 6, 57
Edward, John, 4, 25-26, 141, 182
Eglinton, William, 215
Ehrhardt, Rolf-Dietmar, 85
Einstein, Albert, 6
Electromagnetic Field Device (EMF), 86-88, 96
Electronic Voice Phenomena (EVP), 4, 8, 20, 37, 52, 76-83, 90, 95, 119, 122, 132, 137, 141, 145-46, 148, 169-70, 187, 195, 201, 219, 231, 233
Elijah, 222, 224
ESP (extra-sensory perception), 4, 30, 63, 94, 196
Estep, Sarah, 78, 169-70
Eternal rest, 7, 122
Etheric body, 212, 214
Etheric Council, 28
Everett, Charles, 44

Evil, 2, 7, 111-12, 113, 120, 121, 123, 136, 156-65, 170, 191, 192, 198, 226,
Exorcism, 164, 190
Expanded consciousness, 12, 70, 143-44, 150
Extraterrestrials, 39, 65
Feilding, Everard, 56
Fischer, John Martin, 133-34
Fontana, David, 73
Forgiveness, 6, 107, 115-16, 120, 148, 174, 191-92, 201, 219, 221, 226, 230-32
Fourth R, 134-36
Fox Jencken, Kate, 49, 126-29, 205, 215
Fox, Leah, 126-29
Fox, Maggie, 126-29
Foy, Robin and Sandra, 84-85
Francis of Assisi, 123
Free will, 24, 28, 113, 133, 134, 160, 166, 172
Fullerton, George, 44
Galka, Cindy, 87
Galka, Gary, 87
Galka, Melissa, 87
Geller, Uri, 98
Gibbens, Eliza, 50
Goodwin, Aaron, 21, 87
Gordon, Larry, 133-34
Grey, Margot, 32
Greyson, Bruce, 32, 62, 68
Grierson, Francis, 77
Groff, Nick, 21, 87
Group karma, 28, 172-73, 198
Gurney, Edmund, 44-45, 206-07, 212, 215

Hancock, Maureen, 4, 26, 32, 118, 141, 145-46, 152, 171, 189-90
Hare, Robert, 68
Harsch-Fischbach, Jules, 84, 166, 233
Harsch-Fischbach, Maggy, 84, 166, 233
Harvard Divinity School, 44
Harvard Medical School, 209
Harvard University, 65
Hawes, Jason, 13, 18, 19, 20, 73, 96
Heaven, beautiful settings, 7, 11, 26, 37, 104, 131, 143, 149, 150-55, 182, 186, 201, 211, 225-26, 232, 233
Hell, gray areas of existence, 7-8, 115, 119, 120, 190, 131, 133, 156-66, 191, 218, 224, 231
Hildegard of Bingen, 122-23
Hitler, Adolf, 15
Hodgson, Richard, 46, 50-55, 70-71, 207-08, 210, 213, 214, 215
Hogan, R. Craig, 182
Holt, Henry, 44
Holy Spirit, 199, 218-21, 224, 227
Home, Daniel Dunglas, 41, 47, 48-49, 118, 205
Houdini, Harry, 49, 205
Hubbard, Gardiner, 44
Hyslop, James, 47, 53-54, 70, 71, 208-09, 213
Il Laboratorio, Interdisciplinary Laboratory for the Biopsychocybernetics Research, 80

270

Institute of Noetic Sciences, 61, 90
Instrumental Transcommunication (ITC), 52, 83-87, 95, 137, 162, 201
James, William, 40, 41, 44, 50, 54, 70, 203, 206, 208
Jesus, 14, 116-19, 135-36, 150, 153, 158, 164, 167, 179-80, 212, 221, 222, 223, 226, 232
John Templeton Foundation, 133-34
Jordan, Phil, 4, 26-27, 141, 161
Joseph, Saint, 123-24
Joyeux, Henri, 182
Judaism, 7, 11, 26, 109-13, 114, 150, 228
Judgment, of God unlikely, 34, 113, 121, 144, 161, 226-27, 231
Julian of Norwich, 123
Jürgenson, Friedrich, 61, 77-78, 81
Justinian, 167-69, 195
Kabbalah, 112, 167
Karma, law of cause and effect, 24, 25, 28, 32, 39, 94, 113, 120, 121, 155, 169, 172, 183, 186, 192, 195-98, 200, 201
Kelsey, Morton T., 8, 14, 119, 158
König, Hans-Otto, 84, 147
Langley, Noel, 166-68, 172
Laurentin, René, 182
Leonard, Gladys Osborne, 211
Licinius, 228
Life Reading/s, 23, 119, 123, 172, 179, 212, 220, 221, 222
Life Review, self-judgment, 34, 101-02, 130, 144, 192, 226

Light, Josh, 17
Lincoln, Abraham, 6, 28
Lincoln, Mary, 6
Lischer, Sarah Kenyon, 132
Lodge, Oliver, 50, 54-55, 70, 71, 196, 205, 210-12, 213
Lodge, Raymond, 211
Lombroso, Cesare, 54-55
Long, Jeffrey, 1, 5, 9, 32, 33, 34, 35, 36, 67, 100-02, 144-45, 151
Love, prevalence and power of, 6, 151, 196, 200-01, 232
MacRae, Alexander, 89-90
Macy, Mark, 85
Malhoff, Fritz, 84
Matla, J.L., 58
Medium/s, 3, 4-5, 10, 11, 16-17, 18, 21-26, 28, 29-32, 36, 37, 41, 42, 46-56, 59, 63, 66, 69-71, 84-85, 89-90, 99-100, 105, 110, 112, 118-20, 121, 123, 125, 127, 129, 132, 133, 135, 137, 140-43, 145, 146, 148, 149, 151-52, 155, 157-58, 160-63, 165, 169, 171-72, 175-77, 180, 183-84, 185, 187, 189-90, 193, 196, 201, 205, 207-08, 210, 211, 213-14, 217, 219-220, 226, 228, 229-32
Medjugorje, visionaries of, 91-93, 182, 201, 222
Mel Meter, 86-87
Melton, F.R., 58
Merrell, John, 27
Miller, Lisa, 8-9
Miracle/s, 29, 75, 117-19, 151, 199, 216, 222
Monophysites, 167-68
Monroe, Robert, 5, 13, 16, 28, 36, 37-39, 82, 123, 124, 140-43, 147,

151, 152-53, 155, 159-60, 164, 169, 172, 180, 226, 233
Moody, Raymond, 32
Moon, Chris, 90-91
Morse Code, 58
Moses, 109, 117, 222, 224
Moses, Stainton, 53, 213
Music, Eilfie, 17
Myers, Frederic William Henry, 44, 45, 50-51, 54, 55, 206-07, 212-13, 215-16
Mystics, mysticism, 112-13, 122-23, 139, 151, 182-83, 190, 194, 220, 222
National Public Radio, 13, 61
National Spiritualist Association of Churches, 103, 128-29
Near Death Experience Research Foundation (NDERF), 32, 34, 101, 144, 151
Near-death experience (NDE), 1, 3, 5, 7, 8, 9, 10, 22, 32-37, 52, 62, 66, 69, 94, 101, 105, 119, 122, 140-43, 151, 169, 177, 193, 195, 201, 220
New England Society for Psychic Research, 29
Newcomb, Simon, 44, 206
Newnham College, 45, 54, 214, 215
Nussbaum, Martha, 134
Ochorowicz, Julian, 55
Origen, 167-69
Orso, Renato, 80-81
Out-of-body experience (OOBE), 3, 5, 9, 10, 33, 36, 37-39, 52, 61, 67, 82, 101, 105, 112, 122-24, 135, 137, 140-42, 147, 149, 151,

152, 155, 159-60, 169, 172, 180-81, 201, 219, 220, 226, 233
Ovilus, 88-89
Palladino, Eusapia, 47-48, 54-56, 69, 212-14
Paranormal Research Society (PRS), 17-19, 20, 21, 90-91, 96, 158, 176-77
Paranormal Skeptic Academy, 100
Parapsychology, 4, 7, 8, 36, 41-42, 59, 62-64, 97-99
Parnia, Sam, 66-68
Paul, Saint, 198-201, 231
Pellew, George, 51-52
Penfield, Wilder, 102
Pentecost, 227
Piper, Leonora, 41, 47, 49-54, 207-08, 210, 211-13
Planes or levels of existence on the other side, 119-20, 124, 129, 142-43, 149, 152, 159, 191, 219, 220, 224, 226
Plato, 114-15, 167
Poberezhny, Sergey, 17
Podmore, Frank, 45, 46, 206, 212
Poe, Edgar Allan, 126
Pontius Pilate, 218, 223
Prayer, power of, 120, 148, 154-56, 164-65, 190-91, 229
Pre-birth decision/s, 28, 31, 113, 121, 166, 171-74, 198
Presi, Paolo, 80-81
Price, Robert M., 135-36
Psychic/s, 3, 4, 5, 7, 10, 22, 24, 26, 27, 29, 30, 31, 42, 52, 90, 98, 99, 119, 121, 125, 137, 146, 148, 155, 165, 169, 171, 183-84, 185,

187, 189, 190, 193, 195, 201, 220, 226, 231
Psychometry, 27
Purgatory, 7, 8, 119-20, 156-58, 191, 231
Puryear, Anne, 178, 188, 201
Pythagoras, 167
Radin, Dean, 61-62
Randi, James, 98-100
Rappings, 48, 126-27, 205
Raudive, Konstantin, 61, 77-78, 81
Rawlings, Matthew, 33
Reincarnation, past lives, 6, 7, 9, 11, 12, 22, 28, 31, 39, 94-95, 104, 112, 113, 114-15, 121, 123, 129, 133, 157, 167-72, 173, 182-83, 186, 195-98, 202, 220, 222, 223, 226-27
REM Pod, 87
Renier, Noreen, 4, 27, 120, 141, 161-63, 190
Ressler, Robert, 27
Resurrection, 7, 111-13, 115-17, 119, 135-36, 179-80, 182-83, 212, 218, 219, 222, 232
Reunion with loved ones, 34, 151, 155, 202, 219
Rhine, J.B. (Joseph Banks), 40, 63-64, 71, 97
Rhine, Louisa E., 63-64
Richet, Charles Robert, 55, 213-14
Ring, Kenneth, 32
Roach, Mary, 8-9, 67, 195-96
Rogers, E. Dawson, 213
Sabom, Michael, 32
Sacks, Oliver, 134
Savage, Minot, 44

Schreiber, Klaus, 84
Schwartz, Gary, 65
Scole Group, 84-85
September 11, 2001, 24, 25, 232
Service, as essential to spiritual growth, 6, 152, 157, 182, 198-202, 219, 232
Shaman, 76-77, 103
Shamshak, Tom, 163
Sheol, 110-12
Sidgwick, Henry, 43, 44, 52, 55, 203, 207, 214-15
Sidgwick, Nora (Balfour), 41, 44, 45-46, 54-55, 214-16
Siegel, Ronald K., 100-01
Skeptics, 2, 5, 11, 14, 15, 16, 21, 30, 31, 33, 36, 67, 68-72, 86, 98-102, 133, 135-36, 161-62, 190, 193-96, 212, 216
Slade, Henry, 69, 215
Smythe, Colin, 78
Society for Psychical Research (SPR), 4, 41, 42-56, 96, 207-08
Society for Scientific Exploration, 97
SOPHIA Project, 65-66, 118
Soul (survival of individual on the other side), 2, 4, 6, 9, 11, 12, 16, 30, 37-39, 47, 66, 73, 104, 114-25, 134-35, 141-43, 146, 149, 150, 178-79, 183-84, 185, 192-93, 201-02
Spirit circle/s, 137, 149, 157, 163, 187-88
Spirit Group Cloverleaf, 84
Spiritualism, 4, 6-7, 14, 42, 49, 57, 68, 69-70, 102, 103, 125-29, 142-43, 187, 193, 196, 203, 205, 213, 214, 216, 217

Spong, John Shelby, 9
Stephen, Saint, 229-30
Stephen, son of Anne Puryear, 178, 188, 201, 220
Stevenson, Ian, 40, 42, 61, 64, 71, 94-95, 100-01, 169, 170-71, 173
Stollznow, Karen, 99
Suicide, survival of such souls, 174-79, 188, 220
Sumption, Frank, 90
SUNY Stony Brook, 66
Survival Hypothesis, 83, 102
Swedenborg, Emanuel, 125-26
Taddy, Heather, 17
Tajna, C., 80-81
Telekinesis, validity of, 4, 11, 46, 49, 237
Tennyson, Alfred Lord, 43
Thackeray, William Makepeace, 48
The Atlantic Paranormal Society (TAPS), 17, 19, 20, 21, 95-96, 158
Theodora, 167-69, 195
Theosophical Society, 46
Thiering, Barbara, 223
Thought transference, telepathy, 4, 45, 63, 70, 155-56, 190, 203, 206, 227
Thought-action synchronicity, 38
Time, different on the other side, 155, 158, 219, 224
Tipler, Frank J., 179
Tragic, early death, 25, 32, 82, 137, 156, 173, 187, 211
Tubby, Gertrude O., 209
Tucker, James, 61-62
UNIV-CON, 17-18

University of Arizona, 64-65, 118, 184-85
University of Southampton, England, 66
University of Virginia, 61-64, 94, 184-85
Van Praagh, James, 4, 28-29, 31, 32, 141, 145-46, , 152, 155, 160, 172, 174, 190, 232
Verrall, Helen, 54
Verrall, Margaret, 54
Virgin Mary, 35, 91-93, 123-24, 150, 201, 218, 221-23
Wallace, Alfred Russel, 43, 71, 205, 213, 216-17
Wallace, Edgar, 77
Warren, Ed, 29, 158
Warren, Lorraine, 17, 29, 158
Weber, Nancy Orlen, 4, 29-30, 141, 161
Weidman, Katrina, 17
Weiss, Brian, 170-71
Wenzel, Martin, 84
Westar Institute/Jesus Seminar, 134-35
White Eagle, 147, 179-80, 224, 225
Wikipedia, 14, 67, 98, 128, 185
Wilson, Craig, 132-33
Wilson, David, 58
Wilson, Grant, 13, 18, 19
World Broadcasting Company, 59-60
World ITC, 85-86
Xenoglossy, 94
Zaalbert van Zelst, G.J., 58
Zaffis, John, 158
Zaleski, Carol, 130-32
Zohar, 112

Paranormal – Abrahamsen

[1] As I was completing the writing of this book, I came across Julia Assante, *The Last Frontier: Exploring the Afterlife and Transforming Our Fear of Death* (Novato, CA: New World Library, 2012), which elegantly treats many of the same issues I am considering. She examines three topics that support the existence of the afterlife – historical and religious accounts, near-death experiences, and after-death communication – from her viewpoint as a medium, past-life therapist and scholar of ancient Near Eastern studies. Her perspective is thus somewhat different than but highly complementary to my own.

[2] *Evidence of the Afterlife: The Science of Near-Death Experiences* (New York: HarperCollins Publishers, 2010).

[3] Eben Alexander, *Proof of Heaven: A Neurosurgeon's Journey into the Afterlife* (New York: Simon and Schuster, Inc., 2012).

[4] Reader's Digest Association, *Life Beyond Death: Quest for the Unknown* (Pleasantville, NY, and Montreal: Reader's Digest Association, Inc., 1992) 38-39.

[5] See *Journeys Out of the Body* (Garden City, NY: Anchor Books, 1973) and *Ultimate Journey* (New York: Random House, Inc., 1994).

[6] http://www.monroeinstitute.org/.

[7] Pleasantville, NY, and Montreal: Reader's Digest Association, Inc., 1992.

[8] Milford, OH: Faith Publishing Company, 1997.

[9] New York, Ramsey and Toronto: Paulist Press, 1979.

[10] Reno, NV: AA-EVP Publishing, 2008.

[11] Deepak Chopra, *Life After Death: The Burden of Proof* (New York: Harmony Books, 2006); Lisa Miller, *Heaven: Our Enduring Fascination with the Afterlife* (New York: Harper Collins Publishers, 2010); and Mary Roach, *Spook: Science Tackles the Afterlife* (New York: W.W. Norton & Company, Inc., 2005).

[12] Todd Burpo, with Lynn Vincent, *Heaven is for Real: A Little Boy's Astounding Story of His Trip to Heaven and Back* (Nashville: Thomas Nelson, Inc., 2010).

[13] New York: HarperCollins Publishers, 2009.

[14] New Lands, England: The White Eagle Publishing Trust, 2006.

[15] For those unfamiliar with the scholarly study of the early church and nascent Christianity, it is important to note that the field is based on texts, literary works, and archaeological evidence – including papyri, inscriptions,

buildings, grave monuments, art, material and biological remains – that have survived for many centuries.

[16] http://www.npr.org/series/230697113/what-comes-next-conversations-on-the-afterlife, accessed February 17, 2014.

[17] Morton T. Kelsey, *Afterlife: The Other Side of Dying* (New York, Ramsey and Toronto: Paulist Press, 1979) 9.

[18] Kelsey, *Afterlife*, 10.

[19] Arthur Conan Doyle, *A History of Spiritualism*, two volumes (New York: Arno Press, 1975; a facsimile of the 1924 edition) Vol. II, 247.

[20] See below for shows focusing on psychics and mediums, who also help others.

[21] For the full official history of PRS, see http://paranormalresearchsociety.org/overview-history/ (accessed December 15, 2012) and Ryan Buell and Stefan Petrucha, *Paranormal State: My Journey into the Unknown* (New York: HarperCollins Publishers, 2010).

[22] Buell and Petrucha, *Paranormal State*, 125.

[23] Buell and Petrucha, *Paranormal State*, 125-26.

[24] Sergey Poberezhny as quoted in Buell and Petrucha, *Paranormal State*, 32.

[25] Buell and Petrucha, *Paranormal State*, 52.

[26] See http://paranormalresearchsociety.org/ and http://www.people.com/people/article/0,,20736703,00.html, accessed May 24, 2014.

[27] See, e.g., Jason Hawes and Grant Wilson, with Michael Jan Friedman, *Ghost Hunting: True Stories of Unexplained Phenomena from The Atlantic Paranormal Society* (New York: Simon & Schuster, Inc., 2007).

[28] TAPS events, lectures, books, articles and other information can be found on their website at http://www.the-atlantic-paranormal-society.com/.

[29] Hawes, Wilson and Friedman, *Ghost Hunting*, 13.

[30] Hawes, Wilson and Friedman, *Ghost Hunting*, 14.

[31] Hawes, Wilson and Friedman, *Ghost Hunting*, 14.

[32] Hawes, Wilson and Friedman, *Ghost Hunting*, 263-67.

[33] World English Dictionary, http://dictionary.reference.com/browse/psychic?s=t, accessed March 20, 2014.

[34] The *American Heritage Dictionary of the English Language* (ed. Peter Davies [New York: Dell Publishing Co., Inc. 1970] 440) defines medium as "One thought to have powers of communicating with the spirits of the dead." Hancock refers to herself as a spirit medium and defines the term as "a

person who communicates with spirits telepathically by hearing, feeling, and seeing visual impressions, symbols, and scenes from the spirit world or heaven" (Maureen Hancock, *The Medium Next Door: Adventures of a Real-Life Ghost Whisperer* [Deerfield Beach, FL: Health Communications, Inc., 2011] 259); this definition aligns with how Caputo, who avoids the term "psychic" and uses "medium," characterizes her work. See also Buell and Petrucha, *Paranormal State*, 129.

[35] See, e.g., Buell and Petrucha, *Paranormal State*, 130.

[36] See, e.g., Michelle Belanger, *Haunting Experiences: Encounters with the Otherworldly* (Woodbury, Minnesota: Llewellyn Publications, 2009).

[37] Belanger, *Haunting*, 7.

[38] Belanger, *Haunting*, 250ff.

[39] Belanger, *Haunting*, 234.

[40] See *Long Island Medium* on TLC and her website, http://www.theresacaputo.com/.

[41] Caputo's experience of having many spirits around her all the time is paralleled by the nineteenth-century medium Charles H. Foster of Salem, Massachusetts; see Doyle, *History*, Vol. II, 30-32.

[42] See, e.g., Harmon H. Bro, *Edgar Cayce on Dreams* (New York: Paperback Library, Inc., 1968); Harmon H. Bro, *Edgar Cayce on Religion and Psychic Experience* (New York: Paperback Library, 1970); Hugh Lynn Cayce, *Venture Inward* (New York: Harper & Row, Publishers, Inc., 1964); Jeffrey Furst, *Edgar Cayce's Story of Jesus* (New York: Coward-McCann, Inc., 1968); Noel Langley, *Edgar Cayce on Reincarnation* (New York: Warner Books, Inc., 1967); and Anne Read, *Edgar Cayce on Jesus and His Church* (New York: Warner Books, Inc., 1970).

[43] Langley, *Reincarnation*, 47.

[44] Hugh Lynn Cayce, as quoted in Langley, *Reincarnation*, 10.

[45] Langley, *Reincarnation*, 264.

[46] Langley, *Reincarnation*, 52.

[47] Chip Coffey, *Growing Up Psychic: My Story of Not Just Surviving but Thriving – and How Others Like Me Can, Too* (New York: Three Rivers Press, 2012) xxxi.

[48] See, e.g., *Psychic Kids*, http://www.aetv.com/psychic-kids/, and *Growing Up Psychic*.

[49] Coffey, *Growing Up Psychic*, 196, ellipsis in original.

[50] http://www.pamcoronado.com/.

[51] http://lauriecampbell.net/.

[52] See, e.g., John Edward with Natasha Stoynoff, *After Life: Answers from the Other Side* (New York: Princess Books, a Division of Get Psych'd, Inc., 2003).
[53] Edward, *After Life*, 66; italics in original.
[54] This realization is also described in detail by Assante in *Last Frontier*, 217-19.
[55] Edward, *After Life*, 123.
[56] Edward, *After Life*, 154-55.
[57] Edward, *After Life*, 167.
[58] Edward, *After Life*, 207-10.
[59] Hancock, *Medium Next Door*, 44-52.
[60] Hancock, *Medium Next Door*, 45, 261.
[61] Hancock, *Medium Next Door*, 263-65.
[62] http://www.philjordan.com/, accessed May 24, 2014.
[63] See Noreen Renier with Naomi Lucks, *A Mind for Murder: The Real-Life Files of a Psychic Investigator* (New York: Berkley Books, 2005).
[64] Renier, *Mind for Murder*, 196-218.
[65] See, e.g., James Van Praagh, *Reaching to Heaven: A Spiritual Journey Through Life and Death* (New York: Penguin Books, 1999) and ibid., *Unfinished Business: What the Dead Can Teach Us About Life* (New York: HarperCollins Publishers, Inc., 2009).
[66] Van Praagh, *Reaching*, 40; see also Van Praagh, *Unfinished Business*, 105-08, which specifically discuss the karma of the United States and the presidency of George W. Bush.
[67] Van Praagh, *Reaching*, 75-77; see also Van Praagh, *Unfinished Business*, 83-87 and 99-103.
[68] Some of these issues include abortion (*Reaching*, 83-84), homosexuality (*Unfinished Business*, 29-33, 107-08, 188-89), and religious fundamentalism (*Unfinished Business*, 29-33).
[69] http://www.warrens.net/, accessed April 19, 2014.
[70] http://www.nancyorlenweber.com/, accessed April 19, 2014; http://lightwingcenter.org/, accessed May 26, 2014; and http://aptn.ca/theotherside/, accessed May 26, 2014.
[71] This parallels much of what was discovered by nineteenth-century investigators. See Chapter 3: A Short History of Paranormal Research for a discussion of unsuccessful efforts on the part of the nineteenth-century investigators to disprove readings of mediums Daniel D. Home, Leonora Piper, Eusapia Palladino and others.

[72] Van Praagh, *Reaching*, 76, and *Unfinished Business*, 83-87, 110-15.
[73] See, e.g., http://www.huffingtonpost.com/2013/05/27/long-island-medium-theresa-past-lives_n_3342170.html, accessed March 22, 2014.
[74] See, e.g., Brian L. Weiss, *Many Lives, Many Masters* (New York: Simon & Schuster, Inc., 1988).
[75] Van Praagh, *Unfinished Business*, 111-14.
[76] Hancock, *Medium Next Door*, 70-71.
[77] Jeffrey Long, with Paul Perry, *Evidence of the Afterlife: The Science of Near-Death Experiences* (New York: HarperCollins Publishers, 2010) 1,5.
[78] Reader's Digest, *Life Beyond Death*, 10-17, 22-28.
[79] Alexander, *Proof of Heaven*.
[80] See Burpo and Vincent, *Heaven is for Real*, and also the late 1970s treatment of NDEs by Kelsey, *Afterlife*, 79-91.
[81] Long and Perry, *Afterlife*, 68.
[82] Long and Perry, *Afterlife*, 46.
[83] Alexander, *Proof of Heaven*, 154-55.
[84] Long and Perry, *Afterlife*, 46, 69.
[85] Long and Perry, *Afterlife*, 75, italics in original.
[86] Long and Perry, *Afterlife*, 48, 85-87.
[87] Long and Perry, *Afterlife*, 47.
[88] Long and Perry, *Afterlife*, 104.
[89] Long and Perry, *Afterlife*, 102.
[90] Long and Perry, *Afterlife*, 48-49, 107-15, italics in original.
[91] Long and Perry, *Afterlife*, 123, 129. See also Alexander, *Proof of Heaven*, 169, and Assante, *Last Frontier*, 294-95.
[92] Long and Perry, *Afterlife*, 142; Burpo and Vincent, *Heaven is for Real*, 152-53.
[93] Long and Perry, *Afterlife*, 49, 123.
[94] Long and Perry, *Afterlife*, 49-50, 137.
[95] Long and Perry, *Afterlife*, 145.
[96] Long and Perry, *Afterlife*, 50, 149.
[97] Long and Perry, *Afterlife*, 150, italics in original.
[98] Long and Perry, *Afterlife*, 155, 158-59.
[99] Alexander, *Proof of Heaven*, 185-88.
[100] Reader's Digest, *Life Beyond Death*, 29, 33, 35.
[101] Blackmore website, http://www.susanblackmore.co.uk/, accessed March 22, 2014.

[102] Reader's Digest, *Life Beyond Death*, 35. This does not, of course, explain the thousands of testimonies from around the world of objects, events and people witnessed during an OOBE that can be confirmed by tested means.
[103] http://www.susanblackmore.co.uk/.
[104] Chopra, *Life After Death*, 126-29.
[105] Eternea, http://eternea.org, is the non-profit research, educational and outreach organization that was co-founded by Dr. Alexander following his NDE.
[106] Monroe's early explorations and findings are treated most completely in *Journeys*. The Monroe Institute is located at 62 Roberts Mountain Road, Faber, Virginia 22938; http://www.monroeinstitute.org/.
[107] Monroe, *Journeys*, 171.
[108] Monroe, *Journeys*, 79-80, 111-12.
[109] Monroe, *Journeys*, 114-15.
[110] See e.g., Monroe, *Ultimate Journey*, 11-12: "If you want to prove – to yourself and to no one else – that we survive physical death, you can learn to move into the out-of-body state and seek out a friend, relative, or someone close to you who has recently died. To find them, all you need do is tune in on your memory of what that person was or represented. Several such meetings will be enough."
[111] Monroe, *Journeys*, 124.
[112] Monroe, *Journeys*, 127.
[113] Monroe, *Journeys*, 182; italics in original.
[114] Monroe, *Ultimate Journey*, passim.
[115] See for example Monroe, *Ultimate Journey*, 152-55, 251, 253.
[116] For example, see Monroe, *Journeys*, 81-82, and *Ultimate Journey*, 168-69, 183-84.
[117] Assante, *Last Frontier*, provides explicit techniques on communicating with the departed.
[118] Deborah Blum, *Ghost Hunters: William James and the Search for Scientific Proof of Life After Death* (London: Penguin Press, 2006) 72.
[119] "Society for Psychical Research," *Wikipedia*, http://en.wikipedia.org/wiki/Society_for_Psychical_Research, (accessed November 14, 2013) 1.
[120] "Society for Psychical Research," *Wikipedia*, 2.
[121] Blum, *Ghost Hunters*, 73.
[122] Doyle, *History*. Doyle will feature prominently in Chapter 6: Themes and Findings and Chapter 7: Ethics and Comfort, since he communicated from

the other side, through his medium, for at least two years after his death in 1930. His extensive descriptions of "heaven" are found in *Arthur Conan Doyle's Book of the Beyond* (New Lands, England: The White Eagle Publishing Trust, 2006), written by Ivan Cooke, husband of Doyle's medium, Grace Cooke.

[123] Blum, *Ghost Hunters*, 72. See also "William Fletcher Barrett," *Wikipedia*, http://en.wikipedia.org/wiki/William_Fletcher_Barrett, accessed September 24, 2013; "Edmund Gurney," *Wikipedia*, http://en.wikipedia.org/wiki/Edmund_Gurney, accessed September 24, 2013; and "Frederic William Henry Myers," *Wikipedia*, http://en.wikipedia.org/wiki/Frederic_William_Henry_Myers , accessed September 24, 2013.

[124] Blum, *Ghost Hunters*, 82.

[125] Blum, *Ghost Hunters*, 86.

[126] Blum, *Ghost Hunters*, 87.

[127] Blum, *Ghost Hunters*, 87-90.

[128] "American Society for Psychical Research," *Wikipedia*, http://en.wikipedia.org/wiki/American_Society_for_Psychical_Research, accessed November 14, 2013.

[129] This was one of the techniques objected to by Newcomb.

[130] Blum, *Ghost Hunters*, 126. The survey question read: "Since January 1, 1874, have you – when in good health, free from anxiety and completely awake – had a vivid impression of seeing or being touched by a human being, or of hearing a voice or sound which suggested a human presence, when no one was there? Yes or no?"

[131] Blum, *Ghost Hunters*, 121.

[132] Blum, *Ghost Hunters*, 182-83.

[133] "Society for Psychical Research," *Wikipedia*, 2.

[134] Blum, *Ghost Hunters*, 225.

[135] Blum, *Ghost Hunters*, 227-29.

[136] Blum, *Ghost Hunters*, 245-46.

[137] See Doyle, *History*, Vol. II, 81-82.

[138] Doyle, *History*, Vol. II, 75.

[139] Blum, *Ghost Hunters*, 245-47.

[140] "Daniel Dunglas Home," *Wikipedia*, http://en.wikipedia.org/wiki/Daniel_Dunglas_Home (accessed September 24, 2013) 1-3.

[141] "Daniel Dunglas Home," *Wikipedia*, 4.

[142] Doyle, *History*, Vol. I, 204; "Daniel Dunglas Home," *Wikipedia*, 4.
[143] According to Doyle, *History*, "never in the course of the thirty years of [Home's] strange ministry did he touch one shilling as payment for his gifts" (Vol. I, 189).
[144] "Daniel Dunglas Home," *Wikipedia*, 4.
[145] "William Crookes," *Wikipedia*, http://en.wikipedia.org/wiki/William_Crookes (accessed September 24, 2013) 3.
[146] Blum, *Ghost Hunters*, 229-30. See also Doyle, *History*, Vol. I, 209: "The powers of Home have been attested by so many famous observers, and were shown under such frank conditions, that no reasonable man can possibly doubt them. Crookes's evidence alone is conclusive."
[147] Doyle, *History*, Vol. I, 96, 98. More will be said about the Fox sisters – Leah, Maggie and Kate – in a discussion of Spiritualism in Chapter 5.
[148] Blum, *Ghost Hunters*, 229-30.
[149] "Leonora Piper," *Wikipedia*, http://en.wikipedia.org/wiki/Leonora_Piper, accessed September 24, 2013. This *Wikipedia* article is so heavily biased against the validity of Piper that it is almost unusable. The author refers to Deborah Blum's excellent book, *Ghost Hunters*, but ignores almost everything positive that Blum says about Piper, which is extensive and drawn from many reliable sources.
[150] Blum, *Ghost Hunters*, 97-100. See also Doyle, *History*, Vol. II, 75.
[151] Blum, *Ghost Hunters*, 133-36, 141.
[152] Blum states, "Leonora Piper became Richard Hodgson's personal obsession" (*Ghost Hunters*, 142). The *Wikipedia* article on Piper uses this statement as part of its outright disparagement of both Hodgson and Piper, which is unfortunate, since Hodgson's investigations were highly ethical and methodical and only served to convince himself and others of Piper's validity. The *Wikipedia* article on Hodgson, similarly, refers to Blum but again does not acknowledge the many pages in Blum's work that support Hodgson's growing belief in the survival of the personality after death.
[153] Blum, *Ghost Hunters*, 152.
[154] Blum, *Ghost Hunters*, 159.
[155] Blum, *Ghost Hunters*, 163-64.
[156] Blum, *Ghost Hunters*, 181. We will see more modern examples of this phenomenon in Chapter 4 when we examine the visionaries of Medjugorje.
[157] Blum, *Ghost Hunters*, 185-86. Note that Doyle, *History*, gives this man the name George Pelham (Vol. II, 79-80).

[158] Blum, *Ghost Hunters*, 186-87; Doyle, *History*, Vol. II, 80.
[159] Blum, *Ghost Hunters*, 217.
[160] Blum, *Ghost Hunters*, 218. See also Doyle, *History*, Vol. II, 73: Hodgson, James and Hyslop all became "convinced of the genuineness of the phenomena occurring in [Piper's] presence and all favoured the Spiritualistic interpretation of them."
[161] Doyle, *History*, Vol. II, 81.
[162] Blum, *Ghost Hunters*, 220-21. See also, e.g., Anne Puryear, *Stephen Lives! My Son Stephen: His Life, Suicide, and Afterlife* (New York: Pocket Books, a division of Simon & Schuster Inc., 1992, 1996) passim, on the difficulties of communicating with her deceased son after his suicide, even though she had already been communicating with spirit "guides" for some time previously.
[163] Blum, *Ghost Hunters*, 274. This too has parallels in Puryear, *Stephen Lives!*, and other sources.
[164] Doyle, *History*, Vol. II, 83-84.
[165] Doyle, *History*, Vol. II, 76.
[166] Blum, *Ghost Hunters*, 276. See also an accounting of tests conducted in England by SPR, Lodge and others on "cross-correspondence" that caused Nora Sidgwick to concede in 1913 that these studies "offered real evidence of 'cooperation by friends and fellow-workers no longer in the body'" (277-319).
[167] "Eusapia Palladino," http://en.wikipedia.org/wiki/Eusapia_Palladino, accessed February 14, 2014. See also Blum, *Ghost Hunters*, 167, 192.
[168] Blum, *Ghost Hunters*, 192.
[169] Doyle, *History*, Vol. II, 29.
[170] Blum, *Ghost Hunters*, 193.
[171] "Palladino," *Wikipedia*.
[172] Blum, *Ghost Hunters*, 193. While we will not dwell on the phenomenon of ectoplasm in this book, it should be noted that it is a substance that is occasionally encountered by the *Ghost Adventures* investigators and perhaps others.
[173] "Palladino," *Wikipedia*, and Blum, *Ghost Hunters*, 193-94.
[174] Blum, *Ghost Hunters*, 200-01.
[175] "Palladino," *Wikipedia*.
[176] Blum, *Ghost Hunters*, 319. Note the negative approach to Carrington taken by Mary Roach in *Spook*, 114-17, where she refers to him as a "gizmo geek" and focuses solely on his more dubious experiments and writings.

[177] Doyle, *History*, Vol. II, 28.
[178] Tom and Lisa Butler, *There is No Death and There are No Dead* (Reno, NV: AA-EVP Publishing, 2008), see especially 2-30.
[179] Reader's Digest, *Life Beyond Death*, 82.
[180] As quoted by Butler and Butler, *No Death*, 6.
[181] Butler and Butler, *No Death*, 3-4. Roach, *Spook*, also discusses Matla and Zaalberg van Zelst but criticizes them as having hubris and being arrogant and puts them in the same category as Carrington (114-15).
[182] Butler and Butler, *No Death*, 4-7.
[183] Butler and Butler, *No Death*, 5-6.
[184] Butler and Butler, *No Death*, 7-9; italics in original.
[185] See Butler and Butler, *No Death*, 9-11.
[186] http://www.medicine.virginia.edu/clinical/departments/psychiatry/sections/cspp/dops/home-page, accessed May 28, 2014.
[187] HarperOne, 1997.
[188] Simon & Schuster, 2006. See http://www.medicine.virginia.edu/clinical/departments/psychiatry/ sections/cspp/dops/home-page, accessed May 28, 2014.
[189] http://www.medicine.virginia.edu/clinical/departments/psychiatry/sections/cspp/dops/home-page, accessed May 28, 2014.
[190] http://www.medicine.virginia.edu/clinical/departments/psychiatry/sections/cspp/dops/home-page, accessed May 28, 2014.
[191] http://library.duke.edu/rubenstein/findingaids/paralab/, accessed May 28, 2014.
[192] http://library.duke.edu/rubenstein/findingaids/paralab/, accessed May 28, 2014.
[193] http://www.rhine.org/who-we-are/history.html, accessed May 28, 2014.
[194] http://library.duke.edu/rubenstein/findingaids/paralab/, accessed May 28, 2014.
[195] http://library.duke.edu/rubenstein/findingaids/paralab/, accessed May 28, 2014.
[196] http://www.rhine.org/who-we-are/history.html, accessed May 28, 2014.
[197] http://lach.web.arizona.edu/veritas_research_program, accessed May 29, 2014.
[198] http://lach.web.arizona.edu/veritas_research_program, accessed May 29, 2014. Roach met Schwartz during her research for *Spook* and has high regard for him; however, she focused primarily on experiments that were less

successful and seemed dubious about Schwartz's optimism and tenacity (151-68).
[199] http://lach.web.arizona.edu/veritas_research_program, accessed May 29, 2014.
[200] http://lach.web.arizona.edu/veritas_research_program, accessed May 29, 2014. Interestingly, Dr. Beischel's fellowship was named the William James Post-doctoral Fellowship in Mediumship and Survival Research, and she was its first recipient. Beischel is discussed by Roach in *Spook*, 154-56.
[201] http://medicine.stonybrookmedicine.edu/medicine/faculty/parnia, accessed June 28, 2014.
[202] http://horizonresearch.org/main_page.php?cat_id=38, accessed June 28, 2014.
[203] Participants in the program can be found at http://horizonresearch.org/main_page.php?cat_id=213, accessed June 30, 2014.
[204] http://horizonresearch.org/main_page.php?cat_id=38, accessed June 28, 2014.
[205] http://en.wikipedia.org/wiki/AWARE:_Awareness_during_resuscitation#AWARE, accessed June 30, 2014.
[206] http://infidels.org/library/modern/keith_augustine/HNDEs.html#experiments, accessed June 30, 2014.
[207] http://infidels.org/library/modern/keith_augustine/HNDEs.html#experiments, accessed June 30, 2014.
[208] Doyle, *History*, Vol. I, 138.
[209] Doyle, *History*, Vol. I, 252.
[210] Doyle, *History*, Vol. I, 316.
[211] Doyle, *History*, Vol. II, 199-200.
[212] See e.g., Doyle, *History*, Vol. I, 297-98, and Vol. II, 20.
[213] See Assante, *Last Frontier*, passim, Edward, Van Praagh, Caputo and Hancock, for instance.
[214] See, e.g., Doyle, *History*, Vol. I, 306.
[215] For discussions of skeptics and skepticism pertaining to paranormal research, see Tom Butler, "Why Has There Not Been More Study of the Paranormal?" (http://atransc.org/research/research_funding_nsf.htm, accessed December 27, 2012); Tom Butler, "Concerns with Wikipedia" (http://atransc.org/articles/concerns_with_wikipedia.htm, accessed December 27, 2012); Dean Radin, Review, *Parapsychology and the Skeptics: A Scientific Argument for the Existence of ESP* by Chris Carter, in *The Journal*

of Parapsychology 71 (Spring-Fall 2007) 184-85; David Fontana, "ITC and its Role in Survival Research," *ITC Journal* (April 2007; http://atransc.org/articles/fontana-itc.htm, accessed April 7, 2012). See also Kelsey, *Afterlife*, 7-73.

[216] Butler and Butler, *No Death*, 2-3.
[217] Butler and Butler, *No Death*, 7.
[218] Butler and Butler, *No Death*, 13.
[219] Butler and Butler, *No Death*, 14-15, and R. Craig Hogan, "Applying the Science of the Afterlife," *Journal of Spirituality and Paranormal Studies*, Vol. 32, Issue 1 (Jan. 2009) 14.
[220] See Butler and Butler, *No Death*, 13, 120-21, 177-78.
[221] Butler and Butler, *No Death*, 20.
[222] Butler and Butler, *No Death*, viii, and Coffey, *Growing Up Psychic*, 162; Lisa Butler, "Electronic Voice Phenomena as Evidence for Life After Death," *Journal of Spirituality and Paranormal Studies* (Annual Conference 2007 Proceedings) 130; Thomas Wingert, "Continuing a relation with the deceased: A contemporary choice for coping with grief," http://atransc.org/articles/wingert-greif_mgmt.htm, 2002 (accessed December 27, 2012) 2.
[223] Tom Butler, "Physical Processes Involved in Trans-etheric Influences," originally published in the fall 2009 *ATransC NewsJournal* (http://atransc.org/theory/trans-etheric_influence.htm, accessed March 25, 2012) 1.
[224] See http://atransc.org/theory/terms_a-l.htm#E for an explanation of etheric energy, which can be roughly equated to spiritual energy. Etheric energy is everywhere at once (nonlocal), not time-bound, and influenced by intention. "Trans-etheric" can be defined as "From the etheric aspect of reality to the physical aspect of reality" (http://atransc.org/theory/terms_m-z.htm#T; accessed April 13, 2013).
[225] Tom Butler, "Physical Processes," 2.
[226] Lisa Butler, "Precursor Sounds in Physical Phenomena," as published in the Summer 2002 AA-EVP NewsJournal (http://atransc.org/articles/precursor_sound.htm, accessed April 7, 2012) 1-2.
[227] Lisa Butler, "Evidence," 132.
[228] Paolo Presi, "Italian Research in ITC: The Interdisciplinary Laboratory For Biopsychocybernetics Research (Il Laboratorio)," originally published in *ITC Journal* (March 2000) by Anabela Cardoso

(http://atransc.org/articles/presi-italian_research.htm, accessed April 7, 2012) 2.
[229] See, e.g., Doyle, *History*, Vol. I, 306.
[230] Presi, "Italian Research," 2. See also Anabela Cardoso, "Brief Remarks on the Role of the Recipient in ITC," *ITC Journal*, http://atransc.org/articles/Cardoso-itc.htm, 2002; accessed June 28, 2013.
[231] Presi, "Italian Research," 2-3.
[232] Presi, "Italian Research," 3.
[233] Tom Butler, "Electronic Voice Phenomena: A Tool for Validating Personal Survival," *The Journal of Religion and Psychical Research* (2002) 216; and Butler and Butler, *No Death*, 202-10.
[234] Butler and Butler, *No Death*, 210.
[235] See Monroe, *Journeys*, passim.
[236] Lisa Butler, "Evidence," 132.
[237] See, e.g., Anabela Cardoso, "ITC Contacts with Animals?" Previously published in the August 2008 ITC Journal: www.itcjournal.org. http://aransc.org/articles/cardoso-contact_with_animals.htm, accessed April 7, 2012.
[238] Tom Butler, "What we Know about Life After Death via EVP/ITC," *Annual Conference 2007 Proceedings* (Academy of Spirituality and Paranormal Studies, Inc., 2007) 135.
[239] Tom Butler, "Electronic Voice Phenomena," 223.
[240] Butler and Butler, *No Death*, 76-79.
[241] Butler and Butler, *No Death*, 79-82.
[242] Butler and Butler, *No Death*, 151, 174.
[243] Tom Butler, "What We Know," 144.
[244] Padú Lampe, "Instrumental Communication with the Dead," *The Journal of Religion and Psychical Research*, Vol. 16, No. 2 (April 1993) 147.
[245] See Lisa Butler, "Evidence," 130, for a short discussion of spirit teams.
[246] Anabela Cardoso, David Fontana, and Ernst Senkowski, "Experiment transcript only for Visiting Hans Otto König," *AA-EVP NewsJournal* (originally published in the ITC Journal, No. 24, December 2005; accessed December 27, 2012) 1.
[247] Butler and Butler, *No Death*, 22-23; Lampe, "Instrumental," 147-48.
[248] Lampe, "Instrumental," 147.
[249] Hogan, "Afterlife," 14, 16-17.
[250] Butler and Butler, *No Death*, 154-56.
[251] Butler and Butler, *No Death*, 28-29.

[252] Butler and Butler, *No Death*, 150-52. See also http://atransc.org/examples/itc_bennett_2.htm, accessed May 11, 2013.
[253] Butler and Butler, *No Death*, 23-24.
[254] Butler and Butler, *No Death*, 63.
[255] Butler and Butler, *No Death*, 151, 174.
[256] Coffey, *Growing Up Psychic*," 162.
[257] Coffey, *Growing Up Psychic*," 162, and Hawes, Wilson and Friedman, *Ghost Hunting*, 264. See also *Wikipedia* for a scientific explanation of EMF measurements, http://en.wikipedia.org/wiki/EMF_Detector, accessed April 14, 2013; and Buell and Petrucha, *Paranormal State*, 52.
[258] http://www.ghoststop.com/REM-Pod-EMF-Detector-p/emf-rempod.htm, accessed April 27, 2013.
[259] http://en.wikipedia.org/wiki/List_of_Ghost_Adventures_episodes, accessed April 14, 2013.
[260] http://en.wikipedia.org/wiki/List_of_Ghost_Adventures_episodes, accessed April 14, 2013.
[261] Hawes, Wilson and Friedman, *Ghost Hunting*, 263-64.
[262] Buell and Petrucha, *Paranormal State*, 52.
[263] http://www.ghoststop.com/EVP-Recorders-Ghost-Hunting-s/59.htm, accessed June 22, 2013.
[264] http://www.ghoststop.com/Spirit-Box-B-PSB7-EVP-for-ITC-p/evp-psb7-amfm.htm, accessed April 27, 2013.
[265] Coffey, *Growing Up Psychic*, 169.
[266] http://www.digitaldowsing.com/themes/digitaldowsing/images/DBB.pdf, accessed April 14, 2013.
[267] http://www.digitaldowsing.com/themes/digitaldowsing/images/DBB.pdf, accessed April 14, 2013.
[268] http://www.ghoststop.com/Ghost-Box-Ovilus-X-p/evp-ovilusx.htm?gclid=CKCCx4aL67YCFcfd4Aodvw4Afg, accessed April 27, 2013.
[269] Butler and Butler, *No Death*, 61-62. See also other EVPs detected by MacRae and his device, 103, and http://atransc.org/articles/macrae_2007.htm, accessed June 2, 2013.
[270] Josh Light in Buell and Petrucha, *Paranormal State*, 353.
[271] Buell and Petrucha, *Paranormal State*, 342.
[272] Buell and Petrucha, *Paranormal State*, 342-45, 348.
[273] Buell and Petrucha, *Paranormal State*, 344-45. See also a reference to Frank's Box in Coffey, *Growing Up Psychic*, 23.

[274] This is confirmed many times by Assante, *Last Frontier*.
[275] See http://www.medjugorje.org/, accessed June 11, 2013.
[276] René Laurentin and Henri Joyeux, *Scientific and Medical Studies on the Apparitions at Medjugorje* (Dublin: Veritas Publications, 1987) 6-8; see also 16-17.
[277] Laurentin and Joyeux, *Medjugorje*, 50.
[278] Laurentin and Joyeux, *Medjugorje*, passim.
[279] http://en.wikipedia.org/wiki/Medjugorje, accessed June 11, 2013.
[280] Laurentin and Joyeux, *Medjugorje*, 48-49.
[281] Laurentin and Joyeux, *Medjugorje*, 18.
[282] Laurentin and Joyeux, *Medjugorje*, 26.
[283] Laurentin and Joyeux, *Medjugorje*, 14, quoting Dr. Lucia Capello.
[284] Laurentin and Joyeux, *Medjugorje*, 53-54.
[285] Laurentin and Joyeux, *Medjugorje*, 75.
[286] http://medjugorje.org/ivanse.htm, accessed June 22, 2013.
[287] http://en.wikipedia.org/wiki/Ian_Stevenson, accessed August 27, 2013.
[288] Erlendur Haraldsson, "Obituaries: Ian Stevenson 1918-2007," *The Journal of Parapsychology*, Vol. 71 (Spring-Fall 2007) 159-68.
[289] http://en.wikipedia.org/wiki/Ian_Stevenson, accessed August 27, 2013.
[290] Haraldsson, "Obituaries," 162.
[291] Haraldsson, "Obituaries," 163-64.
[292] Hawes, Wilson and Friedman, *Ghost Hunting*, 14.
[293] Buell and Petrucha, *Paranormal State*, 51-52.
[294] http://www.spr.ac.uk/main/, accessed August 29, 2013.
[295] http://www.spr.ac.uk/main/page/spr-publications-parapsychology, accessed August 29, 2013.
[296] http://en.wikipedia.org/wiki/American_Society_for_Psychical_Research, accessed August 29, 2013.
[297] http://www.parapsych.org/home.aspx, accessed August 29, 2013.
[298] http://www.parapsych.org/section/17/journal_of_parapsychology.aspx, accessed August 29, 2013.
[299] http://www.scientificexploration.org/journal/, accessed August 29, 2013.
[300] http://fromgrieftobelief.com/index.htm, accessed August 29, 2013.
[301] http://fromgrieftobelief.com/About%20Us.htm, accessed August 29, 2013.
[302] Coffey, *Growing Up Psychic*, 129.
[303] http://en.wikipedia.org/wiki/Psychic_detective, accessed August 29, 2013.
[304] http://en.wikipedia.org/wiki/Paranormal#Parapsychology, accessed August 29, 2013.

[305] http://en.wikipedia.org/wiki/James_Randi, accessed August 29, 2013. One obvious and automatic explanation for EVPs and photographic and videographic images of the deceased is fraud: recordings and images are fabricated, air-brushed or otherwise tampered with. Fraud has certainly been perpetrated throughout the entire history of paranormal research; many frauds have been exposed. As we have seen, however, dozens, if not hundreds, of investigators all over the world have, especially in recent decades, completely ruled out fraud in scores of experiments. Scientists and other highly trained investigators from fields of physics, electricity, chemistry and others have conducted controlled experiments and scientifically documented not only their results but also how they eliminated the possibility of fraud or tampering.
[306] http://www.randi.org/site/index.php/swift-blog/1755-long-island-medium-a-tall-story.html, accessed August 29, 2013.
[307] http://paranormalskepticacademy.com/, accessed August 29, 2013.
[308] Buell and Petrucha, *Paranormal State*, 178.
[309] Ian Stevenson, "Comments on 'The Psychology of Life After Death,'" *American Psychologist* (November 1981) 1459-61.
[310] Alexander, *Proof of Heaven*, 185-88. See also Reader's Digest, *Life Beyond Death*, 29, 33, 52-53.
[311] Long and Perry, *Afterlife*, 80, italics in original.
[312] Long and Perry, *Afterlife*, 104. See also Assante, *Last Frontier*, 47-48, 50-52; Chopra, *Life After Death*, 122-26; and Raymond A., Moody,Jr., with Paul Perry, *The Light Beyond* (New York: Bantam Books, 1988) passim.
[313] Long and Perry, *Afterlife*, 117-20.
[314] See, e.g., Spong, *Eternal Life*, 150.
[315] This overview will focus primarily on Christianity, since that is the author's area of expertise, and Judaism. The reader can find helpful discussions of Jewish, Christian, Muslim and other afterlife beliefs and practices in such recent works as Assante, *Last Frontier*, and Miller, *Heaven*.
[316] Old Europe is a term coined by the late anthropologist Marija Gimbutas: "the collective identity and achievement of the different cultural groups of Neolithic-Chalcolithic southeastern Europe. The area it occupied extends from the Aegean and Adriatic, including the islands, as far north as Czechoslovakia, southern Poland and the western Ukraine. See Marija Gimbutas, *The Goddesses and Gods of Old Europe 6500-3500 BC: Myths and Cult Images* (Berkeley and Los Angeles: University of California Press, 1996. First ed.: London: Thames and Hudson Ltd., 1974, 1982. Originally

published in the U.S. in 1974 by University of California Press under the title *The Gods and Goddesses of Old Europe: 7000-3500 BC*. New and updated edition in paperback, 1982) 17.

[317] See for a discussion of the Neolithic nature deity Valerie A. Abrahamsen, *Goddess and God: A Holy Tension in the First Christian Centuries* (Marco Polo Monographs 10. Warren Center, PA: Shangri-La Publications, 2006) 19-45, e.g., and passim.

[318] Marija Gimbutas, *The Civilization of the Goddess*, ed. Joan Marler (San Francisco: HarperSan Francisco, 1991) vii.

[319] Gimbutas, *Civilization*, viii.

[320] Gimbutas, *Civilization*, viii.

[321] Marija Gimbutas, *The Language of the Goddess* (San Francisco: Harper and Row, Publishers, 1989) 125-37.

[322] Gimbutas, *Language*, 195.

[323] Gimbutas, *Language*, 195.

[324] Abrahamsen, *Goddess and God*, 20.

[325] Abrahamsen, *Goddess and God*, 30, and Gimbutas, *Civilization*, 9.

[326] See, for instance, Assante, *Last Frontier*, 119.

[327] Assante, *Last Frontier*, and Miller, *Heaven*, both have helpful discussions of Jewish perspectives on the afterlife.

[328] Michael D. Coogan, "Exodus, The," in Bruce M. Metzger and Michael D. Coogan, eds., *Oxford Companion to the Bible* (New York and Oxford: Oxford University Press, 1993) 209.

[329] Coogan, "Exodus," 210.

[330] Robert North, "Exile," in *Oxford Companion to the Bible*, eds. Bruce M. Metzger and Michael D. Coogan (New York and Oxford: Oxford University Press, 1993) 209.

[331] North, "Exile," 209.

[332] Wayne T. Pitard, "Afterlife and Immortality: Ancient Israel," in Bruce M. Metzger and Michael D. Coogan, eds., *Oxford Companion to the Bible* (New York and Oxford: Oxford University Press, 1993) 15.

[333] Pitard, "Afterlife," 16. See also Assante, *Last Frontier*, 108-09.

[334] Pitard, "Afterlife," 16.

[335] Sidnie Ann White, "Afterlife and Immortality: Second Temple Judaism and Early Christianity," in Bruce M. Metzger and Michael D. Coogan, eds. *Oxford Companion to the Bible* (New York and Oxford: Oxford University Press, 1993) 16. We will hear more about Plato below.

[336] Thomas Francis Glasson, "Heaven," in *Oxford Companion to the Bible*, eds. Bruce M. Metzger and Michael D. Coogan (New York and Oxford: Oxford University Press, 1993) 270.
[337] White, "Afterlife," 17. See also Everett Ferguson, *Backgrounds of Early Christianity*, 2nd ed. (Grand Rapids: William B. Eerdmans Publishing Company, 1993) 520-21, and Assante, *Last Frontier*, 111.
[338] Samuel A. Meier, "Evil," in Bruce M. Metzger and Michael D. Coogan, eds. *Oxford Companion to the Bible* (New York and Oxford: Oxford University Press, 1993) 208. For Biblical passages, see Job 38.8-11, Isaiah 45:7, Jeremiah 4:6, Amos 3:6, 1 Kings 17:20, Lamentations 3:1-106, 1 Samuel 16:14-16, etc.
[339] Miller, *Heaven*, 234.
[340] This compilation is culled from the following sources: Ferguson, *Backgrounds*, 233-34, 314; Miller, *Heaven*, 45-46; Assante, *Last Frontier*, 104-06, 112-16; Alfred Edward Taylor and Philip Merlan, "Plato," *Encyclopaedia Britannica* (Chicago: Encyclopaedia Britannica, Inc., 1963) Vol. 18, 54-56, 63; and Langley, *Reincarnation*, passim.
[341] Taylor and Merlan, "Plato," 54-55. See also Assante, *Last Frontier*, 105-06 and 159-60. We should always resist the temptation to see body and soul in purely dualistic terms – body and material existence are bad, soul is good. Dualistic thinking too often leads to extremes of behavior and thinking that are more destructive than helpful.
[342] Taylor and Merlan, "Plato," 55-56.
[343] We shall trace the history of Christianity's condemnation of reincarnation in Chapter 6.
[344] See discussions of this evolution in Miller, *Heaven*, 60-61, and Assante, *Last Frontier*, 112-15.
[345] See especially Miller, *Heaven*, 105-11.
[346] Ferguson, *Backgrounds*, 151-53, 360-61.
[347] "In that state of purification of the physical form he [Jesus] vanished, when the time came, from the sight of his disciples. . . [T]his can be done by all who have attained to the required degree of initiation into spiritual life" (Cooke, *Book of the Beyond*, 246).
[348] See Miller, *Heaven*, 143-50; "Indulgences," in F.L. Cross and E.A. Livingstone, eds., *The Oxford Dictionary of the Christian Church* (Oxford: Oxford University Press, 1985) 700; and "Purgatory," *Oxford Dictionary*, 1144-46.
[349] Kelsey, *Afterlife*, 247.

[350] See, e.g., "Reducing the use of incarceration: What can we learn from Europe?" Rob Allen, for the Criminal Justice Alliance, May 2012; http://www.prisonpolicy.org/scans/CJA_ReducingImprisonment_Europe.pdf; http://www.crimlinks.com/MurderRateInternational.html; and http://www.theguardian.com/news/datablog/2012/jul/22/gun-homicides-ownership-world-list.

[351] Church Pension Fund, *The Book of Common Prayer* (New York: The Church Hymnal Corporation, 1986) 486.

[352] Miller, in *Heaven*, and Roach, *Spook*, both address this question in different ways.

[353] "Mysticism," in Cross and Livingstone, *Oxford Dictionary*, 952.

[354] New English Bible translation.

[355] Assante, *Last Frontier*, 283.

[356] Monroe, *Journeys*, 203-04.

[357] Chopra, *Life After Death*, 15-16.

[358] Doyle, *History*, Vol. I, 12-13.

[359] Doyle, *History*, Vol. I, 18-20.

[360] Doyle, *History*, Vol. I, 47-49.

[361] Doyle, *History*, Vol. I, 55-59.

[362] Doyle, *History*, Vol. I, 59.

[363] Doyle, *History*, Vol. I, 61-69.

[364] Doyle, *History*, Vol. I, 73-74.

[365] "Fox Sisters," *Wikipedia*, http://en.wikipedia.org/wiki/Fox_sisters, accessed September 24, 2013; Barbara Weisberg, *Talking to the Dead: Kate and Maggie Fox and the Rise of Spiritualism* (New York: HarperSanFrancisco, 2004) 212, 224-46, and passim; and Doyle, *History*, Vol. I, 89-104.

[366] Doyle, *History*, Vol. I, 86-88, 91, 93, 94, 100, etc. Weisberg makes the argument that "Kate is central to the mystery of the Fox sisters," and asserts that her gifts might be attributed primarily to her playful personality, the societal restrictions on women and girls in the nineteenth century, and pre-puberty hormonal changes (Weisberg, *Talking to the Dead*, 242-43, 248 and passim). As modern mediums and psychics have reported time and again, however, their psychic gifts often manifest very early in their lives and only become more refined over time; this certainly seems to be the case with all three Fox sisters.

[367] Doyle, *History*, Vol. I, 90.

[368] Doyle, *History*, Vol. I, 105, and Weisberg, *Talking to the Dead*, 242.

[369] See Doyle, *History*, Vol. I, 108-118. It is noteworthy that the *Wikipedia* article on the Fox sisters quotes Doyle, *History*, several times, yet the author ignores most of the positive conclusions about the sisters that Doyle reaches ("Fox Sisters," *Wikipedia*). The *Wikipedia* author dismisses the findings of the bones in the Foxes' cellar with one statement – "No missing person named Charles B. Rosma was every identified" – yet Doyle provides several plausible explanations about the skeleton and other corroborating information over the span of five pages (73-77). In fairness to *Wikipedia*, and significantly, the author extensively quotes prominent scientist William Crookes in his positive assessment of Kate Fox's abilities.

[370] National Spiritualist Association of Churches, "Foundation Facts Concerning Spiritualism as a Religion," pamphlet (Lily Dale, NY: National Spiritualist Association of Churches, revised April 9, 2002).

[371] Doyle, *History*, Vol. II, 179-80; Cooke, *Book of the Beyond*, 202; "Spiritualism," *Wikipedia*, http://en.wikipedia.org/wiki/Spiritualism, accessed October 12, 2013. Note that Spiritism, a branch of Spiritualism developed in the 1850s and still adhered to today in some parts of the world, does hold to reincarnation (Doyle, *History*, Vol. II, 171, 174; and "Spiritualism," *Wikipedia*).

[372] Carol Zaleski, *The Life of the World to Come: Near-Death Experience and Christian Hope* (New York and Oxford: Oxford University Press, 1996) 34. In the interest of full disclosure, Dr. Zaleski was one of my teaching assistants at Harvard Divinity School in the 1970s and was more recently a colleague of mine at Smith College. I have a great deal of respect for her scholarship and for her as a person.

[373] Zaleski, *World to Come*, 81-82.

[374] Carol Zaleski, "Immortal dreams," *Christian Century* (November 28, 2012) 35.

[375] Rodney Clapp, "Life after life after death," *Christian Century* (May 30, 2012) 45.

[376] Rodney Clapp, "Animals in the kingdom," *Christian Century* (June 27, 2012) 45.

[377] Sarah Kenyon Lischer, "Reports of heaven," *Christian Century* (August 7, 2013) 13.

[378] Craig Wilson, "Publishers in 7th heaven with near-death memoirs," *Christian Century* (March 20, 2013) 19.

[379] Larry Gordon, "Using the here and now to get a handle on the hereafter," http://articles.latimes.com/2013/mar/12/local/la-me-adv-immortality-20130313, accessed July 25, 2014.

[380] Gordon, "Here and now," accessed July 25, 2014. Assante makes an extremely important point about evidence, following a suggestion from Victor Zammit in *A Lawyer Presents the Case for the Afterlife*: "If each [person alive with no links to science] were to submit private testimony about his or her experiences with the world beyond and its inhabitants, the sum total would constitute evidence so overwhelming that we would not even need a lawyer to argue the case" (*Last Frontier*, 32). In other words, our culture uses types of evidence in legal contexts to prove guilt and innocence that are different from but at least as compelling as scientific evidence, yet on the subject of the afterlife, the materialist, secular culture eschews such legal evidence.

[381] Again for full disclosure purposes, I am a Fellow of the Westar Institute and generally respect their excellent work.

[382] Pieter F. Craffert, "Jesus' Resurrection as a Cultural Reality," *The Fourth R*, Vol. 26, No. 2 (March-April 2013) 3.

[383] Craffert, "Jesus' Resurrection," 14.

[384] Cooke, *Book of the Beyond*, 246, and Read, *Jesus and His Church*, 145.

[385] Robert M. Price, "A Response to Pieter Craffert," *The Fourth R*, Vol. 26, No. 2 (March-April 2013) 14. Once again in the interests of full disclosure, I have written a number of articles for Professor Price in *The Journal of Higher Criticism*, which he edited. I am very grateful for his publishing my work and greatly respect his progressive scholarship, even though we might disagree in some areas.

[386] *Book of Common Prayer*, 526, 538.

[387] Assante, *Last Frontier*, is probably one of the best books today that deals constructively with connecting with the deceased.

[388] Arthur Conan Doyle manifested as "himself" through a medium in full, complete paragraphs for several years; we will draw on his many teachings below.

[389] Reader's Digest, *Life Beyond Death*, 32-35, 38-39.

[390] Charles T. Tart, "Introduction," in Monroe, *Journeys*, 4-5.

[391] Monroe, *Journeys*, 116.

[392] Monroe, *Ultimate Journey*, 272, and passim.

[393] In *Ultimate Journey*, Monroe does not use the term Locale II, but it is roughly equivalent to what he called Belief System Territories; see p. 272 and passim.
[394] Monroe, *Journeys*, 272.
[395] Cooke, *Book of the Beyond*, 211.
[396] Cooke, *Book of the Beyond*, 160.
[397] Alexander, *Proof of Heaven*, 154-55, italics in original.
[398] Alexander, *Proof of Heaven*, 169.
[399] Van Praagh, *Reaching to Heaven*, 37.
[400] Long and Perry, *Afterlife*, 14, 113.
[401] Cooke, *Book of the Beyond*, 168.
[402] Cooke, *Book of the Beyond*, 225.
[403] Butler and Butler, *No Death*, 102-03.
[404] Long and Perry, *Afterlife*, 128-29.
[405] Butler and Butler, *No Death*, 69, 111.
[406] Lisa Butler, "Electronic Voice Phenomena," 130.
[407] Hancock, *Medium Next Door*, 79-94.
[408] Van Praagh, *Reaching to Heaven*, 83-84.
[409] Butler and Butler, *No Death*, 108-111.
[410] Anabela Cardoso, "ITC Contacts with Animals?,"2. See also Hancock, *Medium Next Door*, 265.
[411] See, e.g., Monroe, *Ultimate Journey*, 39, 95.
[412] Butler and Butler, *No Death*, 105.
[413] Butler and Butler, *No Death*, 68.
[414] Butler and Butler, *No Death*, 108.
[415] Cooke, *Book of the Beyond*, 247.
[416] Butler and Butler, *No Death*, 144.
[417] Butler and Butler, *No Death*, 106-07.
[418] See, e.g., Butler and Butler, *No Death*, 103-05; Hancock, *Medium Next Door*, 261-62 and passim; Monroe, *Ultimate Journey*, 105-24.
[419] Butler and Butler, *No Death*, 103-05.
[420] Cooke, *Book of the Beyond*, 170.
[421] Luke 1: 26-38.
[422] Long and Perry, *Afterlife*, 130-32.
[423] Alexander, *Proof of Heaven*, 70-71.
[424] Hancock, *Medium Next Door*, 265.
[425] Cooke, *Book of the Beyond*, 165.

⁴²⁶ Cooke, *Book of the Beyond*, 165-66. Doyle says more about the planes at this point, bringing in the Buddhist concept of nirvana: "There are actually twelve planes. Of the seven spheres which we must call astral, the lowest, or seventh, remains so closely interwoven with earth, so identified with earthly interests and influences, that it cannot be included [in a counting of 13 planes]. ¶ [The 12 planes are] six astral and six heavenly. The last mental plane marks the stopping place, or the *nirvana*, where the soul meditates, contemplates and absorbs experiences of the past. This is the resting place after every incarnation before the soul returns to gather fresh experience. ¶ Beyond these mental planes, beyond *nirvana*, awaits – we will not call it the 'third death' – but the final liberation from incarnations. Then the soul goes onward through the 'waiting halls' into the celestial or cosmic consciousness."

⁴²⁷ Cooke, *Book of the Beyond*, 185.
⁴²⁸ Monroe, *Ultimate Journey*, 274; see also 166-67.
⁴²⁹ Cooke, *Book of the Beyond*, 169.
⁴³⁰ Cooke, *Book of the Beyond*, 170.
⁴³¹ http://blog.heritage.org/2013/07/16/family-fact-of-the-week-majority-of-americans-pray/, accessed September 1, 2013.
⁴³² http://www.huffingtonpost.com/howard-s-friedman-phd/where-exactly-is-the-heal_b_838603.html, accessed September 1, 2013.
⁴³³ http://archinte.jamanetwork.com/article.aspx?articleid=216980, accessed September 1, 2013.
⁴³⁴ Cooke, *Book of the Beyond*, 179.
⁴³⁵ Van Praagh, *Reaching to Heaven*, 65.
⁴³⁶ Alexander, *Proof of Heaven*, 143.
⁴³⁷ Monroe, *Journeys*, 74. See also *Ultimate Journey*, 180-81, 185-89.
⁴³⁸ Belanger, *Haunting*, 206-07.
⁴³⁹ Brown, *After Life*, 44.
⁴⁴⁰ Psalm 86:13; Psalm 88; Psalm 116:3-4.
⁴⁴¹ 2 Peter 2:4; Matthew 8:12, 13:42, 50; 22:13; 24:51; 25:30; Luke 13:28.
⁴⁴² Brown, *After Life*, 55.
⁴⁴³ Summerland is a term coined by Spiritualists to describe an astral level of beauty, health and joy; Cooke, *Book of the Beyond*, 109-10.
⁴⁴⁴ Cooke, *Book of the Beyond*, 110.
⁴⁴⁵ Kelsey, *Afterlife*, 247.
⁴⁴⁶ Cooke, *Book of the Beyond*, 168.
⁴⁴⁷ Cooke, *Book of the Beyond*, 125.

[448] Cooke, *Book of the Beyond*, 110.
[449] Cooke, *Book of the Beyond*, 163.
[450] Cooke, *Book of the Beyond*, 165.
[451] Monroe, *Journeys*, 121, italics in original.
[452] Van Praagh, *Reaching to Heaven*, 60-61.
[453] Monroe, *Journeys*, 120.
[454] Cooke, *Book of the Beyond*, 196-97. Also, "There exist *both* destiny and freewill choice. Destiny, so far as man is concerned, stands for certain physical experiences through which you must and will pass: choice lies *in your own reaction* spiritually to these conditions of physical life" (190; italics in original).
[455] Butler and Butler, *No Death*, 87.
[456] Renier, *Mind for Murder,* passim.
[457] For example, see Monroe, *Ultimate Journey*, 110-24.
[458] Butler and Butler, *No Death*, 86-87.
[459] Cooke, *Book of the Beyond*, 159.
[460] Renier, *Mind for Murder*, 294.
[461] Renier, *Mind for Murder*, 299-302.
[462] Renier, *Mind for Murder*, 304.
[463] Coffey, *Growing Up Psychic*, 135-36.
[464] Accessed September 1, 2013.
[465] Coffey, *Growing Up Psychic*, 105.
[466] Buell and Petrucha, *Paranormal State*, 149.
[467] Alexander, *Proof of Heaven*, 83.
[468] Monroe, *Journeys*, 55-57.
[469] Cooke, *Book of the Beyond*, 194.
[470] Cooke, *Book of the Beyond*, 195; italics in original.
[471] Cooke, *Book of the Beyond*, 198; italics in original.
[472] Butler and Butler, *No Death*, 120.
[473] Langley, *Reincarnation*, 165. See also "Metempsychosis," F.L. Cross and E.A. Livingstone, eds., *The Oxford Dictionary of the Christian Church* (Oxford: Oxford University Press, 1985) 908.
[474] Langley, *Reincarnation*, 166.
[475] Langley, *Reincarnation*, 167.
[476] Langley, *Reincarnation*, 179-84.
[477] "Metempsychosis," *Oxford*, 908.
[478] Langley, *Reincarnation*, 179-84.
[479] Langley, *Reincarnation*, 184-88, 195.

[480] Langley, *Reincarnation*, 198.
[481] Langley, *Reincarnation*, 201. Reincarnation was condemned implicitly by the Councils of Lyons in 1274 and Florence in 1439, "which affirmed that souls go immediately to heaven, purgatory, or hell" ("Metempsychosis," *Oxford*, 908).
[482] Butler and Butler, *No Death*, 89-90.
[483] Butler and Butler, *No Death*, 90. Butler and Butler also give an example of a deceased pet dog, Rolf, reincarnating into someone else's pet dog, Wanda (110).
[484] Cooke, *Book of the Beyond*, 202.
[485] This does not mean that each life is linearly more positive or efficacious than the last. Time, as we have seen, is different on the other side than in our earthly lives. As Assante points out, "[M]any different versions of the past, present, and future coexist with, or parallel, those we choose to bring into our awareness, whether we are alive or dead. Yet they are equally real, equally concrete and valid…" (*Last Frontier,* 148).
[486] Hancock, *Medium Next Door*, 135.
[487] Cooke, *Book of the Beyond*, 208.
[488] See e.g., Assante, *Last Frontier*, 213-14, 307.
[489] Cooke, *Book of the Beyond*, 176. See also Assante, *Last Frontier*, 155 and passim.
[490] Monroe, *Journeys*, 181.
[491] Langley, *Reincarnation*, 48.
[492] Langley, *Reincarnation*, 52.
[493] Van Praagh, *Reaching to Heaven*, 40-41.
[494] Assante, *Last Frontier*, 200.
[495] Langley, *Reincarnation*, passim.
[496] Langley, *Reincarnation*, 236-37.
[497] Personal experience with past-life techniques and testimony from a male acquaintance and psychic who resides in Greenfield, Mass. but prefers to remain anonymous.
[498] Van Praagh, *Reaching to Heaven*, 38-39.
[499] Belanger, *Haunting*, 205-14.
[500] Buell and Petrucha, *Paranormal State*, 305-17.
[501] Long and Perry, *Afterlife*, 182-83.
[502] Puryear, *Stephen Lives!*, 184-91 and passim.
[503] Assante, *Last Frontier*, 239.

[504] Frank J. Tipler, *The Physics of Immortality: Modern Cosmology, God and the Resurrection of the Dead* (New York: Doubleday, 1994) 1-5.
[505] Tipler, *Immortality*, 308. It should be noted, though, that the paranormal evidence generally points to the non-existence of "beginning" and "end" of time and the universe.
[506] Cooke, *Book of the Beyond*, 246.
[507] Read, *Jesus and His Church*, 70-72, 142-43.
[508] Reader's Digest, *Life Beyond Death*, 104-07.
[509] Monroe, *Journeys*, 124-25.
[510] See Assante, *Last Frontier*, for an excellent presentation of this subject.
[511] Doyle, *History*, Vol. II, 286-87.
[512] Doyle, *History*, Vol. II, 284-85, quoting Lilian Walbrook, "Case of Lester Coltman," 34.
[513] http://atransc.org/circle/about_the_big_circle.htm, accessed July 4, 2014.
[514] Puryear, *Stephen Lives!*, 146-48 and passim.
[515] Cooke, *Book of the Beyond*, 219-26.
[516] See Assante, *Last Frontier*, 313-25 and passim.
[517] Van Praagh, *Unfinished Business*, 161.
[518] Miller, *Heaven*.
[519] Interestingly, Doyle equates Purgatory with life in the physical word (*History*, Vol. II, 279).
[520] Miller, *Heaven*, 136.
[521] Assante, *Last Frontier*, 4.
[522] These observations address many of the concerns – among Christians, Jews and Muslims – discussed by Miller in *Heaven*, especially pages 105-24. See also Assante, *Last Frontier*, which was written specifically to conquer the fear of death.
[523] Doyle, *History*, Vol. II, 247.
[524] See treatments, for instance, by Assante, *Last Frontier*, 13-18, 26-27, and Chopra, *Life After Death*, 126-29. There are many others available.
[525] Roach, *Spook*.
[526] Roach, *Spook*, 153-54.
[527] Roach, *Spook*, 154-55.
[528] Again, Assante, *Last Frontier*, deals with these issues very elegantly.
[529] We start with Paul, not Jesus, because Paul's authentic writings are the earliest in the New Testament canon, written within a generation of Jesus' death.
[530] King James Version.

[531] 1 Cor. 13:1-13, Revised Standard Version.
[532] "William Fletcher Barrett," *Wikipedia*, http://en.wikipedia.org/wiki/William_Fletcher_Barrett, accessed September 24, 2013.
[533] "Barrett," *Wikipedia*.
[534] Blum, *Ghost Hunters*, 71.
[535] Blum, *Ghost Hunters*, 82.
[536] "Barrett," *Wikipedia*. See also Doyle, *History*, Vol. II, 240.
[537] "Barrett," *Wikipedia*.
[538] Blum, *Ghost Hunters*, 83.
[539] Blum, *Ghost Hunters*, 73-74.
[540] Blum, *Ghost Hunters*, 74.
[541] Blum, *Ghost Hunters*, 172-75.
[542] "William Crookes," *Wikipedia*, http://en.wikipedia.org/wiki/William_Crookes, accessed September 24, 2013.
[543] "Society for Psychical Research," *Wikipedia*, http://en.wikipedia.org/wiki/Society_for_Psychical_Research (accessed November 14, 2013) 3.
[544] "Crookes," *Wikipedia*.
[545] "Edmund Gurney," *Wikipedia*, http://en.wikipedia.org/wiki/Edmund_Gurney, accessed September 24, 2013.
[546] Blum, *Ghost Hunters*, 80-81.
[547] Blum, *Ghost Hunters*, 88-90. See also Chapter 3 above.
[548] Blum, *Ghost Hunters*, 125-26.
[549] "Gurney," *Wikipedia*.
[550] Blum, *Ghost Hunters*, 276.
[551] Blum, *Ghost Hunters*, 83-86.
[552] "Richard Hodgson (parapsychologist)," *Wikipedia*, http://en.wikipedia.org/wiki/Richard_Hodgson_(parapsychologist), accessed September 24, 2013.
[553] Blum, *Ghost Hunters*, 141-42.
[554] Blum, *Ghost Hunters*, 142-43, 180-82.
[555] Blum, *Ghost Hunters*, 181-82.
[556] Blum, *Ghost Hunters*, 181-82.
[557] See, e.g., Theresa Caputo in many episodes of *Long Island Medium*; Hancock, *Medium Next Door*, 104-06, 260 and passim; and Renier, *Mind for Murder*, in the case of clues that help detectives in murder cases.

[558] "James H. Hyslop," *Wikipedia*, http://en.wikipedia.org/wiki/James_H._Hyslop, accessed September 24, 2013.
[559] "Hyslop," *Wikipedia*.
[560] "Hyslop," *Wikipedia*.
[561] Doyle, *History*, Vol. II, 75.
[562] Blum, *Ghost Hunters*, 247-48.
[563] "Hyslop," *Wikipedia*.
[564] Horace Meyer Kallen, "James, William," *Encyclopaedia Britannica* (Chicago: Encyclopaedia Britannica, Inc., 1963) Vol. 12, 883-84.
[565] Kallen, "James," 884.
[566] Blum, *Ghost Hunters*, passim.
[567] Blum, *Ghost Hunters*, 82.
[568] Blum, *Ghost Hunters*, 97-100, and Doyle, *History*, Vol. II, 75.
[569] Blum, *Ghost Hunters*, 170-71.
[570] Blum, *Ghost Hunters*, 310-11, and William James, "The Confidences of a 'Psychical Researcher,'" *The American Magazine*, Vol. 68 (Oct. 1909) 580-89.
[571] "Oliver Lodge," *Wikipedia*, http://en.wikipedia.org/wiki/Oliver_Lodge, accessed September 24, 2013.
[572] "Lodge," *Wikipedia*.
[573] Assante, *Last Frontier*, for one, has many such examples.
[574] Blum, *Ghost Hunters*, 163-67.
[575] Blum, *Ghost Hunters*, 162.
[576] "Lodge," *Wikipedia*.
[577] "Lodge," *Wikipedia*.
[578] Myers worked for many of his 57 years on paranormal research, yet the article on him in *Wikipedia*, "Frederic William Henry Myers" (http://en.wikipedia.org/wiki/Frederic_William_Henry_Myers , accessed September 24, 2013) says virtually nothing about his life or accomplishments.
[579] Blum, *Ghost Hunters*, 121.
[580] Doyle, *History*, Vol. II, 62.
[581] Doyle, *History*, Vol. II, 74-75.
[582] Doyle, *History*, Vol. II, 85.
[583] Doyle, *History*, Vol. II, 64.
[584] "Charles Richet," *Wikipedia*, http://en.wikipedia.org/wiki/Charles_Richet, accessed November 14, 2013.

[585] Blum, *Ghost Hunters*, 225-27.
[586] "Richet," *Wikipedia*.
[587] Doyle, *History*, Vol. I, 184.
[588] "Henry Sidgwick," *Wikipedia*, http://en.wikipedia.org/wiki/Henry_Sidgwick, accessed September 24, 2013.
[589] "Henry Sidgwick," *Wikipedia*.
[590] Blum, *Ghost Hunters*, 83.
[591] Blum, *Ghost Hunters*, 178
[592] Arthur MacDonald, "The International Congress of Experimental Psycology, Held in London, August 1892," in *Science*, Vol. 20, No. 511 (November 18, 1892) 289.
[593] "Eleanor Mildred Sidgwick," *Wikipedia*, http://en.wikipedia.org/wiki/Eleanor_Mildred_Sidgwick, accessed June 7, 2014.
[594] Blum, *Ghost Hunters*, 72. See also "Barrett," *Wikipedia*; "Gurney," *Wikipedia*; and "Myers," *Wikipedia*.
[595] Doyle, *History*, Vol. II, 70-71.
[596] Blum, *Ghost Hunters*, 182-83. Note that the *Wikipedia* article on Sidgwick makes no mention of this significant work of research.
[597] Blum, *Ghost Hunters*, 276.
[598] "Alfred Russel Wallace," *Wikipedia*, http://en.wikipedia.org/wiki/Alfred_Russel_Wallace, accessed September 24, 2013.
[599] "Wallace," *Wikipedia*.
[600] Doyle, *History*, Vol. I, 171, and Vol. II, 134.
[601] Doyle, *History*, Vol. II, 134-35.
[602] Doyle, *History*, Vol. II, 96.
[603] "Apostles' Creed, The," in F.L. Cross and E.A. Livingstone, eds., *The Oxford Dictionary of the Christian Church*, Third Edition (Oxford: Oxford University Press, 1997) 75.
[604] See for example Alexander, *Proof of Heaven*, 156.
[605] See Burpo and Vincent, *Heaven is for Real*, especially 105-09.
[606] Cooke, *Book of the Beyond*, passim, but especially 206-07.
[607] Cooke, *Book of the Beyond*, 186.
[608] See Van Praagh, Puryear, Coffey and others.
[609] Langley, *Reincarnation*, 48.
[610] See, e.g., "Parthenogesis," Colin Blakemore and Shelia Jennett, *The Oxford Companion to the Body*, 2001,

http://www.encyclopedia.com/topic/parthenogenesis.aspx, accessed July 28, 2014.
[611] See especially Jane Schaberg, *The Illegitimacy of Jesus* (Sheffield, England: Sheffield Academic Press, 1995; first published by Crossroad Publishing Co., 1990).
[612] See, e.g., Robert J. Miller, *Born Divine: The Births of Jesus and Other Sons of God* (Santa Rosa, CA: Polebridge Press, 2003) passim.
[613] See, e.g., Valerie Abrahamsen, "Human and Divine: The Marys in Early Christian Tradition," in Amy-Jill Levine with Maria Mayo Robbins, eds., *A Feminist Companion to Mariology* (London and New York: T & T Clark International, 2005) 164-81.
[614] Read, *Jesus and His Church*, passim.
[615] For example, Colton Burpo; see Burpo and Vincent, *Heaven is for Real*.
[616] See, e.g., Edwin A. Judge, "Pilate, Pontius," in Bruce M. Metzger and Michael D. Coogan, eds., *Oxford Companion to the Bible* (New York and Oxford: Oxford University Press, 1993) 594-95; "Pilate, Pontius," in *Oxford Dictionary*, 1090.
[617] See, e.g., Read, *Jesus and His Church*, 130-31.
[618] Michael Baigent, Richard Leigh, and Henry Lincoln, *Holy Blood, Holy Grail* (New York: Bantam Doubleday Dell Publishing Group, Inc., 1982, 1983).
[619] Barbara Thiering, *Jesus and the Riddle of the Dead Sea Scrolls: Unlocking the Secrets of His Life Story* (New York: HarperCollins Publishers, 1992).
[620] Read, *Jesus and His Church*, 132-35.
[621] See, e.g., John Dominic Crossan, *The Birth of Christianity* (New York: HarperCollins Publishers, 1998) 544-45.
[622] Cooke, *Book of the Beyond*, 168. I find androcentric language, e.g., using "man" and "men" generically to refer to both men and women, offensive, but I have chosen to leave it intact when quoting Doyle.
[623] Barbara G. Walker, *The Woman's Encyclopedia of Myths and Secrets* (San Francisco: Harper and Row, 1983).
[624] Read, *Jesus and His Church*, 13.
[625] Cooke, *Book of the Beyond*, 246.
[626] Read, *Jesus and His Church*, 142-44.
[627] Read, *Jesus and His Church*, 145.
[628] See, e.g., Monica Sjöö and Barbara Mor, *The Great Cosmic Mother* (San Francisco: Harper & Row, Publishers, 1987) 157-58.

[629] Burpo and Vincent, *Heaven is for Real*, 100-02.
[630] Cooke, *Book of the Beyond*, 160-61, italics in original.
[631] Acts 2:4, Revised Standard Version.
[632] Read, *Jesus and His Church*, 108-09.
[633] Church Pension Fund, *Book of Common Prayer*, 854.
[634] F.E. Peters, *The Harvest of Hellenism* (New York: Simon and Schuster, 1970) 684.
[635] Cooke, *Book of the Beyond*, 216-17.
[636] See, e.g., Coffey, *Growing Up Psychic*, 138-42; and Hancock, *Medium Next Door*, 261.
[637] Alexander, *Proof of Heaven*, 148.
[638] Michael E. Tymn, "St. Stephen Communicates," http://www.aspsi.org/feat/life_after/St. Stephen.html, accessed March 29, 2013.
[639] E.g., Romans 5:12-21.
[640] Karen Armstrong, *A History of God* (New York: Random House Publishing Group, 1993) 307, 354.
[641] Abrahamsen, *Goddess and God*, 136-46.
[642] Read, *Jesus and His Church*, 136.
[643] Van Praagh, *Reaching to Heaven*, passim; and Coffey, *Growing Up Psychic*, 195-97.
[644] Cooke, *Book of the Beyond*, 239.
[645] Alexander, *Proof of Heaven*, 146.
[646] Butler and Butler, *No Death*, 23.
[647] Butler and Butler, *No Death*, 76.
[648] Monroe, *Journeys*, 123-24.
[649] This column includes evidence from the medical examinations of the visionaries of Medjugorje.
[650] This column includes evidence from Edgar Cayce and postmortem Arthur Conan Doyle.

www.ingramcontent.com/pod-product-compliance
Lightning Source LLC
Chambersburg PA
CBHW070048080526
44586CB00013B/959